Religion, Race, and Justice in a Changing America

Civil Rights in a New Era

A series of Century Foundation Books developed in conjunction with the Civil Rights Project at Harvard University. The volumes in the series assess the prospects for justice and equal opportunity under law for racial and ethnic minorities in the United States.

Religion, Race, and Justice in a Changing America

GARY ORFIELD AND
HOLLY J. LEBOWITZ, *editors*

with Vignettes from the Field by Michal Kurlaender

A CENTURY FOUNDATION BOOK
1999 • THE CENTURY FOUNDATION PRESS • NEW YORK

The Century Foundation, formerly the Twentieth Century Fund, sponsors and supervises timely analyses of economic policy, foreign affairs, and domestic political issues. Not-for-profit and nonpartisan, it was founded in 1919 and endowed by Edward A. Filene.

LIBRARY OF CONGRESS CATALOGING-IN-PUBLICATION DATA

Religion, race, and justice in a changing America
/ Gary Orfield and Holly J. Lebowitz, editors.
   p.   cm.
Includes bibliographical references and index.
   ISBN 0-87078-433-1 (cloth: alk. paper)   ISBN 0-87078-435-8 (paper: alk. paper)
   1. Civil rights—Religious aspects.   2. Civil rights—United
States.   I. Orfield, Gary.   II. Lebowitz, Holly J.
   BL65.C58   R45   1999
   291.1'77—dc21   99-18241
                                                    CIP

Cover design and illustration: Claude Goodwin
Manufactured in the United States of America

Contents

Preface

L ove, justice, compassion. These universal values are endorsed by every major world religion. Yet contemporary American society is still beset by bigotry, discrimination, and racism, and there has been little leadership working to devise new solutions to these basic problems. Political solutions often carry little moral weight, and the legislative civil rights victories of the 1960s leave many, even in religious communities, with a sense that the battle has been waged and won. What is to become of these religious universals in this climate? Acknowledging that the ground has shifted since the 1960s, we are looking for a place where we can locate universal religious values in our new multiracial, pluralistic society.

We must wrestle with what this new milieu means for civil rights discourse. This book contains a collection of essays, most of which are arguments for each author's own religion's theologies, with suggestions for social priorities. But these various voices do not regard themselves to be in a vacuum; rather, they understand that their views are among many articulations of the universals. The question arises: How deep is each tradition going to be in its self-understanding as one player in discussions concerning race? The essays assembled here indicate that we no longer have a religious consensus for the orientation we came close to in the days of Martin Luther King, Jr. In the absence of that consensus, racial justice, when related to religious traditions as well as the values we espouse as a democratic society, becomes even more difficult to achieve. Further, the entrance of religion into the public sphere is not going to make a political consensus easier, but only more difficult. It is even conceivable, given the contentiousness of race issues and the urgency of racial problems, particularly in the nation's inner cities, that these issues may generate the same sort of controversies that have arisen around abortion, sexuality, and a litany of other matters.

However, in the 1960s, perhaps we did not have as widely accepted a consensus as we might imagine in retrospect. Martin Luther King's letter to the three clergymen in Birmingham exists alongside the "I Have a Dream" speech. Agreement among religious activists from various traditions that racism and discrimination in the American South were wrong did not always translate into a moral consensus about the appropriate action that the government should take to combat these evils. Furthermore, some religious organizations did not agree upon their own role in the movement, and often abandoned the effort when it spread outside of the South. But for all of these complexities, this period of temporary cooperation and genuine desire for consensus did make a difference at the time, and it leaves us with lessons for today.

The contemporary situation is one in which those who protest the racial status quo—questioning the deepening racial and economic polarization in our cities—are often dismissed by political leaders and ignored by the judiciary. Religion, meanwhile, has become a force in conservative politics. Religious activists are therefore left with the task of calling on Americans of faith to reaffirm their commitment to racial justice and initiate discussions with this aim in mind. The papers in this book are meant to be a first step in this conversation by suggesting that perhaps unbroken consensus is not the standard by which we should judge the state of religious involvement in civil rights activism. To demand unquestioning adherence to a single party line would, in fact, be counter to the very project that we are undertaking. On the contrary, democracy demands that we suggest another framework for extracting the universalities common to our traditions in a way that will help us become a "movement" again.

These essays reflect the massive complexity that religion adds to our public discussions, but they also reveal the illumination that public discussions give to the presumed conceptions of universalism and religious teachings. In this balance, they tell us that those of us who take religion seriously have a job to do if we expect our traditions to be supportive of universal values of equality and justice and compassion. This book does not make specific policy recommendations for future action, but we do ask that our readers recognize that they have an obligation to apply religious principles to contentious issues of public policy. We are hoping that they will be willing to understand each other's approaches to life and citizenship, a responsibility that involves an openness to learning and a commitment to being honest in one's reflections.

The civic community is part of God's creation and, as religious people, we have to affirm this conviction in our daily lives. The pluralism of religions makes that task more difficult, but we can work to overcome this difficulty by reading and becoming more aware of the various theologies. This book begins this process by setting forth the larger contexts in which the various traditions and understandings are placed, with the hope and belief that these will raise some fresh questions and issues.

Not all religions approach the race question from the same position. Several of our authors argue that Buddhism and Islam are freer from racism than Christianity, because the one began by repudiating the caste system in India, and the other speaks about the central religious event as one in which people come together and transcend the category of race. This implies that Christianity may have to confront racism in ways that other religions do not. By the same token, Christianity may have the advantage of existing in a more realistic way with the hard facts of the political and economic system.

King argued that the fundamental core of all religions is love. He believed that adherence to this core belief would enable religions to work together and bring about a universal community. King attempted to create a religious consensus built around the principle of love. But all the while, he clung to his Christian faith. The pursuit of a similar balance in the new context goes on. All religions need to understand and follow the universals at the core of their traditions, cleaving to the particular set of beliefs that sustain them even as they consider their universals. That is today's struggle.

If we genuinely expect this to happen, we have to work harder at persuading our citizenry of the significance of this endeavor. We have to rearticulate our goal of the good life, both spiritually and materially, and rekindle the urgency of our need to pursue that goal in the contemporary context.

As history has shown us, the closer we get to the prize, the more challenging the struggle. When people's consciousness is raised and new freedoms are revealed, fragmentation inevitably follows. This leads us to the issues of power and how power might be controlled—by love, justice, and compassion or by prejudice or indifference. Even as the situation progresses and we become significantly closer to racial equality than we were in the 1950s, our new pluralism is going to beget possibly greater tensions. So we are going to have to build ever wider coalitions of groups. And while just and moral policies should always be sought, it is impossible to legislate cooperation of this sort. The only way to achieve this cooperation is through the democratic process of continuing dialogue.

We hope these essays give us a better understanding of how the various religious traditions view the struggle for civil rights. The desire of these traditions to assert in a more vigorous way their historic orientations in the public square leads to the need for a more complex and nuanced approach to civil rights issues. The stated concern of all groups to do good and avoid evil in the end unites us in this struggle. Public policies that carry out that desire will be arrived at only after much debate, conflict, forgiveness, and reconciliation.

Preston N. Williams
Holly J. Lebowitz
Cambridge, Massachusetts

Acknowledgments

The editors have found it a special blessing to work with so many people who see so clearly the links between the basic values of their religious traditions and the issues of racial justice in American society at a difficult time of serious reversals in civil rights policy. First and foremost, we are deeply indebted to The Century Foundation for investing staff resources and support in the publication of this book, and for their commitment to working with us on the important issues in this volume and the others in the series of which it is a part. We are also grateful for the support provided by the John D. and Catherine T. MacArthur Foundation, the Charles Stewart Mott Foundation, and an anonymous donor.

We express our appreciation to an exceptionally responsive set of authors and activists and to the Interdenominational Theological Center and the Harvard Divinity School for cosponsoring the conference that led to this book. Preston Williams of the Harvard Divinity School and Robert Franklin of the Interdenominational Theological Center provided wise counsel from the outset of this project as did a number of theologians across the country. Christopher Edley, Jr., added important questions to the discussions. Michal Kurlaender, Marilyn Byrne, and Suenita Lawrence helped greatly with many aspects of this enterprise. We also extend our appreciation to Missy Daniel of the Harvard Divinity School and Richard Parker from the Kennedy School of Government for their input.

Introduction
Religion and Racial Justice

GARY ORFIELD

The most famous civil rights leader of the twentieth century was a minister, Martin Luther King, Jr. The most powerful images of the civil rights movement show marchers singing hymns as they faced violent resistance, and clergy of many faiths joining hands to challenge the deep traditions of communities divided for centuries by race. Diverse religious communities seemed united by a goal that was at the same time a fundamental civic goal and a deeply spiritual quest. Those who were religious often felt their religion with a new intensity.

Those who were not religious were caught up in a force they couldn't quite understand but that gave a transcendent and unifying dimension to a long and exhausting struggle. They reached across the color line, holding hands in small black churches that were suddenly swept into the tide of historic change. The movement changed the country. Without committing a single act of violence, this movement and the tide of conscience it aroused, ended apartheid in seventeen states that maintained laws separating blacks and whites in many key aspects of life. The movement went far beyond the church, but church was central in many ways to what seemed like an irreversible movement for racial justice.

At its peak the movement stirred hope and demands from other groups that had experienced a history of discrimination and prejudice. Latinos and American Indians had long struggled for justice in the courts and against discrimination by government and private interests, but now their struggles received more attention and more help. In his last major effort, Martin Luther King, Jr., was trying to assemble groups from many backgrounds into a grand coalition for what they called the "Poor People's Campaign."

King would have led the movement had he lived, bringing along his allies, including many religious groups. When the campaign came to Washington after King's assassination and the resulting riots in scores of cities, it was unorganized and had little impact. The black coalition split during King's last years, urban riots terrified the country, and an angry white electorate, aroused by Richard Nixon's Southern strategy, captured the White House. Churches were criticized for becoming too political and neglecting the spiritual needs of their people. Many preachers promised salvation on a strictly personal level, disregarding the sins of racism. Often their churches prospered while the old Protestant mainstream congregations declined. Hard feelings arose between blacks and Jews, particularly in the political and social turmoil that beset New York City. Some black Muslims openly challenged King's dream of a common society.

The stream of energy that activated the movement for racial justice split and drained away. Many looked back and concluded either that the work was done or that it was a mistake to try to push further. Others stayed with the issue, but often without carrying their communities with them. Only the conservatives seemed to be able to bring religion into politics effectively, capitalizing on intense issues like abortion, school prayer, and the decline of public morality to undercut the liberal agenda. A conservative political alliance turned against activist government, and, within a generation, redirected the courts to cut back sharply on civil rights.

The great days of the civil rights movement have vanished. The deaths of Martin Luther King and Robert Kennedy, the serious third-party presidential candidacy of segregationist governor George Wallace, and the election of President Nixon—all in the same year—marked the end to an era. Yet, the country is fundamentally different because of that movement, particularly the South, which has become much more like the rest of the nation. The religious leaders and believers who played a central role in that struggle remember it as the time when their faith and their action touched history. Faith became a powerful force in the real world and religious tactics succeeded in challenging the morality of a system backed by overwhelming local power. The South changed and, in many ways, its people accepted the change peacefully.[1] The movement was a light to the world, a marvel of peaceful transformation. It is no wonder that protesters in East Germany clamoring for the Berlin wall to come down at the end of the Soviet regime would often meet in churches and sing "We Shall Overcome," and that King's sermons resonated across the world.

The movement did not stop because the problems had all been solved. On the contrary, much was left undone. Martin Luther King's last great protest, against housing segregation in Chicago, ended without significant change in this system of racial exclusion, often called "the white noose." King wrote sadly in his last book *Where Do We Go From Here: Chaos or Community?*[2] that he was stunned that urban segregation, the Northern form of inequality defined by residential exclusion rather than state law, was defended with even more ferocity than the segregation laws of the South. The Poor People's Campaign ended in profound defeat in a bedraggled encampment called "Resurrection City" on the Mall in Washington—the same place where the crusade against Southern apartheid reached its great peak with his "I Have a Dream" speech five years earlier.[3] In celebrating King, most Americans do not hear about the parts of his work that are still undone.

Out on the West Coast, César Chávez was leading a struggle to gain basic rights and living conditions for Latino farm workers. He became the first great hero of the Mexican-American protest movement, drawing heavily on the religious symbols of his people. He confronted Governor Ronald Reagan, an opponent of all the major civil rights laws, whose rise reflected a major turn against the social movement for racial justice. At the same time, American Indians were mounting explosive protests over treaty rights and land. What had seemed morally clear in the South became bitterly controversial as new demands were made and as the conservative movement grew in power and asserted its claim to be the legitimate expression of Christian morality in American society.

Why did many churches drop out or pull back as the movement turned toward Northern forms of imposed segregation and discrimination? Where were the churches when the Reagan administration successfully reversed civil rights policy? Why didn't the major reversals in the rights of immigrants and non-English speakers in the 1990s provoke greater indignation? Certainly, there were protests by some religious leaders, but no social movement and little public visibility. Many churches turned inward, away from the big problems of society.

The conference and the papers that led to this book were commissioned by the Civil Rights Project at Harvard. This university-based interdisciplinary research project founded in 1996 by me and my codirector, Professor Christopher Edley, Jr., of Harvard Law School, aims to help fill the vacuum of constructive thought and research about many race relations issues after three decades of political domination by critics of the civil rights revolution who have often engaged in strategies of racial polarization. We have watched the erosion of the scholarly, legal, and political dimensions of civil rights support and worried about the lack of work that helps explain the problems and define the possibilities of a society with deep racial problems, which differ greatly from those of the South a half-century ago. One of our basic strategies has been to commission leading scholars in various fields to write new studies for the general public, and to discuss ideas critically in conferences with people from many backgrounds. We have found scholars in many disciplines and in many parts of the country very eager to participate in this endeavor.

The Civil Rights Project was founded to stimulate serious scholarly examination of the civil rights realities and the issues of a generation transformed by rapid changes that have turned America into a metropolitan multiracial society of extraordinary racial and ethnic diversity and profound economic and racial stratification. One of our central missions is to learn what scholars and thinkers in various disciplines can contribute to understanding the nature and possibilities of our society's racial dilemmas.

We do not conceive of the race issue in America as a matter for examination by social scientists or lawyers or activists alone. Obviously what we do about discrimination and inequality in our basic institutions reflects the nature of the values we hold. America is a deeply religious country and it is impossible to understand American values without understanding the role of religion. One of the riches of our culture is theology, systematic thought that examines the nature and implications of our religious traditions.

This book is an effort to learn from theologians and those involved in religious-based civil rights work about those values and their implications for the larger society. We did not choose to study churches as sociological groups or as political actors, but we aim to examine religious ideas for their intrinsic value. We believe that religious ideas and visions for the future matter a great deal in working out the destiny of American society.

This book is not an effort to find a single world view or ideology, and the authors are not official spokesmen for their religions. Their chapters are thoughtful commentaries growing out of their religious understandings. Our intent is to generate serious consideration of the implications of religion for racial justice and contemporary civil rights policy. It is not to prescribe an answer, to suggest that everyone within a given religion has the same view, or to assume that the answer to the social question is a uniform one.

Many people enter into public life with values from their religious traditions and use religion-based arguments in discussion of public issues. Many candidates, for example, promise to work to restore "traditional values," reflecting a widespread sense of loss of moral moorings in community life. By the same token, religious leaders and institutions engage in some public debates, with recent examples ranging from abortion to gay rights to physician-assisted suicide, human cloning, and publicly funded vouchers for religious schools.

Politicians, of course, will often use religious ideas and symbols hypocritically. One of the traditional critiques of Southern culture was the jarring contrast between strong Christian religious institutions and overt racial oppression. The Gospel message of love and justice seemed to disappear outside the walls of the all-white churches. Pastors may preach a universal message, but their congregations are highly segregated and their parishioners are powerful actors in many institutions that reinforce social inequalities. In the ugliest example of using religious symbols to thwart racial justice, the Ku Klux Klan (KKK) used the burning cross to terrorize blacks working to secure their rights.

THE HISTORIC ROLE OF RELIGION

The civil rights era was a unique time, but there is a long tradition of religious ideas influencing politics in the United States. Although there is a strong wall of separation between church and state in American law, religion is a powerful force in American public life. Millions came to America as religious exiles to a nation that guarantees freedom for all religions and officially supports none. This history has helped produce a vigorous and autonomous set of religious communities. We have not seen the secularization that has taken hold in many other advanced societies. New religious movements are constantly arising and old ones redirecting their energies.

There have been religious critiques of racial injustice in American society from the time of the American Revolution. Sometimes religious people have become major actors in struggles over those issues, which they see as deeply related to their basic beliefs. When a broad consciousness of the religious dimension of racial justice emerges, the politics of the issue are transformed.

Many students of American history and politics have noted that our diverse nation is held together by a political structure that lays out only a minimal set of goals for government. We have the oldest surviving written constitution and there is a deep acceptance of the idea of limited government. The American consensus strongly values freedom and individualism but offers little agreement on what government should do to solve common problems. Our consensus is mostly about the methods we use to make decisions and about needed limits on government.

Many of the civil rights embodied in the Constitution were enacted in the aftermath of the Civil War. Prohibitions against slavery, disenfranchisement, and racial discrimination by state and local governments became part of our fundamental law. The meaning of these civil rights is often bitterly controversial. Enforcement of those rights was vastly strengthened by the civil rights laws adopted in the 1960s and then weakened by courts increasingly dominated by conservative jurists.

When there are deep divisions within society, it is often impossible to go from procedural consensus to substantive solution, or to derive from the Constitution the solution to a problem never imagined when the words were written. When the country was founded, it was assumed that values needed to establish goals would come not from government structure and documents but would rather derive from Protestant religious ideas deeply embedded in the culture.

The biggest moral issues left unresolved in the Constitution were, of course, slavery and the rights of minorities. Citizenship, for example, was automatic for everyone born in the United States except blacks and Indians. These issues profoundly divided the country, and many churches split into separate denominations over slavery. Religious leaders and institutions played extremely important roles in the abolitionist movement before the Civil War, as they would a century later in the second great movement for racial justice in American history—the civil rights movement—in the 1950s and 1960s.

New England religious leaders played powerful roles in establishing the national abolitionist movement.[4] Ironically, the greatest leader of the battle against slavery, Abraham Lincoln, was not a formal church member, but his ideas and language were deeply shaped by the Bible. The anthem for the Union side was not accidentally the "Battle Hymn of the Republic," which resounded with the certainty that God was in the fight against slavery. "He hath loosed the fateful lightening of his terrible swift sword. His truth is marching on."

Many of those from the North who went down to reconstruct the South after the war were inspired by religion, and religious groups played a powerful role in some of the lasting accomplishments of that era, such as the creation of black colleges. (Religious leaders were also among the most important critics of the war against Mexico and the treatment of Indians on reservations, problems whose consequences remain with us today.)

If abolitionism drew much of its sustenance from the moral certainty of New England Protestants, the twentieth-century civil rights movement was rooted deeply in the Southern black church. Many of its leaders were preachers reflecting the core values and traditions of the black experience.[5] Although civil rights lawyers and leaders framed the issues, the mobilization of the churches turned the struggle into a great moral crusade. Black religious leaders found ways to transform a religion of consolation in oppression into a mighty movement for equality. The courage of leaders deeply committed to answering violence with prayer and peaceful protest galvanized a profound response across many parts of the American religious spectrum.

In the historic congressional battles for legislation to reverse state-imposed apartheid in seventeen states, many churches mobilized to support civil rights laws, providing a constituency and leaders for reform even in Middle Western and Western states with few minority residents. It was one of the great moments of mainstream Protestantism, made even stronger by the support of a powerful black-Jewish coalition. American Catholicism was also strongly supportive. Religious leaders of many denominations marched arm-in-arm for racial justice and played a decisive role in the outcome of the greatest legislative civil rights battle of the twentieth century, the enactment of the 1964 Civil Rights Act. Robert Mann describes the climactic period of the most important legislative battle in the history of civil rights:[6]

> On Saturdays and Sundays the rabbis, ministers, and priests sermonized in favor of human rights. By week's end senators received hundreds, sometimes thousands of letters urging them to support the bill. . . . Undecided senators could no longer ignore the issue. Father John Cronin, a staff member of the U.S. Catholic Conference of Bishops, worked especially hard . . . calling many bishops across the country. One such phone call went to a bishop in South Dakota, home of Republican Karl Mundt. . . . When Mundt finally supported the civil rights forces on a key vote, he reportedly emerged from the Senate chamber and grumbled, "I hope that satisfies those two god-damned bishops that called me last night."[6]

After the breakup of the civil rights coalition, under the pressure of riots, the Vietnam crisis, the black power movement, and the division and defeat of the Democratic Party in 1968, organized religious involvement in civil rights rapidly receded. Although some national church organizations regularly participated in the civil rights legislative battles that ensued in Washington over the following decades, as conservative movements fought to weaken the laws and reverse court decisions, there was no social movement and often little or no discussion of the issue in local churches.

POLITICAL REACTION AND RELIGIOUS RETREAT

When the liberal coalition of the 1960s was replaced by the conservative coalition whose great leaders were Richard Nixon and Ronald Reagan, there was a major and highly successful effort to bring conservative Christians into the political realm. Driven by cultural issues that brought together whites across social class lines, particularly in the South, they became supporters of the Republican Party's "Southern strategy." Emphasizing issues like abortion, homosexuality, and prayer in the schools, conservative Christians helped create a majority in combination with the anti-government, pro-business wing of the GOP, whose basic issues were about economics. The Christian Coalition and other organizations became part of a movement that had few black members, that believed that racial change had gone so far that it was hurting whites, and that much of the welfare system should be cut back. The Southern Strategy from the beginning included promises of a rollback of elements of the civil rights revolution. Though this was never a central goal of religious conservatives, they were very active in the political coalition that accomplished the goal. In its period of maximum power, in the early Reagan administration, the conservative movement controlling the agenda decided to move on economic issues and to delay the religious issues.[7] It succeeded in transforming the economic and social policy agenda for the rest of the century but failed to deliver on the religious changes.

All five successful conservative presidential campaigns from 1968 to 1988 called for a battle to make the courts more conservative through the appointment power, thus giving hope to the religious conservatives that decisions on abortion and school prayer, among other issues, would be reversed. Although the crusades against abortion and for school prayer failed in the courts, the transformation of the courts led to sweeping reversals on civil rights law issues ranging from affirmative action to school desegregation. Conservative presidents appointed judges who favored limiting the powers of government to promote social justice, but some of these judges had a libertarian streak concerning the key issues of the religious right.

By the 1980s the conservatives clearly dominated the national agenda and political activism in the name of religion was largely in the conservative direction. The Christian Coalition became a major force in the Republican Party and a conservative minister, Pat Robertson, became a serious presidential candidate. The religious conservatives became one of the basic power centers in the GOP. They had an important voice in politics, and the support of a growing number of think tanks financed by religious conservatives.

THE CONTINUING CENTRALITY OF RELIGION IN AMERICAN LIFE

In dramatic contrast to a number of other advanced societies, religion retains a strong hold in American life. Forty-two percent of Americans said in 1998 that they go to religious services at least once a week. Another 34 percent went at least a few times each year. Fifty-eight percent prayed at least once a day, and another 24 percent once or more a week.[8] There was also widespread agreement on what many would see as a basic religious principle—"it is important to me personally to help others who are less fortunate." Sixty percent of Americans agreed strongly with this statement, and 32 percent more said that they "agreed somewhat."[9] University of Michigan surveys of those voting in elections between 1980 and 1994 found that at least three-fourths said that religion was an important part of their lives. A July 1997 Gallup Poll showed that "churches and organized religion" are held in relatively high regard by Americans. Religion received the high confidence of 35 percent of the public, compared to 9 percent for Congress, 15 percent for newspapers, and 25 percent for the Supreme Court.

Even teenagers expressed a strong connection with religion in a 1998 national survey of thirteen- to seventeen-year-olds. Ninety-four percent said that they believed in God. Forty-one percent said that "developing a meaningful philosophy of life" was a very important goal, and 32 percent said the same about "helping to promote racial understanding."[10] It is clear that a very large group of Americans take their faith seriously, try to express it in some way almost every day, and are concerned about helping those in need in their society. In American culture, religion retains a powerful shaping influence and is an important source of legitimacy for views about society and justice.

THE RELIGIOUS AND POLITICAL VACUUM ON RACE: A PERSONAL VIEW

During the nearly three decades since the civil rights movement came apart in the late 1960s, I have been saddened by the passivity of most religious leaders and by the claims of the conservative anti-government Christian movement to represent the Christian tradition.[11] The dominant contribution of Christian activists to shaping mainstream politics during the past two decades has been to spur support for "family values" and to limit government. Family values refer mostly to cultural issues. All religions, of course, have a profound interest in family and cultural values, but the conservative movement separates these issues from the economic and social context of family and community life and often attempts to legislate its views on religion or personal morality with regard to such issues as abortion and school prayer. The ideas that government should be used to enforce the moral value of racial justice or to lessen family-destroying poverty in minority communities are rarely mentioned in this movement. When the Christian Coalition,[12] for example, functions as a component of the Republican Party coalition, it ends up backing legislators who support programs that take from the poor and minorities and give tax breaks and special treatment to the rich. It is as if Christ had said that riches were a sign of virtue, as if he had invited the money changers into the Temple, as if his parables had emphasized taking away the shelter of the poor to make them shape up for their own good. It is as if Christ had condemned the Good Samaritan for helping a stranger from another land.

Liberals have lost many elections to conservatives who use racial wedge issues. Many liberals and moderates are reluctant to discuss race and uncomfortable in using religious arguments to promote racial justice. The fact that Carter and Clinton, the only two Democrats elected president in the last third of the twentieth century, were white Southern Baptist moderates from politically conservative branches of Protestantism may help explain this avoidance of moral arguments in racial matters.

While Christianity has no simple or agreed-upon political theory, it contains rich traditions of theological thought on obligations that go beyond markets and individual satisfaction. Moreover, it shares these aspirations with other world religions. The confident attack on racial barriers that resonated in many religious communities in the 1960s is seldom heard now in public debates. Today one might get the impression that religion is restricted to issues within the household and that there is no moral dimension to problems of increasing tension and inequality in the community and nation. In this setting, it is not surprising that many religiously inspired activists pursuing racial justice tend to operate on a local level without a vision that goes beyond their own communities. One might hope that religion would be independent of political trends, but it often tends to reflect those trends.

I've been working for the past thirty years on issues of civil rights and racial justice, carrying out studies across the country on many issues and participating in dozens of law suits and efforts to strengthen civil rights policy. Every day I see evidence in government statistics, in reports and studies and court decisions, of deep and often intensifying inequalities and discrimination. What remains of the fabric of civil rights policy and law, after three decades of intense conservative attack, has been badly frayed by cuts in government programs and by a successful conservative effort to staff the federal courts with judges who believe that too much has been done already.

I watch this incessant attack on civil rights and on government social policies and study the shrinking opportunities for minority youth as the doors of opportunity are pulled shut. I listen to leaders of both parties proposing popular ideas that ignore issues of race and class and are likely to further harm minority opportunities. I see surveys that show that the great majority of whites favor no more help for minorities, that they believe that minorities already enjoy equal opportunity in many ways, even though gaps remain large and are widening in some key respects. Many whites and others who have made it into affluent suburbs simply deny any responsibility for those left behind. They and their families have no contact with the dispossessed but hold strong stereotypes, and they go to churches that do not challenge their ideas that what the country needs is still another tax cut and that poor minorities are poor and isolated because they chose to be or because they deserve to be. Often the attitudes verge on contempt for those left behind, for the teachers and others who work with them, and for the "do-gooders" or "big spenders" who try to help. Millions of Americans have no capacity to imagine living on the other side of the lines of color, language, and poverty and face no moral challenge to understand and love and help those denied the opportunities they have received.

I see a country where for two decades there have been massive cuts in federal and state aid to cities, where the budget is being balanced partly through further cuts in services to the poor and their communities. I see the world's richest country consumed with selfishness and self-indulgence, convinced that it cannot afford any more help to the poor, that it must cut what is already the Western world's most limited system of social protection, while increasing the huge subsidies that flow to the affluent through the tax system. I see a fearful country where people cross the street when they see young men of a different race approaching, a country that puts more of its young people in prison than any other industrialized society and that cuts programs to rehabilitate those who have served their terms. I see a level of poverty for children that no other advanced society tolerates and that goes virtually unnoticed and millions of minority families working full time and still living in poverty. I study and report on the policies that produce deepening segregation and inequality in our schools and that cut off access to college for many poor and nonwhite students.

I go to Mass on Sunday and listen to words from Scripture about God's love for the poor, about the obligations of those who have been given much, and about Christ's challenges to stereotypes and his reaching out to those who were excluded. As a member of the largest church in the world's richest and most religious industrialized society, I feel a terrible disjuncture between the values at the core of my tradition and those of the society I live in. I look across the pews and wonder how people can listen to these words and pray about Gospel messages and then drive back across the searing divide between city and suburbs without sensing the dissonance. I sometimes think that today's big-city residents have become as blind to the realities of our social system as were many of the religious whites of the South before the civil rights crisis.

I know the disjuncture is linked to the history of recent decades. Despite the triumphs of the civil rights movement in the 1960s, the decade ended with the movement in tatters and the churches in retreat. Racial inequality, discrimination, and polarization continue, however, to be fundamental challenges today. Recent studies point to continuing discrimination, intensified segregation in schools, and deep racial inequalities, but opinion surveys show widespread denial of these problems among the white public. Sweeping demographic, political, and social changes are transforming a white society with an excluded black minority into a multiracial society with new dimensions of discrimination and layers of inequality.

The rising generation is often criticized as uncaring and selfish, but it has rarely been challenged. There is no Martin Luther King and there is no president like Lyndon Johnson willing to spend his political capital to act strongly against racial injustice. In this period of neglected and deepening social problems, the responsibilities of moral leaders are great. In this situation, what is the role of America's religious communities? Are they a source of vision and new ideas or do they have little or nothing to contribute?

I believe that we need new religious insights to understand our current form of racial stratification in metropolitan areas and to find ways to bring down barriers within our society. I know that there is no way to draft urban policy out of parables or psalms, but I think that our traditions are rich with principles that are rarely taken seriously in our public debates and that can provide a context to persuade many Americans to confront issues of injustice they shut out or accept as inevitable. In a society where racial inequality has always been a central fact, it is easy to accept the status quo as natural, or even to become blind to it, unless the contradictions are illuminated by contrasting the realities with what we claim to believe. Religious principles are genuinely important to many millions of people in this country and should be taken seriously in thinking about ways to achieve a more just society. This is why I asked theologians to put aside their other work for a time and reflect on this issue.

The book is mostly by theologians; only brief passages are about initiatives that individual churches are undertaking. It begins with the basic beliefs of the religious communities. The content of the faith becomes important because churches and synagogues are communities bound and defined by belief. Analysis of the last, often unhappy, phase of the civil rights movement shows that many of the problems arose when church activists lost contact with the beliefs of their tradition and with the lives and experiences of their congregations. When, for example, leaders of a mainstream Protestant church in a tradition committed to nondiscrimination and universalism became allied with a movement that embraced black nationalism and began to abandon the nonviolent protest tradition of Dr. King, they acted in disregard of the beliefs of their communities.

Religious communities are not political institutions, but they can have considerable political influence in a religious society. They can be important sources of social and political values, particularly when there is a genuine and understood connection between the issue and their beliefs. So we have to start with what is essential to the religion before we can understand the potential and limits of its contributions. If there is no appeal to a system of beliefs, then we would merely be talking about a political movement using religious language, not something likely to have lasting significance.

When theologians think about the way religious beliefs might interact with current and historical issues of racial justice, we have learned through this project, they speak not only of religious principles but also of their understanding of the possibilities and limits of current political and community conditions. Applying theological premises effectively to contemporary civil rights issues requires at least an implicit view of what the problems and possibilities of the present situation are. Developing a theory or an argument about these issues necessitates clarification not only of the value premises but also of premises about the facts. Going from a belief that the damage done by the sin of racism should be repaired to conclusions about what policies believers should support requires conclusions about the effects of present and past discrimination and the impacts of various policies. The assumptions about the facts may be implicit or explicit, and they may be right or wrong.

We learned that most of the people whose lives are devoted to working on civil rights don't keep up with theology, though they may have deep religious beliefs, and that most theologians concerned with racial justice don't keep up with data and research on the realities of American race relations. To move from a value or a belief to a policy that accurately reflects that value and works in practice requires factual information. Understanding whether a market approach will, for example, produce greater racial justice in health care, would require understanding what is known about what kind of market information various groups of people have, whether or not the market actually produces a fair supply of options in minority communities, and a number of other factual relationships. To reach a valid policy in a complex society, it is not safe to rely merely on personal pastoral or community experience, though that should be carefully considered. A great deal of research is available that can illuminate some of the factual premises, but it is often not known to the theologians. Much is known about these issues, and other parts of the Civil Rights Project are commissioning new scholarship to learn more.

Eventually, it will be important to bring together theologians with scholars working to understand social realities for a searching examination of each other's premises. Before that can be done, it is important to think through some of the basic value issues. That is the primary purpose of this book, to examine religious principles as the authors see them operating on issues of racial justice.

SOCIAL TRANSFORMATIONS

Social problems arising from huge racial changes attracted surprisingly little attention from religious leaders during the conservative era. After the 1965 immigration reform, ending overtly racist restrictions on immigration for the first time, the United States began to receive a large and overwhelmingly non-European immigrant population that created the kind of multiracial communities that had never before been seen. The nation's two largest states already have a majority of nonwhite school-age children, and in many others the nonwhite population is growing rapidly. The nation's white population will begin to decline if existing demographic trends continue. The society is changing rapidly in a time of increasing economic polarization and race and class separation within metropolitan areas where 80 percent of Americans live.

At the same time, diversity has been growing rapidly among and within America's religions. The establishment Protestant churches, which so powerfully shaped America's culture, are in a long-term decline. White Protestant growth has been concentrated in evangelical and Pentecostal churches, which preach a much more fundamentalist and individualist view of the Bible, with less emphasis on public racial justice and other social issues. But some of their organizations have begun to raise racial justice concerns. The male "Promise Keepers" movement, for example, whose mass meetings attract huge groups of men, has spoken strongly of the need for racial reconciliation, though the leaders offer no concrete proposals.[13]

With the growth of immigration, Islam surpassed Judaism, eastern religions grew rapidly, and a "new age" consciousness spurred many new forms of religions expression. Often older Protestant congregations in big cities share their churches with people holding services in another language. The vast Latin immigration and migrants from Haiti and Southeast Asia brought American Catholicism a surge of members, and much greater racial and cultural diversity than it had ever before experienced. Churches and synagogues and mosques try to reach across racial lines in unprecedented ways.

As American society has become more diverse, we were also experiencing the most dramatic rise in inequality of income in the Western world, an inequality particularly affecting children. In the past generation, nearly half of the nation's black and Latino children were born into poverty.

Churches, however, had a lot of other major changes to worry about. What had been the leading establishment churches in the cities often experienced drastic declines in congregations as suburbs grew and middle-class white families left the cities. The dramatic increase in divorce, the decline of the two-parent family, and other changes in society created serious challenges to communities and their church leaders. Deindustrialization, globalization, downsizing, and the collapse of older neighborhoods created huge stresses. Such dramatic dislocations provoked anxiety and anger as long-established expectations crumbled. The conservative movement offered explanations that proved extremely popular. The problems, it said, grew from too much competition from immigrants, unfair advantages to minorities, too many "welfare queens," and too much money going to the government through taxes. Minorities and the laws protecting them became easy scapegoats.

Poor people were increasingly blamed for their own poverty and ignorance, and punitive measures to force them to change replaced many of the support systems of previous decades. Programs for the elderly were preserved, but most of the rest of the social policy agenda was radically reduced. Welfare, housing, and job training programs suffered huge cuts. The rights of immigrants were sharply curtailed.

Some religious leaders protested the moral issues raised by these changes, but the churches for the most part remained silent. Though some became involved in the fights, for example, over the welfare reform and the anti-immigrant legislation, it was nothing like the mobilization of the 1960s. There were no great demonstrations, just statements from leaders. Many other religious leaders said nothing.

REFORMULATION

Because the moral challenges raised by these issues are complex, it is not easy to understand them and to decide what to do; this book is not about figuring out all the answers to those problems. Its basic question is whether our religious traditions can help us sort out the values questions that can help inform and generate a policy debate.

Racism is widely seen as a sin today, across a broad spectrum of American religions. That is a legacy of the civil rights movement. Very little that happens in American society today, however, is attributed to white racism. The safest sin to be against is one that was practiced mainly in the past. Americans have accepted the comfortable view that racism existed in a flagrant way only in the pre-civil rights era, that current racial differences are largely the product of cultural differences and choices, that we have done everything that can work (and maybe too much), and that somehow the schools or a gradual improvement in attitudes will provide opportunity for all. Even when it is recognized that nonwhites fare poorly in this society, there is a deep skepticism in this conservative era about the capacity of government to do anything about it. If discrimination is rare and nothing would work anyway, there is no moral responsibility for addressing race.

White America may attribute something terrible, like bombings of black churches, to racism, but otherwise give it little attention in national policy debates. Being against the sin of racism, defined this way, is like being against slavery; it generates good feelings, but it doesn't recognize or resolve present issues of discrimination and unequal opportunity. The new public myth is that there was racism until Martin Luther King, but then changes in the law and public attitudes ended racism except in rare and extreme cases. Persisting inequality was attributed to other factors, for example, failings within the group or well-intentioned but misguided policies. These arguments, central themes of the Reagan administration, have been widely accepted. The sin of racism seemed to disappear almost as soon as it was widely recognized.

In any case racism is not a very useful term, since it implies animus against minority members. Most current discrimination, however, results more from blindness to the racial consequences of institutional practices than from a personal intent to discriminate. Richer and less judgmental concepts are needed to support efforts to explore and understand the roots of contemporary inequalities. We must move beyond the superficial to clarify principles and more systematically assess the social facts.

This book represents an essential but far from sufficient step toward reengagement of religious leaders with issues of racial justice. For religion to make a difference, three things must be present: (1) an understanding of the implications of basic religious views for the goals of racial policy; (2) an understanding of the nature of racial problems and their possible solutions; and (3) an understanding of the link between religious values and policy choices, probably mediated by church leaders putting the issues before their congregations. This book is mostly about the first step and about the efforts of some groups of religion-based activists to find answers to the two remaining questions in their local circumstances.

STEPS TOWARD A NEW VISION

A first step in giving contemporary meaning to the sin of racism is to translate it into contemporary settings and to change its name to discrimination, defined as knowingly taking actions that are virtually certain to have negative racial consequences. Racism refers to a belief that people are inherently different because of their skin color and that it is legitimate to treat people differently on the basis of their race. Since there is no scientific basis for relevant intrinsic differences related to skin color, racism, and the discrimination based on it, is often illegal and is widely seen as a sin.

This principle is easy to apply when someone denies another person a job or a house on the basis of race alone or harasses him when he asks for a legal right guaranteed to all. Recent studies show the persistence of employment and housing discrimination, in which people reporting the same qualifications are treated differently because of their race.[14] There is still a great deal of direct discrimination long after the passage of civil rights laws.

The most common form of contemporary discrimination, however, is more complicated. It arises from a denial of the continuing impact of the history of racism against a group and passive acceptance of institutional practices and policies that intensify or perpetuate the impact of discrimination and unequal opportunity.

In formulating an ethical analysis of contemporary civil rights issues, it will be important for theologians and religious leaders to come to terms with two well-documented realities: the persistence of overt discrimination in some important areas of American life, and practices that, given the existing inequalities among racial groups, perpetuate and intensify those differences. Well-documented examples of current discriminatory practices include:

1. discrimination in selling, renting, and financing housing;

2. racially polarized voting in which substantial shares of the public vote on the basis of the race of the candidate not qualifications;

3. differential treatment of black and Latino students in schools;

4. denial of basic services to immigrant families; and

5. unequal risks of arrest, prosecution, and punishment for minority youth compared to whites engaged in similar offenses.

Practices that perpetuate or even intensify the consequences of previous discrimination are much more common and tend to go unnoticed. Many institutional practices have powerful racial consequences. Suppose, for example, in a community where blacks have always had inferior schools and have been systematically shut out of white neighborhoods that the school board consistently decides to build its best new schools, and to assign its best teachers to them, in outlying new all-white suburban neighborhoods, while allowing older schools in poorer neighborhoods to decay. This pattern is, in fact, the norm in many communities. The racial results are usually never assessed, and the decisions appear to be a legitimate response to the need for new schools for growing communities. Consider, also, the realities of the housing market. Because of the previous history of discrimination, many black families lack the knowledge and the resources to buy into the white housing market. As a result, the best schools are reserved for the children on the richest periphery of suburban development. Ignoring the racial impact of such decisions has much the same effect as making a decision to help perpetuate racial inequality. Before this can be seen as a sin or as a target for policy change, it has to be recognized and identified in the community and to be connected to values.

Since the Reagan administration we have also been rapidly moving to abandon the civil rights policies formulated in the 1960s.[15] The conservative courts are cutting back on affirmative action, voting rights, school desegregation, college access, and other policies. Increasingly, they reject the basic premise that reforms need explicit racial goals, that discrimination had such deep impacts that merely opening the door of opportunity would not produce significant change. If it turns out that the conservative assumptions are wrong and inequality grows, the new policies may severely intensify existing inequalities.

Since it is not the goal of this book to solve policy arguments, I will illustrate the challenge with a set of "what if" statements that address the kind of issues that must be confronted in considering the relationship between social conditions and values.

1. What if there are massive public subsidies that help to create all-white affluent suburbs, and then policies requiring those communities to provide some affordable housing are canceled?

2. Voting rights policies promoted unprecedented levels of minority representation. What if political power is severely curtailed by reversal of those policies?

3. What if minority students do substantially better in getting ready for college in integrated schools, but school officials send them back

to inferior segregated schools, where they do much worse? And what if college entrance requirements are raised while affirmative action is abandoned at the same time?

4. What if the best research suggests that welfare mothers want to leave welfare but need training, health care, and day care and that minority families will be disproportionately hurt by the lack of jobs and support systems in their communities when welfare deadlines are reached without needed support systems?

If these things are true, what are the implications of the basic beliefs outlined by our theologians for public policy discussions? The larger question is the following: Given that we have a history of inequality based on discrimination, genuinely equal opportunity has not yet been achieved, and we know policies that can help, do we have a responsibility to support those policies? Is it moral to accept what are presented as racially neutral policies when they have the demonstrable effect of perpetuating or even intensifying racial inequalities? Should we passively accept the decisions of conservative courts limiting civil rights, or do we have a responsibility to criticize them on moral grounds as, for example, the conservative Christians have criticized the abortion and school prayer decisions and as Abraham Lincoln assailed the Dred Scott decision upholding slavery? What about decisions denying the rights of Indian tribes or immigrants? These are hard issues, both factually and spiritually, and they pose difficult institutional and political choices. But they are the kinds of issues that a serious examination of current racial patterns will bring to the forefront.

THE FUTURE OF CIVIL RIGHTS: POSSIBLE ROLES OF RELIGION

There was a clear recognition in the papers and discussions leading to this book that religion is not some kind of flexible, vague, progressive thing that can be used for political purposes unrelated to the spiritual activities of churches. Churches must not be treated like political precincts. This was a mistake of some activists in the 1960s, and it may well be a serious mistake of some of the conservative religious coalitions now. If they are detached from their own traditions and from their members' spiritual needs, churches cannot succeed. When some religious leaders became civil rights leaders and adopted policies that did not have an authentic link with their traditions, religious participation in civil rights came under bitter attack.

It was very clear in the conversations at our conference that religious thinkers and leaders today think much more about the possibility of entering coalitions and movements within their own traditions that are closely linked with their church. They see their churches as institutions that must challenge injustice in the world, even if in little ways.

In recent times there have been some racial issues where the moral dimensions seemed clear. When black churches in the South were burned, the situation was unambiguous. For many churches, the immorality of South African apartheid was patently clear, and it was not difficult to support sanctions to force dramatic change. But the issue of metropolitan apartheid built on residential discrimination in most of America's great urban communities usually receives little or no attention in most congregations.

Large numbers of Americans contribute to causes in other lands that help provide things to children that their families cannot afford. Many helped settle refugees. Yet, at the same time, many of the same people vote for representatives who cut programs providing food, shelter, and other basic necessities to large numbers of poor children living a few miles away in inner-city ghettos and barrios. They see the children of the Third World as deserving a better chance but cannot extend that vision to the children in our own Third World. This myopia is a failure of spiritual imagination, of the ability to put ourselves in others' shoes, to see people from other races as our sisters and brothers, to examine our responsibility to share our harvest with those who need. A new vision is needed.

Obviously, it would be unrealistic to expect theologians to offer any specific answers about college admissions, or how to fairly draw election districts to increase minority representation, or how to decide what kind of a school tracking program is racially fair. Any answer to a complex problem must come out of a consideration of both the values that the policy is supposed to promote and the factual relationships that must be understood to figure out how to realize those values in a complex setting. But if the problem is to be recognized, if it is to be given priority, and if there is going to be a political will to answer those difficult questions, the contribution of strongly held values can be extremely important.

The next step will be much harder. Suppose one starts with a widely shared value—it is wrong to deny opportunity to an entire group of people because of their skin color. This belief may be based on a religious conviction—everyone is a child of God and is equal before God—while it also relates to our legal value of equal justice under law.

Then try, however, to apply those values to a problem like metropolitan housing discrimination by real estate salesmen, rental agents, and mortgage lenders. Since survey data show that few minority families actually prefer to live in segregated areas, and research shows that even blacks with high incomes are highly segregated, and that segregated neighborhoods offer inferior education and fewer jobs, you have a set of difficult moral, legal, and policy issues. By showing that housing segregation is linked to inferior education, diminished wealth from gains in housing values, less access to good jobs, less safety, etc., this issue takes on moral importance. Religious people holding the value of equal justice might then face these moral choices: (1) What should I do myself if I am a participant in one of the institutions with practices that work against minority housing opportunity? (2) What should my fellow believers, religious organizations, and my church do? (3) Should I raise the issue? (4) What public policies need to be changed?

This suggests the many ways in which a relatively simple basic value can interact with social facts to produce new questions and new challenges. One of the important questions for organized religion is to what extent it should raise such issues and become involved in their solution. Beyond that are the questions of what are the limits on what a church can do without threatening other parts of its religious mission and how it can best foster justice authentically within its particular tradition. Obviously, the answers differ depending on the structure of the church, the presence or absence of social elements in its theology, who its members are, how much risk the leaders are willing to take, and whether or not the church community itself is directly implicated in or affected by the racial problem.

THE CHALLENGE OF BRINGING BELIEFS INTO A DISINTERESTED WORLD

Seeing these papers develop and witnessing the intense interest in our conference and ongoing discussions was extremely exciting. It validates our belief that there are great resources for civil rights work in our religious traditions. What is lacking is a framework for political dialogue to support this effort. That may be why most of the energy that has surfaced so far in recent years is focused on limited local efforts.

In a way, though, the responsibilities of religious leaders are greater today than in the past. The decline of respect for political leaders and public institutions means that the institutions that retain legitimacy have even more responsibility for raising the sensitive but fundamental questions about our common future.

We have no Dr. King and thus will have to find our own language to work in a society that has grown more complex. Clarity about values is essential. If religion is to play an appropriate role again in helping address some of our fundamental dilemmas, it must be informed rather than paralyzed by past problems and armed with the best available information on the social realities. Religious leaders must be clear about the values they are pursuing, since they will be pushed in many ways by pressures from various groups and political forces. Part of the price of adhering to principle is being willing to stick to that principle when the situation changes and the policy becomes unpopular. If religion matters enough to engage opponents on the grounds of principle, it matters enough to be willing to be unpopular and attacked by friends who shy from confrontation. Religious leaders can function effectively as religious leaders only when they continue to act within their religious traditions.

WHERE DO WE GO FROM HERE?

This book is not a manifesto for a program of action. Its essays are a manifesto for serious thought. It is a powerful reminder that some of the most fundamental values of our religious traditions raise serious questions about some of the most basic structures of our society. Glaring inequalities and social polarization, apparent immediately to outsiders visiting the United States, are so taken for granted that they become virtually invisible and virtually unmentioned in public life. Viewing them in the light of our religious values makes them visible and raises many disturbing questions.

We must remember that the only two movements in U.S. history to profoundly change racial injustice, the abolitionist movement and the civil rights movement, had very deep religious roots. So did protest movements of the Chicano community. Churches exist, in good measure, to challenge people to think about things that are uncomfortable and difficult but that must be grasped if we are to have a good life and a good society. Racial injustice is one of those things. Our society has been flawed by it from its founding, and we are far from resolving the effects on our communities. After a generation of erosion of the promise of the civil rights revolution and deepening multiracial polarization, it is important to reactivate the dialogue between our faith and civil rights communities that helped change the country a third of a century ago.

This book is a promising beginning. It opens the ground for a searching encounter between theologians, church leaders, those who know about the racial facts of our society, and the activists, lawyers, and government officials who are trying to address the continuing and changing forms of racial and ethnic injustice.

As society becomes more multiracial, inequalities of race and class deepen, separation intensifies, and fragmentation becomes manifest, it is important to reflect on these issues again and again. The essays in this book and the stories of the activists who struggle for racial justice growing out of their religious values are an important step in that direction. There must be more.

PART I

THE CIVIL RIGHTS TRADITION: THE 1960s MOVEMENT AND TODAY'S REALITIES

When Reverend Sylvester Laudermill first became the pastor of St. Peter's African Methodist Episcopal Church (AME) in St. Louis, Missouri, two members approached him about a problem in the community. Postal services were being stopped in this poor area on the north side of St. Louis, and there was little transportation to get people to the next closest post office. Laudermill, a new resident of St. Louis, also discovered that the area he was living in and serving had only one supermarket, no small businesses, and no sit-down restaurants.

After successfully leading an effort to keep the postal services, Laudermill became president of a congregation-based and community-centered organization, Congregations Allied for Community Improvement. This organization is made up of about twenty congregations on the north side of St. Louis. When the organization began to research and explore the history of the community, they brought in policymakers and demographers to look at statistics of the inner city. Laudermill explains, "We were agitated, knowing that soup kitchens, food pantries, and shelters were not solutions for the long term; we needed a structure, that was not random, or arbitrary, but that was organized, thoughtful and deliberate, and rooted in faith."

Laudermill has been affiliated with AME all of his life, but it was not until his early twenties that he began to feel that religion was more than just traditions and faith. Now, as a leader in his denomination, he finds that he preaches less about heaven and the hereafter and more about how to live day-by-day. His congregants may have looked or acted as though everything in their lives was under control, when in fact there were many problems that the church was not addressing. Today, as pastor of a black congregation in the inner city, he has built a platform on which he provides leadership, opinion, and direction on many civic issues and community concerns. His congregation expects him to be more than just a spiritual leader.

Laudermill asserts, "We must admit that the worship hour is the most segregated time in American life, but this segregation is not only by race, it is also by class and belief; and that this is a result of many systems that for a long time have, and continue to, separated us." With the help of the Gamaliel Foundation, Laudermill's organization joined two other sister organizations and formed the Metropolitan Congregations United for St. Louis, of which Laudermill is president. The organization now makes up over sixty congregations throughout the north and south sides, and also the county of St. Louis.

Laudermill has been deeply involved in organizing efforts to renew the St. Louis inner city. Teaming up with the St. Louis Reinvestment

Corporation, he helped form a group whose goal is to assist people, through low-interest home loans and small-business loans, to stay in the inner city. Laudermill's activism has always been rooted in faith. He explains: "In looking at Jesus we see that he didn't just spend time in the Temple, but among the people, calling for justice and naming systems that oppress people." Thus Laudermill believes that the organizing table cannot consist only of congregations or faith-based groups. He has widened his organizing net to include partnerships with environmental and other community improvement organizations.

Laudermill argues that his efforts are about the "racial and economic disparities that cause there to be no development in the inner city except for stadiums, concert halls, and malls; our efforts are about affordable housing, tax revenue sharing, and putting a halt to white flight." In reflecting on the church's role, Laudermill feels grateful that churches have remained in the inner city and have hung on to their communities. "Seventy percent of my congregation resides outside of the inner city, but still come back to worship and support the church, and its efforts in the community."

Laudermill believes that there are many issues that we must attack to eradicate segregation, two of them being urban sprawl and the increasing concentration of poverty. In Laudermill's words: "The churches have been and continue to be the foundation of communities. Metropolitan Congregations United for St. Louis has not yet arrived, and we have just put the key in the door in an attempt to place on the agenda of civil rights the simple question: How can we live together?"

In Boston, Leonard Zakim, executive director of the Anti-Defamation League (ADL), explains, "People in the civil rights community know each other and have been intentional about knowing each other." A few years ago, when minority students were attacked at South Boston High School, a group of religious leaders from the Catholic, Protestant, and Jewish communities, as well as from other faiths, came together to speak out against the violence and discrimination. What made such an action so novel is the fact that Jews were speaking out, not just against anti-Semitism, but against racism and violence directed at blacks and Asians, and that Asians and blacks were speaking out against anti-Semitism and other forms of bigotry. The fact that religious groups were focused not just on their individual parochial interests attracted the attention of the media and of key policy and school leaders, leading to the initiation of changes at South Boston High School.

Leonard Zakim has been organizing in the Boston area for over twenty years. He grew up in a town with very few Jews, and there was a good deal of anti-Semitism, both on a personal and political level. He explains, "In the Jewish tradition we are told never to separate your self from the community, and we haven't done enough in this country to build bridges between people of the same community and other communities— neither happens by itself." Zakim has always been an organizer. In high school he organized around dress codes and behavior codes; in college he lobbied against housing and racial discrimination; as a law student and upon completion of law school, he provided legal services in a predominantly minority and low-income community in the city of Boston.

Always interested in civil rights, Zakim recalls being aware of Dr. King and his work even before he fully knew about the tragedy of the Holocaust. He began to learn more about the social justice aspect of Judaism, the teachings of the prophet Isaiah, and the historical status of the Jewish people. Today Zakim finds spiritual comfort in the Scriptures, in particular the Prophets. While he believes very strongly in the separation of church and state, he fears the building and maintenance of a wall can be an obstacle between individuals and spirituality. He finds the secular message of social justice, which is central to Judaism, very provocative, explaining, "There are many Jews who are active in pursuing civil rights and social justice, but [they] are not necessarily religious or devout, yet that very same secular message is rooted in the Scriptures and in the Torah. There is this belief among many Jews that if there is a threat to any minority group then it's a threat to all of us, history has taught us that connection is strong."

Zakim believes that religion and religious institutions must find a way to make "civil rights, in a sense, a theology unto itself." He argues, "This theology of activism, of 'repairing the world,' should know no boundaries with respect to race, religion, ethnicity, or sexual preference; it should be the theology of the common deed."

A year ago in Massachusetts two Catholic racetrack workers were fired for refusing to work on Christmas. The owner of the racetrack was a noted philanthropist in his particular religious tradition. The workers approached the ADL, and Zakim helped organize the Jewish community and others as an inter-religious coalition representing the workers.

This organizing effort led to a court decision and new legislation on religious freedom. Moreover, people representing different racial, religious, and ethnic groups came together to discuss common problems of religious freedom. For Zakim, the episode reaffirmed his belief that organizing becomes a powerful tool when religious or racial groups stand up not just for themselves but also for others, and with others, over specific issues or about common injustices that cross racial and religious lines. Such coalitions are no longer just an option, they are the best way to proceed. "People committed to the movement have to rethink what needs to be done. If ADL's mandate is to combat bigotry, then I want to mobilize and collaborate with any organization that has the same goals. For example, the ADL has established a hate-crime hotline which it operates in collaboration with Protestant churches across the state."

Zakim also believes that organizing and outreach has to be community-based, working from neighborhood to neighborhood. He fears civil rights organizing today has become too much of an intellectual discussion and not enough of an activist challenge. For younger people, he explains, it's more of a discussion of "us versus them" and less about changing America and holding it accountable to fulfill its promise of equality. "It is not enough to concentrate on political lobbying, we have to mobilize public opinion, and we have to be intentional about challenging people personally, in the same way that we have to be intentional about finding a diverse school for our kids. Dr. King was intentional and his success was a direct result of this strategy. Today, the goals may still be the same, but the strategy is gone. We have to make civil rights relevant to people today, it's got to become personal again."

Zakim describes, "When there's division between religious groups there are headlines, when we work together it doesn't get covered. Sustained interest in the work is also hard; how can you get people to work in the absence of a hate crime or a crisis? Crisis intervention will draw thousands, but the ongoing day-to-day collaboration is harder, it requires patience and determination."

Zakim believes that the majority of people never really translate their religious faith into action. "We have both the best and the worst within our religious traditions, and therefore you have to choose what you want to do, you have to be intentional about this, you have to choose to be an ally."

He goes on to explain, "Translating prayers into action is a two-thousand-year-old problem—Isaiah would talk to people who were fasting and ask why are you fasting, God would want you to be feeding the hungry." In explaining how Judaism fits into this concept of religious action, Zakim refers to Rabbi Abraham Joshua Heschel. "Heschel told us that Judaism is not the theology of the word, it's about the theology of the deed, and therefore we have to be judged and measured by what we're willing to translate. We have to look within ourselves to see if the prayers we say match with our actions."

CHAPTER ONE

Another Day's Journey:
Faith Communities Renewing American Democracy

ROBERT M. FRANKLIN

As a concession to a culture profoundly shaped by televised images, I invite you to consider my nomination for the nation's most significant icon depicting religion as a positive force in securing civil and human rights. It is the familiar portrait of Dr. Martin Luther King, Jr., delivering his "I Have a Dream" oration from the steps of the Lincoln Memorial. The image is so familiar that we may fail to grasp its extraordinary, multidimensional character. The black Baptist preacher standing at the foot of the monument to the emancipator is a stunning, riveting symbol suggestive of many values and issues that interest those of us who think about religion and civil rights.

For instance, in the portrait one encounters religion restraining its sectarian energies and harnessing them in the service of public order. Also, one sees a representative of a particular, Christian view of human nature and destiny standing in solidarity with other faith traditions. And one perceives in the King/Lincoln juxtaposition the graceful and mysterious power of religious faith to transform imperfect human beings into courageous exemplars of moral citizenship.

In that 1963 portrait, Lincoln is but a figure carved in marble, his complexity and contradictions concealed in cold stone. Before the stone stood a vibrant incarnation of the indomitable African-American spirit of authentic freedom. Recall the manner in which King began the famous speech: "Fivescore years ago, a great American, in whose symbolic shadow we stand today, signed the Emancipation Proclamation. This momentous decree came as a great beacon light of hope to millions of Negro slaves who had been seared in the flames of withering injustice. It came as a joyous daybreak to end the long night of their captivity. But one hundred years later, the Negro still is not free. . . ."[1] With those words, King paid respect to one of the nation's sacred ancestors, underscored the rude fact that Lincoln's agenda was unfinished, and positioned himself as a moral successor to the slain president.

Also in that extraordinary speech, King drew upon the two major philosophical traditions that have shaped the American culture and character: the covenant tradition based upon biblical notions of American exceptionalism; and the Enlightenment tradition of Immanuel Kant, John Locke, Thomas Jefferson, and others who asserted the inviolable rights of the individual. No one was more skilled than King at interweaving the great and noble ideas from varying intellectual traditions.

Recall his words that day as he placed his dream in the context of the hard work that lay before his listeners. "Even though we must face the difficulties of today and tomorrow, I still have a dream. It is a dream deeply rooted in the American dream that one day this nation will rise up and live out the true meaning of its creed—we hold these truths to be self-evident, that all men are created equal."[2] King believed that a dream inspired by references to particular biblical sources could live in dialectical and fruitful tension with ideals embraced by nontheistic rationalists. "I have a dream that one day every valley shall be exalted, every hill and mountain shall be made low, the rough places shall be made plain, and the crooked places shall be made straight and the glory of the Lord will be revealed and all flesh shall see it together."[3]

King did not merely search for common ground, he sought to create it out of the stuff of living traditions. In so doing, he was able to use theology and ethics as resources for renewing American public life. He used theology to prompt people to vote, to run for office, and to be concerned about the moral state of the society. A person who seeks to create common ground, build traditions, craft narratives, and negotiate coalitions exemplifies a quality of character that moral education should seek to inculcate.

We should also acknowledge that using theology and ethics as resources for renewing public life can have unforeseen negative consequences. For instance, many religious people who regard the concept of grace as central and significant to their faith may construe it to mean that they are acceptable to God despite their admitted racist behavior and attitudes, or their indifference to racial justice. Some people suggest that America in the post-civil rights movement era has come a long way through hard work and heroic effort, and that to push further might be counterproductive. We should now focus on celebrating our progress rather than rousing bitter feelings by advocating additional progress. Grace, thereby, becomes a psychological mechanism that absolves responsibility for the contemporary condition of race relations and civil rights. This is the double edge of grace. Ironically, the theological shift from "salvation by works" to "salvation by grace" encourages complacency with the racial status quo. King understood, clearly, that the Bible and theological concepts could be misappropriated to justify social evil and felt that an important check upon this tendency would involve keeping the Bible and human reason in mutually critical dialogue.

In the pages that follow, I will provide: (1) a brief sketch of the character of black church culture that illustrates how a marginalized and particular religious tradition helped to renew democracy during the modern civil rights movement; (2) an analysis of King's concept of the "beloved community" as an ethical norm that should be used to critique, guide, and inspire public policy and individual behavior; and (3) a brief overview of the heroic role that faith communities are now playing to promote a more just society.

THE REVOLUTION LED BY PREACHERS, CHURCH WOMEN, AND SUNDAY SCHOOL CHILDREN

In order to understand Dr. King's journey from Atlanta to the steps of the Lincoln Memorial in 1963, we need to understand something about the culture that produced him, and, thereby, revisit the ways in which culture is a vehicle of moral education. Paul Tillich said that culture is the form of religion, and religion is the substance of culture. If these claims are true, what system of values is available to children being reared in neighborhoods that are scarred by violent crime, adult joblessness, multigenerational dependence, aimlessness, disease, hopelessness, and wretched schools?

King's biographers all note that the black church and family were the context in which the boy King learned something about racism, poverty, and religion as a resource for mobilizing social change. James Cone has gone further, noting that the culture of the black church included theological concepts that played a critical role in shaping King's worldview and moral compass. These included notions of human freedom, social justice, black self-love, and collective power.

Historians such as Albert Raboeau (Princeton), the late James Melvin Washington (Union), and Evelyn Brooks Higginbotham (Harvard) have noted that black church culture is an amalgam of numerous symbolic and ritual traditions, including African traditional religions (ATR), Catholic popular piety, Protestant evangelicalism, and Islam. This collection of religious traditions infused the core practices of progressive African-American Christianity that produced King.

These core practices include the following:

1. A multisensory worship experience in which all of a human being's capacity to respond to God is engaged. Worship is conceived to be a sacred drama, a dance with the gods. Hence, drums are present to orchestrate the antiphonal call and response between the people and the deity. Colorful choir robes and clergy vestments provide visual stimulation. Brass horns, electric guitars, tambourines, and clapping hands electrify the air with sound. Usually, the church kitchen is in operation, sending aromas of soul food wafting throughout the neighborhood. And, this sacred space is animated by lots of touching, hugging, holy kissing, and high-five greetings that bridge the social distance that is common in secular gatherings.

2. Intimate communal prayer, when led by a skilled leader, succeeds in weaving lonely personal concerns into a community of pain, struggle, reconciliation, and hope. Worshippers who approach the altar as separate individuals experience a transformation that sends them away as members of the body of Christ.

3. Choirs give triumphant voice to the church's confidence that it will not be vanquished by evil in the world. Triumphal songs are situationally rational and appropriate if those who sing them regard themselves as warriors in the midst of a great and bloody conflict between good and evil.

4. Prophetic preaching in the black church tradition is the focal point of worship. It is the high, holy moment in the liturgical drama. The brilliant historian of religion, Mircea Eliade, has observed that "for people in traditional societies, religion is a means of extending the world spatially upward so that communication with the other world becomes ritually possible, and extending it temporally backward so that the paradigmatic acts of the gods and mythical ancestors can be continually reenacted and indefinitely recoverable."[4] Eliade helps to illumine

the genius of black preaching as he reminds us that words can be deployed to mediate an encounter with the holy. Words can usher the imagination into a transcendent realm where one may be empowered to give one's life on behalf of a noble cause. The black preacher, through the virtuosity of imaginative, narrative, lyrical, and poetic language and the co-creativity of a responsive congregation, unites the sacred and the human realms. Stated briefly, the entire liturgical culture of progressive black churches nurtures political sensibilities. These are the congregations that shape moral character and teach people to care about the moral condition of the society.

The biblical scholar Walter Bruggemann offers a cogent observation about such transformative liturgy: "Every act of a minister who could be prophetic is part of a way of evoking, forming, and reforming an alternative community. This applies to every facet and every practice of ministry. It is a measure of our enculturation that the various acts of ministry (for example, counseling, administration, even liturgy) have taken on lives and functions of their own rather than being seen as elements of the one prophetic ministry of formation and reformation of alternative community."[5]

Bruggemann's comment about "alternative community" reminds us again of King's dream narrative, and the fact that it was crafted in the genre of a sermon rather than as an essay, philosophical argument, or lecture. King and his counterparts were products of a liturgical culture that cultivated the capacity to engage in utopian discourse and to act boldly to achieve moral causes.

I shall have more to say about utopian discourse, black Christian preaching, and political theology when we consider King's notion of the beloved community.

CONGREGATIONAL CULTURE AUTHORIZES A VARIETY OF POLITICAL RESPONSES

We should note briefly that blacks reared in the congregational context that I have described here, and on which I elaborate in my book, *Another Day's Journey: Black Churches Confronting the American Crisis* (Fortress Press, 1997), opted for a variety of political responses rather than simply the one embraced by King. I have characterized five major responses. They include the pragmatic accommodationists who cooperate with the political and economic status quo in the interest of maintaining social order. In that context, they believe that they can maximize their acquisition of goods. This was the political agenda of Booker T. Washington and the National Baptist Convention leader, Dr. Joseph H. Jackson. Accommodationists tend to embrace a theology of creation that emphasizes abundance in the natural order. A second response is that of the prophetic radicals who challenge the system to improve the life prospects of marginalized people. This was the orientation of W. E. B. Du Bois and Dr. King. Radicals tend to develop a theology of liberation and a view of God as an ally of oppressed people.

A third response could be characterized as redemptive nationalism, aimed at avoiding the conventional power structure in order to create a separate, ethnically pure order. This was the social vision of Marcus Garvey and of the young Malcolm X and Nation of Islam. Nationalists work from a theology of redemption in which God seeks to restore and redeem the halcyon days of the past, when ethnic kingdoms were distinct and uncontaminated by diversity. The fourth response is characterized as grassroots revivalism, which condemns and avoids the political systems of this world and focuses instead upon individual salvation and moral reform. This agenda was advanced by William J. Seymour, the father of black Pentecostalism. In this theological arena, God is working to save individuals by transforming them one by one. Faith does not have social consequences. Finally, the fifth response is positive thought materialism, which is indifferent to social justice and concerned primarily with opportunities to maximize individual health, wealth, and success. This is spirituality for the upwardly mobile classes who lack a social conscience. This is the outlook of Reverend "Ike," the New York religious showman, an outlook that may lack a full-blown example earlier in black history. Materialists work from a theology of prosperity in which God is a provider of material bounty.

This typology of political theologies should serve to remind us that black church culture is not a monolith, that it fosters and celebrates diversity. I am simply making the point that a variety of political responses emerged from the ecology of black worship culture. Those responses produced a variety of theological reflections upon the nature of the state, political objectives such as voting, citizenship, and running for office, and the relationship between religious and civil obligations.

THE UNDERSIDE OF AMERICAN CHRISTIANITY

It is perplexing to consider that Christianity has had two thousand years to eradicate the multiple and overlapping forms of oppression based upon ethnicity, race, creed, culture, region, class, and gender, but has failed to do so. Why is this the case? And, more to the point of our dis-cussion, why haven't Protestantism and Catholicism succeeded in can-celing the power and grip of racism on the minds and behavior of the masses of their adherents? Is this a theological crisis? Does the tradition possess the resources to address racism in a compelling manner? Is it a human and cultural crisis that represents, yet again, the depths and vari-ety of sinful human nature? King framed it poignantly when he noted the following in his "Letter from a Birmingham Jail":

> I have traveled the length and breadth of Alabama, Mississippi, and all the other southern states. On sweltering summer days and crisp autumn mornings I have looked at her beautiful churches with their lofty spires pointing heavenward. I have beheld the im-pressive outlay of her massive religious education buildings. Over and over again I have found myself asking: "What kind of people worship here? Who is their God? Where were their voices when the lips of Governor Barnett dripped with words of interposition and nullification? Where were they when Governor Wallace gave the clarion call for defiance and hatred? Where were their voices of support when tired, bruised, and weary Negro men and women decided to rise from the dark dungeons of complacency to the bright hills of creative protest?"[6]

Although prophetic religion should hold the state accountable for the moral exercise of power, when religion goes astray who can call it back to its foundation? This is where King's methodological and symbolic eclecticism in drawing up various traditions proved valuable. The biblical and the Enlightenment traditions could critique and correct each other.

Returning to my earlier comments about King's preaching as an in-stance of utopian discourse, I would like to briefly discuss the central thrust of King's political theology.

THE BELOVED COMMUNITY AS A POLITICAL AND ETHICAL NORM

Moral philosopher and former Clinton domestic policy adviser William Galston has noted that "utopian thought is the political branch of moral philosophy" and that "among its many functions it guides our deliberation in devising courses of action, justifies our actions so that the grounds of action are reasons that others ought to accept, and serves as the basis for the evaluation of existing institutions and practices."[7] Utopian discourse becomes moral discourse as it seeks to guide action. It enables us to "imaginatively reconcile and transmute" the "contradictions of experience."

In his final book, *Where Do We Go From Here: Chaos or Community?*, King noted that the "good and just society is neither the thesis of capitalism nor the antithesis of Communism, but a socially conscious democracy which reconciles the truths of individualism and collectivism."[8] He characterized his political philosophy with the term "democratic socialism." In his November 1966 Gandhi Memorial Lecture at Howard University, he said, "Public accommodations did not cost the nation anything; the right to vote did not cost the nation anything. Now we are grappling with basic class issues between the privileged and underprivileged. In order to solve this problem, not only will it mean the restructuring of American society but it will cost the nation something. . . ."[9]

King had always been attentive to the economic dimensions of authentic liberation. At the end of his life, his public ministry focused upon the nation's moral obligation to improve the economic plight of the least advantaged members of the community. When he was killed in Memphis, King was working on behalf of sanitation workers, and he was headed back to Washington, D.C., to lead a national "Poor People's Campaign." Had he lived, there would have been another great speech and another iconic photograph to juxtapose with the 1963 image.

FAITH COMMUNITIES IN PURSUIT OF THE BELOVED COMMUNITY

Today, many of the nation's 320,000 communities of faith are stepping up to tackle Dr. King's unfinished agenda. This includes the more than 70,000 African-American congregations that were part of the coalition of conscience that sustained the Civil Rights Movement and expanded democracy. In many distressed neighborhoods, churches are the only indigenous institutions that have significant assets: talented leaders, credibility, track records of service, armies of potential volunteers, physical space, financial resources, and the spiritual resources necessary to sustain courage and hope amidst adversity. Long after other secular nonprofit service agencies disappear for lack of funding, or employers disappear because of the cost of doing business, or government agencies disappear due to devolution, churches are there to pick up the pieces of people's lives, affirming their dignity and feeding bodies and souls.

Congregations provide basic charity, sustained nurture, social services, political advocacy, and comprehensive community development, on behalf of the poor. Congregations and clergy are helping to sustain civil society and resisting the nihilism of which Cornel West speaks.

Faith communities are working to renew American democracy and, as such, have earned a seat at the table of future public/private ventures. The most creative leaders of the black church tradition understand that the future of the beloved community will depend upon expanding our notion of civil rights to include basic economic rights and the fruits of our labor. Churches and clergy are working overtime to become leaders and partners in the community development enterprise.

To ensure that there will be thoughtful religious leaders capable of moving the nation forward, a number of institutions are engaged in exciting and noteworthy projects. Harvard Divinity School's Summer Leadership Institute trains clergy and lay leaders in the art of innovative community economic development. Through a new initiative called "ITC FaithFactor," the Interdenominational Theological Center provides training, technical support, and vision to the vast army of religiously motivated volunteers who reside, work, and worship in and around this nation's most distressed neighborhoods. The "Sojourners" organization has helped to nurture a broad coalition of religious leaders (Call to Renewal) concerned with the moral decay as reflected in the resurgence of racism and other social evils.

Despite these resources and many others, the larger question remains: Can religion provide something unique and significant to the pursuit of a just society? Many of the revolutionaries of the 1960s, tutored by the writings of Karl Marx, answered negatively. Religion was (is) an opiate that enables people to tolerate injustice in pious quietude. Ironically, many black revolutionaries of the period had to admit that it was the black church and prophetic Christianity that were mobilizing people to risk their lives in the pursuit of freedom. Although many found escape and refuge in the church, others felt that authentic biblical religion is inescapably wedded to God's concern for a just social order. In fact, it is impossible to read the Hebrew prophets of the Hebrew Bible (Old Testament) without recognizing that God seems to have a lot to say about how people who enjoy privilege and power should relate to less advantaged people. God does not ignore politics, and politics involves a proactive concern for people with limited options and few material goods.

As religious leaders today have sought to apply this biblical agenda, or what the late theologian John Howard Yoder called "the politics of Jesus," they have felt the frustration of talking about justice, equality, and love in purely theological terms. Our largely secular society has found it possible to ignore such theological appeals, preferring instead the rhetoric of politics and law. Politicians and lawyers often ignore the contentious and fragmented presence of sectarian religious people. And many religious leaders have reconciled themselves to a marginal role in public life and public policy.

However, some ministers and lay people have resisted marginalization. Although some ministers have elected to run for public office—William Gray, Father Robert J. Drinan, Jesse Jackson, among others—and bring religious rhetoric into the public square, the majority have sought to find ways to talk about the biblical political agenda in their local parishes. It is at that level that tough decisions have to be made about what one will and can say in public about the "hard questions" affecting national life.

Frustration with being regarded as "a marginal voice" often encourages clergy to embrace the language of the modern state. Preachers begin to talk like politicians, and while gaining some credibility as political power brokers, in the process they tend to lose the prophetic edge that they can and should bring to the political debate and the process of creating a better society. This is a temptation to which Dr. King never yielded. He consistently employed theological concepts and language to challenge the modern state to be more just and inclusive. He gave opinions on practical and concrete political matters, but only insofar as they were outgrowths of the theological and ethical principles he espoused.

It is humbling, hopeful, and empowering to consider that preachers, church women, and Sunday school children led a revolution in our lifetime. They marched, prayed, voted, and challenged the nation to, in the words of Arthur Schlesinger, Jr., "conform America's political reality to her political rhetoric." They have now passed the baton to us.

In the words of a great rabbi, "the world is equally balanced between good and evil, our next act will tip the scale."

CHAPTER TWO

The Jewish Basis for Social Justice

Reuven Kimelman

The Jewish theological involvement in the civil rights struggles of the 1960s had its most prominent and articulate spokesman in Abraham Joshua Heschel. He played a similar role in most of the ethical passions of the Jews during the 1960s, including the advocacy of the cause of Soviet Jewry, the promotion of the spiritual relevance of the State of Israel, the amelioration of Christian-Jewish relations, and, above all, the forging of a trans-denominational and moral opposition to the war in Vietnam.[1]

Since this year marks the twenty-fifth anniversary of his death, let us consider his contribution to the struggle for civil rights and its contemporary resonance. His perspective was articulated most forcefully on two occasions. The first was the opening address at the National Conference on Religion and Race, in Chicago on January 14, 1963, entitled "Religion and Race." The second occasion was an address presented to the Metropolitan Conference on Religion and Race, February 25, 1964, entitled "The White Man Is on Trial."[2]

In both presentations, Heschel wove together biblical citation and later Jewish material with sources from the American experience. The implication of such interweaving was that Jewish and American ethical ideals, especially when expressed prophetically, can so converge as to reinforce one another.

Typical of his approach of analyzing the contemporary situation through a biblical matrix are his opening remarks at the National Conference on Religion and Race:

At the first conference on religion and race, the main participants were Pharaoh and Moses. Moses' words were: "Thus says
the Lord, the God of Israel, let My people go that they may celebrate a feast to Me." While Pharaoh retorted: "Who is the
Lord, that I should heed this voice and let Israel go? I do not
know the Lord, and moreover I will not let Israel go" (p. 85).

Heschel continued:

The outcome of that summit meeting has not come to an end.
Pharaoh is not ready to capitulate. The exodus began, but is far
from having been completed. In fact, it was easier for the children of Israel to cross the Red Sea than for a Negro to cross certain university campuses.

In one stroke, Heschel placed the issue of religion and race in a biblical context wherein opposition to civil rights is drawn in Pharaonic
hues. The Negro is identified with ancient Israel except that he is faced
with the task of crossing a university campus, a crossing more daunting
than that of the Red Sea. The rhetoric of seeing the present as continuous with the biblical narrative repeats itself in the second essay. There
he also sought to justify the demand for better education, housing, and
employment by claiming that "The Negroes of America behave just like
the children of Israel" (p. 101). Indeed, again using the biblical
metaphor, he says that "It was easier for the children of Israel to cross
the Red Sea than for the civil rights legislation to pass the floor of the
United States Senate" (p. 103).

To return to the first essay, Heschel next cited the words of William
Lloyd Garrison:

I will be as harsh as truth, and as uncompromising as justice.
On this subject [slavery] I do not wish to think, to speak, or to
write with moderation.
    I am in earnest—I will not equivocate—I will not excuse—I
will not retreat a single inch—and I will be heard (p. 85).

With the sanction of the Bible and the uncompromising words of an
abolitionist, the way is paved for Heschel's prophetic critique of racism
as a remnant of slavery.

Heschel's opening salvo is against the title of the conference. "Religion and Race." "How," he asks, "can the two be uttered together?"

After all, "To act in the spirit of religion is to unite what lies apart, to remember that humanity as a whole is God's beloved child." On the other hand, "To act in the spirit of race is to sunder. . . . Is this the way to honor a father: to torture his child?" (p. 86). Racism not only tears apart that which religion unites, it also casts aspersions on the father-hood of God. Indeed, Heschel cites Proverbs 14:31 (p. 97), which says that "He who oppresses a poor man insults his Maker," holding, as he does, that "To be arrogant toward man is to be blasphemous toward God" (p. 93).

For Heschel there can be no religion and racism, only religion or racism. Playing on Deuteronomy 30:19, he declares, "I call heaven and earth to witness against you this day: I have set before you religion and race, life and death, blessing and curse. Choose life" (p. 86). Clearly a religion of life and blessing can have nothing in common with the death and curse of racism.

Not only is racism for Heschel "the maximum of hatred for a minimum of reason," it is also outright blasphemous in its rejection of the biblical idea of humanity:

In several ways man is set apart from all being created in six days. The Bible does not say, God created the plant or the animal; it says, God created different kinds of plants, different kinds of animals (Genesis 1:11–12, 21–25). In striking contrast, it does not say, God created different kinds of man, men of different colors and races; it proclaims, God created one single man. From one single man all men are descended (pp. 86–87).

It follows, according to Heschel, that "The redeeming quality of man lies in his ability to sense his kinship with all men. Yet . . . there are people in our country," he claims, "whose moral sensitivity suffers a blackout when confronted with the black man's predicament. . . . Thus the problem is not only how to do justice to the colored people, it is also how to stop the profanation of God's name by dishonoring the Negro's name" (p. 87).

How, one may ask, are the names of God and of the Negro linked? Simply: Since "God is One, and humanity is one"; defame man and "God's name may be desecrated." (p. 95). "The image of God" means that every human represents God in the way an ambassador represents a country. Thus an affront to man is an affront to God. According to Heschel, human equality is not a factor of his being, but a factor of his relationship to the divine. As he says, "Equality of man is due to God's love and commitment to all men" (p. 94). We are equal because we all are beloved by God. It is precisely such a position that makes Heschel aghast at racism. His moral and theological horror at racism induced him to coin one of his most often-cited expressions—"the monstrosity of inequality" (p. 93).

In addition to seeing racism as blasphemous, Heschel makes a pragmatic moral case. He asserts that "all of humanity has a stake in the liberty of one person [for] what begins as inequality of some inevitably ends up as inequality of all" (p. 87). Accordingly, "we must . . . keep equally in mind the plight of all individuals belonging to a racial, religious, ethnic, or cultural minority. . . . What we need is an NAAAP, a National Association for the Advancement of All People" (p. 87).

Once the situation has been generalized beyond racism, Heschel argues that the problem exceeds that of physical injury or economic privation. Indeed, for him the nub of the problem is "public humiliation," intentional and unintentional. Indeed, in a society permeated by racism, the face of the white man, "instead of radiating the likeness of God, has come to be taken as an image of haughty assumptions" whose "very presence inflict[s] insult."

Let us now turn to some of Heschel's programmatic suggestions. He critiques the following six ways of dealing with a bad conscience (p. 88):

1. We can extenuate our responsibility.
2. We can keep the black out of our sight.
3. We can alleviate our qualms by pointing to the progress made.
4. We can delegate responsibility to the courts.
5. We can silence our conscience by cultivating indifference.
6. We can dedicate our minds to issues of a far more sublime nature.

With regard to (1): Heschel argues that nothing prevents the conscience from growing while simultaneously dissipating a sense of guilt more than by explaining away crime as a product of circumstances. Relativize the crime and you will relativize the conscience. With regard to (2): He mocks those who would avoid transgressing the demand "Love thy neighbor" by preventing the black from being a neighbor. Indeed, he denounces the ghettoization of the Negro in American society as "A partial apartheid" (p. 90) and sees restricted housing as making the Negro "an exile in his own land" (p. 91). With regard to (3): Pointing to the progress made reflects the smugness of the sensitive person who does not personally feel the hurt. When you are not in pain you can afford to be patient, but woe to the man who so preaches to those hurting.

With regard to (4): Heschel argues that letting the courts handle the issue is inadequate. The biblical demand to pursue justice is incumbent upon the individual, not just the professional, and thus "one that cannot be fulfilled vicariously." After all, "Who shall prevent the epidemic of injustice that no court of justice is capable of stopping?" (p. 91). It was precisely of the individual that Isaiah (1:17) demanded: "Seek justice, relieve the oppressed, judge the fatherless, plead for the widow." With regard to (5): Heschel develops the idea that "indifference to evil is as insidious as evil itself" by underscoring that "it is more universal, more contagious, more dangerous. A silent justification, it makes possible an evil erupting as an exception becoming the rule and being in turn accepted" (p. 92). With regard to (6): The focus on more sublime matters is to him irreligious. It is a betrayal of the prophets to argue that "The job of the minister is to lead the souls of men to God, not to bring about confusion by getting tangled up in transitory social problems" (p. 93).

Heschel refuses to exonerate any of us, for "the individual is in some measure conditioned or affected by the public climate of opinion, an individual's crime discloses society's corruption. In a community not indifferent to suffering, uncompromisingly impatient with cruelty and falsehood, racial discrimination would be infrequent rather than common." Thus, in our society, he concludes, "Some are guilty, but all are responsible" (p. 92).

In the second essay, "The White Man Is on Trial," Heschel expatiates on the meaning of equality. He does not consider equality to be the equivalent of conformity:

> Equality must not be equated with enforcement of conformity. The demand for equal dignity must not be confused with a demand for general leveling. Equality is not a mechanical concept. It implies the right to be a conformist as well as the right to be different (p. 106).

He then asks, "What is the meaning of integration?" and answers, "To integrate means to unite, to form into a whole. Integration means fellowship, mutual respect, and concern." He warns, "Let us not reduce the great idea of integration to an empty togetherness. Our vision is not of white and Negro in integrated saloons" (p. 92).

For Heschel, "Integration means relating and adjusting individuals to a society and to a system of values" (p. 107). But to what values of white Americans should the black be integrated? Do we hold up our family values, our moral and spiritual sensitivities? On the contrary, blacks could become the source of the moral regeneration of society:

> The problem is not only what the white man will do for the Negro, but above all the regeneration of the moral vigor of the Negro. Great spiritual resources of the Negro still lie untapped. A new source of spiritual strength will be opened to all of us by the integration of the Negro (p. 105).

Heschel was apprehensive that in the integration of the black, American society would lose exactly what it could learn from them. He asks, "Will it be a gain if the Negro churches, many of which are rich in simplicity of faith, in discipline, and in devotion, will be dissolved and integrated into the sophisticated bourgeois institutions, into churches with a swimming pool?" (p. 107).

He warns against the dilution of their distinctive moral contribution:

> In this hour of spiritual scarcity, dominated as we are by powers of pompous vulgarity, we must hope and pray that the precious spiritual qualities of the Negro people, their deep religious faith, their love of the Bible, their power to pray, their commitment to nonviolence may continue to live on. Integration must not mean liquidation of the treasures of the soul (p. 109).

Indeed, the black man could become the white man's moral hope:

> Mankind lies groaning, afflicted by fear, frustration, and despair. Perhaps it is the will of God that among the Josephs of the future there will be many who have once been slaves and whose skin is dark. The great spiritual resources of the Negroes, their capacity for joy, their quiet nobility, their attachment to the Bible, their power of worship and enthusiasm, may prove a blessing to all mankind (p. 99).

It is this admiration for black morality and spirituality that induces Heschel to lament the failure of white America to realize its redemption through the black:

The tragedy of Pharaoh was the failure to realize that the exodus from slavery could have spelled redemption for both Israel and Egypt. Would that Pharaoh and the Egyptians had joined the Israelites in the desert and together stood at the foot of Sinai! (p. 103).

In these two essays Heschel laid the groundwork for a biblically based Jewish theology of human equality in general and a moral basis for privileging the blacks in the civil rights struggle. In the 1960s, for Heschel as for many Jews and blacks, the parallel between the ancient Israelites and the modern blacks was obvious. Indeed, the 1960s saw the phenomenon of the "black" Passover Seder, where black liberation was celebrated along with Jewish liberation. Both could sing "Let My People Go" with similar gusto and picture King as a revived Moses. Some Jews even argued for preferential treatment for the blacks based on the biblical legislation for freeing Hebrew slaves, namely:

When you set him free, do not let him go empty-handed: Furnish him out of the flock, threshing floor, and vat, with which the Lord Your God has blessed you. Bear in mind that you were slaves in the land of Egypt and the Lord Your God redeemed you; therefore I enjoin this commandment upon you today (Deuteronomy 15:13–15).

As we enter into the twenty-first century, the question is how much of this maintains its resonance in the ears of both African and Jewish Americans. The issue is both moral and cultural. Morally, the question is whether the parallels articulated in the 1960s between Israelites and Negroes still ring true at the turn of the millennium. Culturally, the question is the role of the Bible in contemporary cultural literacy. Much of Heschel's rhetoric was predicated on listeners whose ears rocked to biblical rhythms and whose minds responded to biblical allusion. This allowed him to articulate cogently a doctrine of human equality based on the biblical assumption that we are all created in God's image. Our question is whether such moral alliances forged on the anvil of the Bible can sustain themselves in a culture where biblical memory is ever-receding. If not, we will be left with competing, fractious groups struggling for their self-interest alone.

CHAPTER THREE

The Beloved Community:
An American Search

CHARLES MARSH

There they stand, a band of sisters and brothers lost in ecstasy, arms raised in praise, blinded by the resplendence of the moment, tears pouring down their faces, the uniforms of denim soaked with sweat. You never know what dangers lurk in the Southern summer outside. Their singing has sealed the room against the night. Their energies are focused; their spirits emboldened. Hand-claps, hallelujahs. These are the righteous and the proud, a perfect circle of black and white, the beloved community.

Soon the staff members, organizers, and student volunteers would scatter. Some would seek solace in Africa. Some would head west to San Francisco, or to desert communes, or across the Pacific to Japan, Tibet, India. Others would travel north to work the urban streets, or to the Ivy League, or to free D.C. Some would just go home, "rotate out," it was called. But they would all move on. Only the local people stayed behind, with a new power to vote and be voted for, with new protections under the law, still surrounded by the same old cloud of resentment and hate.

But for one brilliant moment, the impossible happened: blacks and whites locked hands in solidarity across the treacherous centuries and showed America something better than division and clamor. You could see them gathered together in freedom houses and black churches, or on buses and in city parks, or sitting in drugstores with their sights on the promised land. And then, like a lightning flash across the night sky, darkness quickly returned.

INTRODUCTION

Until 1966, the civil rights movement in the South defined its mission as the pursuit of the "beloved community." Martin Luther King, Jr., and the Southern Christian Leadership Conference (proclaiming their mission "To Redeem the Soul of America") understood the goal of political action informed by love as the creation of a new sociality.[1] Herein ethical relations would stand in sharp contrast to those of the prevailing culture shaped by racial and economic privilege. "If I respond to hate with a reciprocal hate," King said, "I do nothing but intensify the cleavage in broken community. I can only close the gap . . . by meeting hate with love."[2] People would be loved "not because we like them, nor because their ways appeal to us, nor even because they possess some type of divine spark. . . . We love every man, because God loves him."[3]

Although such organizations as the Student Nonviolent Coordinating Committee (SNCC) and the Conference on Racial Equality (CORE) have often been described as the secularizing wave of the movement, a clear religious self-understanding had been articulated in one of SNCC's founding documents. In the staff meeting of April 29, 1962, members of the organization had resolved their firm commitment to the creation of "a social order permeated by love and to the spirituality of nonviolence as it grows from the Judeo-Christian tradition."[4] Love was affirmed as the "central motif of nonviolence," the "force by which God binds man to himself and man to man," which "remains loving and forgiving even in the midst of hostility."[5]

There were plenty of SNCC activists whose moral energies were driven by purely humanistic ideals. Still, the progressive, grass-roots organization—and the larger movement itself—was anchored firmly in the language, imagery, and energies of the black church, committed to what John Lewis described as a "circle of trust, a band of sisters and brothers, the beloved community."[6] But after 1966, and despite an impressive slate of civil rights legislation enacted in 1964 and 1965, the vision of the beloved community began to fragment in ways that continue to shape and frustrate the prospects of racial peace and unity in America.

The reasons are complex and disputed. Nonetheless, the factors include an emergent black separatism,[7] the diversion of white student energies toward anti-war activism (and away from racial matters),[8] the burgeoning women's liberation movement,[9] the search for new religious experiences and an alternative consciousness,[10] and the persisting segregation of the Southern white evangelical church.[11] At the end of 1968, Martin Luther King, Jr., was dead. SNCC, having fired all remaining white members the year earlier, was, as historian Clayborne Carson writes, "scattered like seed to the wind after [its] radicalism could no longer find fertile ground in the Southern struggle."[12] The story of the civil rights movement in America concludes with this final period of disintegration and disillusionment.

Yet there is a different story of the "beloved community" that has not been fully told. This story centers around the more modest, yet the more enduring and more focused pursuits in particular contexts of shared confessional or religious beliefs. The story of these initiatives in racial unity (or "reconciliation") reads as a kind of parallel history (though at times an overlapping one) to the story of the American civil rights movement and racial policy of the post-civil rights years. This story includes the activities of the numerous intentional interracial communities and faith-based social justice initiatives created throughout the South and United States in the decades since the civil rights movement of the 1960s.

In my essay, I wish to stimulate discussion of two important facets of the narrative sketched above: first, the theological commitments and religious convictions that sustained the ideal of the beloved community in the 1960s (well illustrated in the rich religious imaginations of such activists as Fannie Lou Hamer and John Lewis), as well as the conditions and causes of its demise; and second, the theological commitments and religious convictions that continue to shape conceptions of racial unity and civic responsibility as demonstrated in the recent flourishing of intentional interracial communities and faith-based social justice initiatives in the United States.[13] The questions raised at the conclusion concern whether the beloved community is best left in the ruins of the late 1960s, an inspiring though quaint reminder of a vanished idealism, or can be reclaimed (along with its accompanying moral and spiritual energies) as an enduring vision for social movements and campaigns. As I see it, sustainable racial unity requires shared contexts of religious beliefs and values. The debate about racial healing in America must reckon with this difficult fact.

INTERRACIALISM IN THE MISSISSIPPI MOVEMENT

In the fall of 1963, the voter registration drive in Mississippi had reached an impasse. "Too little money was coming in," Kay Mills writes, "and too many sharecroppers were out of work."[14] The Student Nonviolent Coordinating Committee had been a presence in the state for two years without making much progress either in voter registration or in stirring the conscience of white America. At the same time, racist violence against both local black people and civil rights workers had surged to a new level of intensity. Beatings and jailings, death threats and murders, church burnings and bombings of freedom houses became all too familiar features of the state's threatening climate. And white terrorists were not the only ones hard at work in the terrifying business of massive resistance. Conservative whites pursued more insidious forms of retaliation, such as withdrawing food and medical supplies from black communities and tightening Jim Crow laws. White supremacy organizations like the Mississippi State Sovereignty Commission and the Citizens' Council (the "uptown Klan" in the words of the Greenville *Delta-Democrat* editor Hodding Carter) were in full force, defending the practices of racial separation with a neurotic vigilance, investigating rumors of interracial sex, monitoring the activities of black leaders and local people, of white liberals—of anyone who seemed unhappy with the Southern "Way of Life."[15] In historian John Dittmer's view, a siege mentality had taken shape that was "so pervasive it encompassed virtually every citizen and institution."[16] The organization named Help, Inc. created by a group of middle-class whites in McComb, Mississippi, developed a network of self-defense groups based in white neighborhoods and purchased high-decibel sonic whistles to alert families to the coming invasion. Inspired by fantasies of Northern black communists descending on Mississippi to desecrate the Magnolia State's sacred traditions, Help, Inc. advised all concerned Mississippians to "keep inside during darkness or during periods of threat . . . know where small children are at all times . . . [and] do not stand by and let your neighbor be assaulted."[17] Further compounding the difficulties of civil rights organizing was the fact that reprisals from extremists and moderates alike went largely unchecked by Justice Department officials. To disconcerted civil rights activists who sought greater federal protection against pervasive harassment and criminal assaults, the FBI repeated the stock phrase like a mantra, "We are an investigative not a law-enforcing agency." "The Old Mississippi seemed to be winning," journalist Kay Mills writes.[18]

Movement organizers began discussing the possibility of a more dramatic form of protest—a tactic that would shake the foundations of the white power structure and direct the national spotlight on Mississippi, "the middle of the iceberg" of Southern segregation as SNCC's Bob Moses put it. In November of 1963, the Council of Federated Organizations (COFO) inaugurated the "Freedom Ballot Campaign," a mock election aimed at empowering black voters and showcasing black

Mississippians' determination to vote without hindrance. At its convention in Jackson, COFO nominated Aaron Henry, the respected Clarksdale pharmacist and state representative of the National Association for the Advancement of Colored People (NAACP), as its gubernatorial candidate and Reverend Ed King, the white Mississippi Methodist minister who served as the chaplain at historically black Tougaloo College, as lieutenant governor. On election day, 83,000 blacks and a few whites cast their ballots for Henry and King. Although the number fell short of COFO's goal of 200,000, the turnout gave credibility to the claim that blacks were ready to move in large numbers to the polls. Mississippi "nigras" were not content after all, as white politicians had been nervously telling the media, their constituents, and themselves.

The strong turnout invigorated the movement like a shot of adrenaline, demonstrating the effectiveness of extensive grass-roots organizing by the various civil rights groups in the state. As activists Lawrence Guyot and Mike Thelwell later concluded, the experience "took the Movement, for the first time, beyond activities affecting a single town, county, municipality, or electoral district, and placed us in the area of state-wide organization."[19] An often contentious relationship between SNCC and the NAACP had even been cast aside for the moment. (SNCC, along with CORE, commonly regarded the NAACP as overly cautious and fearful of direct acts of social protest.)

The strong vote was also a credit to the small cadre of white student volunteers recruited to assist the registration campaign. This inspired Bob Moses, the Harvard-educated philosopher and movement visionary, to discern in the Freedom Vote the outlines of a much more ambitious voter registration initiative—one that would connect local activists with a larger group of student volunteers in a comprehensive civil rights campaign. In partnership with activist lawyer and teacher, Allard Lowenstein, Moses began to think in more detail of the initiative that would be called the "Mississippi Summer Project," later more popularly rendered "Freedom Summer."[20]

Still, there were controversial issues to iron out. Above all, many SNCC staffers raised the question of what would happen to indigenous black activism when white college students, most of whom were financially and educationally privileged, inundated the state eager to save the Negroes. Would it not be difficult to maintain the fragile balance among the various black coalitions with "a bunch of Yalies running around in their Triumphs," as one person worried?[21] Some SNCC members argued that white college students would be reluctant to take orders from local African-American men and women. Did not the invitation to Northern white students only perpetuate the presumption that blacks needed whites to solve their problems? Local activist Willie Peacock tapped into the source of this concern when he explained, "If you bring white people to Mississippi and say, 'Negro, go and vote,' they will say, 'Yassah, we'll go and try to register and vote.'"[22] But when the oppressor tells the oppressed to do something, Peacock said, that's not commitment or movement towards liberation; it is "the same slavery mentality." "I know that's not permanent," he added.

However, John Lewis along with Bob Moses, Fannie Lou Hamer, Victoria Gray Adams, and most of the local black people in the struggle, made the case for a highly visible interracial initiative. And what better place to situate the initiative than in the great state of Mississippi, the solid-most core of Southern segregation, where the commitment to a brutal pigmentocracy was equaled only by a fervent belief in Jesus Christ. You defeat Jim Crow on his own turf, the thinking went, and you would be well on the way to transforming America in the process.[23] The state was in crisis at every level, with nearly 450,000 blacks of voting age living in a constant state of oppression, and with fewer than 7,000 blacks registered to vote in early 1964.[24] Lewis explained the strategy: "We had to find a way to dramatize the crisis and the best way to do this was not only to organize black people, but to bring a large number of young whites to the state, and let people live alongside each other, and in the process, educate not only ourselves and the volunteers, but, perhaps more importantly, the whole nation about Mississippi. It was a very dangerous effort but it was something that had to be done."[25]

For his part, Bob Moses reminded fellow staffers (which included several white women and men) that the one thing SNCC could do for the country that no one else could was "be above the race issue."[26] He said: "I am concerned that we do integrate, because otherwise we'll grow up and have a racist movement. And if the white people don't stand with the Negroes as they go out now, then there will be a danger that after the Negroes get something they'll say, 'Okay, we got this by ourselves.' And the only way you can break that down is to have white people working alongside of you—so then it changes the whole complexion of what you're doing, so it isn't any longer Negro fighting white, it's a question of rational people against irrational people."[27] The civil rights movement needed to display a new social possibility, to seek, as Moses said, a "broader identification, identification with individuals that are going through the same kind of struggle, so that the struggle doesn't remain just a question of racial struggle."[28] Moses also invoked the vision of the beloved community, the ideal of a universal brotherhood and sisterhood of humankind, which Martin Luther King, Jr., had eloquently proclaimed in his recent sermons.[29] Moses' position was principled and philosophical and ultimately persuasive.

The controversy regarding white involvement in SNCC was far from resolved; nonetheless, with the Summer Project fast approaching, organizers agreed to move ahead with an interracial initiative, and Fannie Lou Hamer's axiom became the rule of thumb. "If we're trying to break down this barrier of segregation, we can't segregate ourselves," she said.[30] For many organizers like Hamer, Lewis, and Moses, the Summer Project's interracialism gained acceptance on moral and religious grounds. For others, however, the interracial campaign was justifiable for the pragmatic reason that white volunteers would bring with them "channels of publicity and communication."[31] These privileged students would generate widespread interest, essential for awakening the nation's conscience, and help create a climate conducive to greater federal involvement in the movement.

By April of 1964, SNCC had drafted a proposal that was posted on campus kiosks and bulletin boards throughout the nation. The document announced a program "planned for this summer" and solicited "the massive participation of Americans dedicated to the elimination of racial oppression."[32] Stated like this, the invitation to white student volunteers was no failure of nerve on the part of local blacks, but a cooperative appeal to "the country as a whole, backed by the power and authority of the federal government."[33]

On the first day of the Summer Project, CORE workers Michael Schwerner and James Chaney, along with summer volunteer Andrew Goodman, were murdered by klansmen in Neshoba County. Cleveland Sellers, who had come to Mississippi as a student volunteer with his Howard University roommate Stokely Carmichael and who had accompanied one of the search parties dispatched to Neshoba County after the three men's disappearance, described the summer as his "longest nightmare," living in a constant state of tension, "always stretched like a tight steel wire between the pit of the stomach and the center of the brain."[34] But the summer also proved exhilarating and empowering, and a strategic success, even aside from the defeat of the Mississippi Freedom Democratic Party at the Democratic National Convention in Atlantic City. By the time of the 1968 Democratic National Convention, 42 percent of the black people living in Sunflower County had registered to vote. In other Delta counties like Leflore, Coahoma, and Issaquena, the percentage was even higher. Compared to the early 1960s when only 250 blacks were registered in Leflore County and fewer in Sunflower, the hard work and sacrifices of the summer had translated to "the coming of political age of Black people in Mississippi in a way that had not been seen since Reconstruction," according to political scientist Leslie McLemore.[35]

THE BELOVED COMMUNITY
IN THEOLOGICAL PERSPECTIVE

What role did religious convictions and theological commitments play in sustaining the interracial character of the movement?

Historian Charles Payne, in his absorbing narrative of civil rights organizing in the Mississippi Delta, *I've Got the Light of Freedom,* offers a helpful analysis of the religious character of the mass meetings with lessons applicable to the question. Payne recounts a meeting at Tougaloo College with the electrifying presence of Fannie Lou Hamer at its center.[36] Hamer had taken the pulpit by storm, as was her custom, delivering a testimony of her civil rights life that included a darkly comic description of the harassments she had encountered. The most recent took the form of night visits from policemen and their barking dogs, an occurrence so regular she had grown accustomed to it. "Look like now the dogs help me to get to sleep," she exclaimed.[37] Her thoughts then became more sobering, more evangelistic. People need to be serious about their faith in the Lord, she said.

> It's all too easy to say, "Sure, 'I'm a Christian,'" and talk a big game. But if you are not putting that claim to the test, where the rubber meets the road, then it's time to stop talking about being a Christian. "You can pray until you faint, but if you're not gonna get up and do something, God is not gonna put it in your lap."[38]

Hamer proceeded to survey the wonderfully diverse ways in which movement people were bearing witness to their faith. She told how much the 17th chapter of Acts meant to her, where it is said that "[God] hath made of one blood all nations of men for to dwell on all the face of the earth," that all races are as one in God's sight.[39] She then concluded with the song:

> I'm on my way to the freedom land
> If you don't go, don't hinder me
> I'm on my way, praise God, I'm on my way.[40]

Combining praise and prophetic provocation, Hamer and all those in attendance set their eyes on the freedom land, the conjured resolve of their solidarity leading them onward together.

In Payne's account, the mass meetings looked a lot like church; they followed the familiar rituals of intercessory prayer, music, testifying, prophesying. The Greenwood rallies, for example, would often begin with a benediction by local activist Cleve Jordon, whose riveting prayers were "part-chant, part-song," evoking in the audience "murmuring assent and agreement at the end of every line."[41] "Grounded in the religious traditions and esthetic sensibilities of the Black South,"[42] these movement-services forged a dynamic union of the sacred and profane wherein pulsing soulful music and bold testimonials of the liberating God coalesced in a "kind of litany against fear."[43] The meetings were a "very powerful social ritual," establishing a "context in which individuals created a public face for themselves, which they then had to try to live up to."[44] In this way, Payne concludes, they were not too different from Alcoholics Anonymous or Weight Watchers, from support groups that try to change the behavior of their members "by offering a supportive social environment."[45] As SNCC staff member Jean Wheeler Smith said of the meetings' effect on her own nascent activism, "The religious, the spiritual was like an explosion to me, an emotional explosion. . . . It just lit up my mind."[46]

Payne's helpful analysis may be taken one step further and slightly revised in the process. While faith played an important role in motivating social protest, solidifying a palpable sense of community and camaraderie, Hamer's faith—like that of most of her local sister and brother travelers—was far greater and infinitely more complex than the utility it offered. Hamer helped create a great reservoir of moral energy; experiences of joy, as well as the dark nights of the soul when glad emotions were spent, were sustained by the spiritual energies radiating outward. But there is much more to the meetings' resiliency than psychological empowerment. What is lost in assessments that emphasize utility over content is not only the theological particularities shaping people's visions of the movement, but also the shared religious perception of those very social realities local black people sought to change—indeed that they believed God was working to change!

In Hamer's mind, the black struggle for justice received its inner sense from the language of the Gospel. The imagery of the biblical narrative—both proclaimed and enacted—placed the people's struggle in a familiar and beloved narrative, refocusing the goal of the faith-journey from the life hereafter to the nitty-gritty of the here and now. She said, "We have to realize just how grave the problem is in the United States today, and I think the sixth chapter of Ephesians, the eleventh and twelfth verses helps us to know . . . what it is we are up against. It says, 'Put on the whole armor of God, that we may be able to stand against the wiles of the devil. For we wrestle not against flesh and blood but against principalities, against powers, against the rulers of this world, against spiritual wickedness in high places.' This is what I think about when I think of my own work in the fight for freedom."[47] The meetings were not simply pep-rallies for wearied foot soldiers or "a very powerful social ritual."[48] As one of Hamer's movement colleagues put it, "These meetings were church, and for some who had grown disillusioned with Christian other-worldliness, they were better than church."[49] Only in church could local people apprehend with such intensity both a theological account of society's wrongs and the hope for decisive change; only there were the memories of the past and the promises of the future secured by trust in God.[50]

Fannie Lou Hamer, who had left the cotton fields in 1962 at the age of forty-four to "work for Jesus" in voter registration, liked to describe the civil rights movement—and salvation itself—as a welcoming table, like the kind you might find in the back yard of her home church in Ruleville, where fried chicken and collards and corn bread and blackberry cobbler and all the soulful food of the deep South would be spread out for special dinners or on Homecoming Sundays. And at God's own welcoming table, like Hamer's at the Williams Chapel Baptist Church, everybody was invited to come and eat, even Governor Ross Barnett and Senator James O. Eastland; but they would have to learn some manners real quick! She gave voice to a distinctive Christian discourse, evangelical in the most vigorous sense of the term, a robust and exuberant love of Jesus of Nazareth, of the whole scandalous story of life, death, and resurrection. At the same time— and no doubt because of this—her love was a great big love, reserved for everyone who cared for the weak and the poor.[51]

Throughout her life, Hamer spoke of the experience of the Summer Project as "the beginning of a New Kingdom right here on earth."[52] She compared the student volunteers to the Good Samaritan, reading Jesus' parable as a description of the New Kingdom emerging amidst the scorched summer fields of the Mississippi Delta. Like the self-righteous priest and the Levite in the biblical account who passed by the wounded man without concern for his welfare, Southern white Christians had turned their sights from black suffering—and "never taken the time to see what was going on."[53] But this was not true of the summer volunteers who came to Mississippi. Although strangers like the Samaritan in Jericho, they never hesitated to act with compassion toward people they found hurting and oppressed. "Although they were strangers, they were the best friends we ever met," Hamer said. "This was the beginning of the New Kingdom in Mississippi. To me, if I had to choose today between the church and these young people—and I was brought up in the church and I'm not against the church—I'd choose these young people. They did something in Mississippi that gave us the hope, that we had prayed for so many years. We had wondered if there was anybody human enough to see us as human beings instead of animals. These young people were so Christlike."[54]

The volunteers, often boasting secular ideals of justice, appeared to Hamer as instruments of divine grace and compassion—their naïveté, bookish agnosticism, and habitual patronizing notwithstanding.[55] In her view, their commitment was quite simply a beautiful and holy thing. "If Christ were here today," she said, "he would be just like these young people who the Southerners called radicals and beatniks."[56] In Hamer's keen theological imagination, the radical, beatnik Christ was taking shape in the compassionate service of others in "the beloved community." This far outweighed, in her mind, the contentious matter of whether the students had purged themselves of whatever racial stereotypes continued to distort their self-perceptions and their perceptions of local people. Clearly a rich and complex theological vision is implicit in the generous imagery of the welcoming table, one that illustrates an expansive and embracing sociality grounded in the particular theological commitments of the black church. The hospitality of the welcoming table was particular to a belief in the reconciling God of Jesus Christ, and at the same time generously set, making room for anyone with her or his sights on justice. Was there not a contradiction between these two images—the theological and the civic? Not for Hamer, who displayed a synthetic ingenuity born of experience, as adept as the most sublime philosopher in weaving apparent contradictions into an integrated whole.[57] The two images fit together as naturally as greens and pork.

Consider the way she combined the spiritual, "Go Tell It on The Mountain," with the song, "Go Down Moses":

Paul and Silas was bound in jail, let my people go.
Had no money for to go their bail, let my people go.

Paul and Silas began to shout, let my people go.
Jail doors open and they walked out, let my people go.

Go, tell it on the mountain, over the hills and everywhere.
Go, tell it on the mountain, to let my people go!

Here is Hamer's answer. My sins are forgiven; my life is made new; the angel of death has passed me by, rescuing me from an eternal perishing. Still, much more is at stake than the fate of my individual soul. For since the good news is proclaimed, I can stand up to Pharaoh, look him in the eyes and say, "Let my people go." There is a land beyond Egypt, as Michael Walzer once put it.[58] The song builds momentum until the final verse repeats the phrase, but now no longer as a plea but as a demand of the Gospel, "Let my people go." The Gospel "go tell it" becomes the theological framework for the liberation of people from oppression.[59]

Thus, the death for which Christ has atoned—my death, humanity's death—is also the death of bondage to fear and oppression—a resounding "No" to Jim Crow.[60] And importantly, both deaths, the atoning death of the cross and the death to slavery, can and must be claimed in the here and now. In Hamer's mind, this is what Moses—that is, Bob Moses—had tried to explain when he said, "The thing was not how you're going to die, but how you're going to live."[61] The solitariness of one's own death—of one's own self—is taken up in the historical unfolding of the demand, "Let my people go," a demand that is also a promise, that also gathers up the particularities of our individual stories into the spirit's movement toward freedom. The Good News is this: The core of who we are as men and women is no longer enslaved in the cotton fields of the Mississippi Delta. It is open toward life, free to all, black and white. For Hamer, this is the Good News that gives life to and nourishes the beloved community.

Hamer emerged as the pillar of strength to local people in the struggle. As one of her fellow activists in the Mississippi movement, Annie Devine, said, "Myself with others realized that there is a woman that can do all these things. . . . Why not follow somebody like that? Why not just reach out with one hand and say, just take me along?"[62] Hamer gave eloquent witness to a faith that both liberates and reconciles, shaped by a jazz-like fusing of African-American spirituals, prophetic religion, and an indefatigable belief in Jesus as friend and deliverer of the poor.[63]

RECENT RETRIEVALS
OF THE BELOVED COMMUNITY

Is it too simplistic to say that the beloved community collapsed as its theological vision was abandoned? Clearly, there were many factors involved in the disintegration of interracialism in the final cataclysmic years of the late 1960s, as I mentioned at the outset. Nevertheless, after

1966, reconciliation took a back seat to liberation, though not simply to black liberation, but to the liberation of women, to speech, to the constraints of Western consciousness, and so on. What shall we then do with the beloved community?

There has been some recent bantering in academic conversation about the beloved community and its possible resurgence in civic life, though most of these references appeal to some undefined global awareness or ethical resolve as grounding sources and seem largely deracinated from social experience.[64] Academics must certainly continue to bring the ideal of beloved community to our conversations about race, religion, and the common good. Nevertheless, I would like to point us elsewhere for an example of social activism reminiscent in many important ways of the civil rights struggle.

In the past two decades a fascinating story has unfolded in the inner cities of America. Many white Christians have joined hands with local African-American religious leaders and formed interracial alliances to combat poverty and homelessness and the prevailing spiritual despair. In some cases, African-American pastors and community developers, seeking to initiate racial healing and reconciliation, have invited white Christians to relocate to urban neighborhoods and live in common with poor blacks.[65] In others, white Christians, often living in middle-class suburbs, have sold their homes and moved to black ghettos—apart from any affiliation with black churches—as a way of bearing witness to the reconciling love of God. These alliances, initiatives, and spontaneous stirrings of the spirit have often led to the building of intentional interracial communities and coalitions.

A good example of this new cooperation is the Summerhill Community, Inc., in Atlanta. Set in the neighborhoods east of the site of the 1996 Olympic Stadium, Summerhill is the most ambitious initiative of its type. What distinguishes the project from other exercises in urban renewal are two interconnected goals: first, the intention of the white and black organizers to move to the Summerhill neighborhood and live in common with the community's mostly black residents; and second, the hope of changing not only the physical but also the spiritual environment of the community. The director of the Summerhill project, Douglas Dean, explains, "We have to revitalize the community on the same basis it was started, where churches set the moral principles that made this a place people wanted to live."[66] In fact, the theological vision is as ambitious as its hopes for full-scale economic and social transformation. By modeling the beloved community in a highly visible manner to the city's otherwise segregated religious communities and social worlds,

Summerhill hoped to inspire nothing less than the refiguration of religious, community, and civic life in Atlanta. As organizer Robert Lupton says, "Of all the usual reasons why people select their homes, absent is proximity to racial diversity and where they're needed most. Our motivations clearly grow out of a belief system that says I need to be rightly related to my neighbor."[67] Thus, as the Summerhill planners claim, the only adequate theory of community is one that attends to Jesus' question, "Who is my neighbor?" Summerhill well illustrates the pursuit of the beloved community in a partnership of black and white mainline Protestant churches in the context of massive corporate involvement.

Baltimore's New Song Community is another helpful example, founded in 1986 in the inner-city neighborhood of Sandtown-Winchester. A recent graduate of a Reformed Presbyterian seminary (who had worked as a summer volunteer at Voice of Calvary) and his former Sunday School teachers moved from their suburban homes into low-income rental housing in a neighborhood where unemployment soared above 50 percent, median incomes averaged $8,500 per household, and teenage pregnancy rates were the highest in the country. The ruinous streets and abandoned row houses displayed the battle scars of a neighborhood ravaged by crack cocaine and urban violence. Even so, Mark Gornik and his co-founders, Allan and Susan Tibbels, brought with them no strategic plan or blueprint for change. "We came here out of repentance," Gornik explained, "to learn from our neighborhoods and just to be a part of the community. As white Christians, we believed it was vital that we turn from our complicity in a culture that is anti-black, anti-poor, and anti-urban and turn to the biblical obligations of justice and reconciliation."[68] An interracial church affiliated with the Presbyterian Church of America eventually took shape, growing to a membership of 125 by 1991. In turn, the community formed a comprehensive health center, job-placement, and youth counseling programs, a private Christian school, and a Habitat for Humanity housing project (which Jimmy Carter inaugurated in 1992). One of the founders summed up the rationale, "Christians missing out on this are missing out on the front lines of God's urban agenda, the gospel of community, and the Lord's reconciliation purposes."

The urban movement's umbrella organization, the Christian Community Development Association (CCDA), when founded in 1989 counted among its membership 37 organizations and 200 individuals. At a recent annual conference in Birmingham, Alabama, founder John M. Perkins (a former civil rights activist in Brandon, Mississippi) announced that the CCDA now has 500 participating organizations and

5,000 individuals. "The CCDA has become the place for Christians who are working in our most forgotten communities to come together, learn from each other, encourage each other, and take the vision of Christian community development and racial reconciliation back to the streets," Perkins explained.[69]

The success of these initiatives may tell us a lot about the prospects for racial peace in America. The most significant, and at the same time perhaps the most perplexing, lesson is that racial healing and reconciliation require a context of shared beliefs and values. As the CCDA emphasizes in its literature, this ought not to be taken as evangelical hostility to the 1960s ideal of the beloved community.[70] Many of the new inner-city activists and developers, like Perkins, have personal connections to the civil rights movement. Most speak with great admiration of their forerunners in SCLC, SNCC, and CORE. Still, there is a strongly felt sense that the civil rights movement of the 1960s eventually abandoned its own best spiritual resources—resources that might otherwise have helped sustain the beloved community over the longer haul.

Spencer Perkins, the son of John Perkins, and Chris Rice, the son of a former white volunteer in the Summer Project, lived together in an intentional interracial community called Antioch in Jackson, Mississippi, until Spencer's untimely death on January 30, 1998, at the age of forty-two. Antioch was comprised of a few "official" buildings—houses converted for a law office, a counseling center, and a magazine devoted to reconciliation issues—and a steadily changing number of houses where residents of the community live. In their 1993 book, *More Than Equals: Racial Healing for the Sake of the Gospel* (now in its seventh printing), Perkins and Rice argued that the civil rights movement's greatest legacy to black and white southerners was its ability to display a distinctive form of religious community. In their view, the movement eventually lost anchor in the prophetic witness of the black church and splintered into activist groups whose spiritual vision was limited by concerns for their own flourishing. This proved devastating because people are by and large not inclined toward radical acts of social relocation, economic redistribution, or racial reconciliation unless they can see their own life-stories as part of a larger theological narrative. "The civil rights movement was an overwhelming success. But it failed to inspire our nation to move beyond integration to reconciliation."[71] In the view of Perkins and Rice, the motivation to move beyond integration to reconciliation must stem from a theologically specific belief in God.

The current growth of interracial and faith-based social justice initiatives offers provocative models for the ongoing pursuit of the beloved community. The CCDA leaders point to their own successes as proof that the primary condition of racial reconciliation is a spiritual solidarity of a highly specific sort.[72] Whites and blacks are not joining hands across the bloodstained centuries of racism in response to some vaguely defined cosmic good. When asked directly, almost every person swept up in this quiet revolution will appeal to St. Paul's second letter to the Corinthians as the theological heart of their mission. "All this is from God, who reconciled us to himself through Christ, and has given us the ministry of reconciliation" (II Corinthians 5:18). As Perkins and Rice say, "Our hope is that we who follow Jesus will take our rightful place as the light—a city on a hill—in the dynamic multicultural society that is emerging in America. We hope that the people of Christ will no longer follow the world's lead, but will move beyond the simple quest for equality to live out the higher call of reconciliation."[73] And it is hard to argue with the successful track record of their service in Mississippi. In West Jackson, African-American and white Christians living in beloved community have formed a cooperative neighborhood that includes a family health center, a community center and freedom house, a nonprofit housing cooperative, a Bible training school, a communications and printing office, a library, a homeless shelter, a hospitality house for volunteers, and a cavernous thrift store and clothing distribution center.

Still, the objection one might raise is that defining reconciliation in such pervasively evangelical terms leaves too many people out of the process.[74] Muslims, Jews, liberal Protestants, liberal Catholics, and atheists (and certainly other kinds of religious and non-religious persons as well) become marginal to the work of racial healing, a regrettable consequence given the extent to which Jews and liberal Christians in particular played courageous and vital roles in the black struggle for equality under the law. The sources of racial peace must be more broadly defined in a pluralistic society; otherwise, there is very little these communities can teach Americans about the common good. In fact, there are early indications that the current movement's potential for wider success in healing social divisions faces some serious limitations. In many intentional interracial communities, the same spirit of compassion extended to whites by African Americans, and vice versa, has not been extended to gay Christians, or to the task of correcting gender inequalities.[75] Moreover, these communities' dependence on corporate dollars and gifts from mainline churches may sometimes weaken their capacity to speak the hard truth about capitalism's role in fostering greed and racial division.

The objection is well taken. The difficult work of racial reconciliation must challenge all Americans, not only those who share common beliefs about God, human dignity, and the meaning of life. Fannie Lou Hamer's genius—and that of the movement in its church-based years—was to display a mutual reciprocity between particular theological commitments and a broader civic good. In the CCDA's vision of the beloved community, we sometimes have the former without the latter—the particular theological commitment of interracial community without a larger civic generosity.

Nonetheless, the successes of faith-based interracial initiatives offer the "national debate on race" some sobering conclusions. Above all, the Christian interracial movement's theological exclusivism and highly developed confessional identity appear to be the very conditions for the durability of its initiatives. "Racial healing for the sake of the Gospel" becomes the first order of business in a faithful ecclesiology, the reparation of what poet Elizabeth Sewell once called "the tigerish divisions of God's body." Christ's body—the Church—must be healed of the sins of white racism. As John Perkins has written, "When blacks and whites who have worked and shopped and studied and eaten side by side all week go to segregated churches on Sunday morning at 11 A.M., the gospel itself is betrayed."[76] Therefore, the theological mandate—"be ye reconcilers"—grounds the pursuit of the beloved community in an ontology of reconciliation. Human reconciliation becomes an instantiation or reenactment of God's reconciliation of the world to himself.

CONCLUSION

Do the faith-based communities of the CCDA best illustrate the ongoing pursuit of the beloved community at the end of the twentieth century? I think so, for in the end the power that animated the civil rights movement's pursuit of the beloved community was the power of the church, the visible witness of the reconciling God. Victoria Gray Adams, one of Fannie Lou Hamer's sister travelers in Mississippi, offered a marvelously complex and nuanced description of this point: "I see the civil rights movement as the journey toward the establishment of the kingdom of God. That's how I understand it now and that's how I understood it then. We were seed people; no matter how bleak the terrain looked out there, we were planted for a rich harvest. And it was the church houses themselves out of which we had to move; these were the center of our lives. We didn't have much of anything really except the church, and as we put our faith in these, they were burned down. But the church was there for us; the church as the representation of the spirit of love—of God. We were a seed people and a spirit people; I don't care whether you call yourself a Christian, Jew, or Muslim. What happened back there in the 1960s with ordinary people could not have happened without an understanding of ourselves as spirit people."[77] Those of us who tell the story would do well to remember not only the faithful who overcame, but also the faith itself; for this faith—exuberant, embracing, full of subversive undercurrents and iconoclastic impulses, spirited with energy, moving into action—might be the civil rights movement's greatest legacy in the American search for the beloved community.[78]

CHAPTER FOUR

Religion, Civil Rights, and Civic Community: The Public Role of American Protestantism

ROBIN W. LOVIN

The civil rights movement of the early 1960s marked a high point for religious leadership in the transformation of American society, and the culmination of many years of religious activity in the public realm. Beginning in the period of racial unrest that followed World War I, Protestant, Jewish, and Roman Catholic religious groups worked together to improve race relations, end segregation, and erase the results of past discrimination. Support for this movement was by no means unanimous in the churches and synagogues, nor was it evenly distributed geographically. Nevertheless, by the 1950s the influence of national religious bodies was solidly arrayed in favor of racial equality. Each religious community found leaders to articulate the theological basis for the social transformation it was advocating: John LaFarge and John Courtney Murray for the Roman Catholics, Robert Gordis and Abraham Heschel for Judaism, and Reinhold Niebuhr and Martin Luther King, Jr., among many others, for the Protestants. This religious coalition played a decisive role in bringing about the Civil Rights Act of 1964, and it seemed that religious commitment to civil rights would shape the American agenda far into the future.

Yet within a few years, the power of that religious coalition had dissipated, and new voices had begun to question the connection between faith and justice on which the coalition had been built. Three decades later, it is not to be taken for granted that religious groups will take the lead in advocacy for civil rights. It is not even certain that the concept of rights has any religious legitimacy.

My aim in this paper is to examine the present state of the connection between religion and civil rights in relation to that consensus that dominated the scene three or four decades ago. What was the link between religion and civil rights that the leading voices in religious ethics developed during the 1950s and 1960s? What caused that consensus to disappear so rapidly? And what would be the connection between religion and civil rights now, if we were able to revive the consensus in a form relevant to our present situation?

To be sure, the past thirty years have seen important changes in legal and political thinking about civil rights. Questions about affirmative action, "reverse discrimination," and the extension to many new groups of civil rights and remedies framed primarily for African Americans have revealed differences among the supporters of civil rights that went largely unnoticed during the 1960s. But to understand how religious commitments to civil rights have changed, it is most important to explore changes in American religion itself, especially changes in the ways that American religious communities think about civil society.

The civil rights movement rested in important ways on religious idealism. Convictions about the equality of all people as children of God, a faith in the ultimate, inevitable triumph of justice, and a disciplined commitment to nonviolent resistance all relied on religious beliefs, and these beliefs provided powerful motivation to individuals who ran great risks and heroically worked for social change. The leaders of the movement, however, expected little from religious idealism taken by itself. They understood that social transformation requires political organization. They knew how to organize religious commitment into public demonstrations. They knew how to argue in terms of constitutional law as well as religious duty, and they understood how to deploy their supporters in ways that would get the attention of the city council, the state legislature, or the U.S. Congress. The civil rights movement was politically effective, as well as morally serious.

In this, the civil rights movement of the 1960s differed from earlier religious movements, which expected social transformation to follow rather more directly from the strength of religious conviction. But it also contrasts sharply with forms of religious political activism that have appeared more recently on the American scene. This new religious activism sometimes approaches the political process instrumentally, as though politics were merely a means to achieve religious ends.

What stands out about the civil rights movement in retrospect is the seriousness with which its religious leaders attended to civil law and the political process. Constitutional government was more than just a means to an end.

To be sure, deference to law and government authority was not absolute. The movement began with a challenge to legal segregation, and it employed civil disobedience as a tactic to call attention to injustice and to obtain changes in the law. The logic of civil disobedience refuses to treat the existing order of law as ultimate, but civil disobedience does not seek to escape civic community. It seeks moral recognition by one's enemies, not isolation from them.[1]

Understanding the changed relationship between civil rights and religion in the United States requires an understanding of how these religious attitudes toward law and politics have changed over the past thirty years. To reduce the inquiry to manageable proportions, I will concentrate in this essay on Protestant social ethics, and especially on the work of Reinhold Niebuhr, who formulated a religious approach to political problems that he called "Christian Realism." My own work as a scholar and educator in a mainline Protestant denomination has been shaped by this way of thinking. Others will find closer or more distant resemblances to their own religious traditions, but it would be hard to overstate the role of Niebuhr's Christian Realism in shaping the religious consensus that supported the civil rights movement. By the same token, I think there is a relationship between Niebuhr's eclipse in American religious thought after his death in 1971 and the subsequent decline of the civil rights consensus. Most important, I believe Niebuhr's work offers important clues for a reconstruction of the connection between religion and civil rights that would serve us well today.

SHAPING THE CONSENSUS

Niebuhr's Christian Realism tempered the religious idealism and youthful optimism of the early civil rights movement with a realistic assessment of the need for power and political strategy. To understand why Niebuhr's generation introduced this cautionary note, we have to recall their earlier disappointment with the religious optimism of the "Social Gospel." American Protestantism at the turn of the twentieth century shared the general sense of its surrounding culture that humanity was on the verge of a new age of prosperity and progress. Walter Rauschenbusch, a Baptist theologian who became the leading exponent of the Social Gospel, predicted in 1907 that if the pace of social progress he saw around him could be sustained, the generation of his grandchildren would look back on his own era as "semi-barbarous."[2]

The Social Gospel theologians were not blind enthusiasts for modernity. They were among the most severe critics of the social inequality and human misery that rapid industrialization was bringing to the cities, but they believed that the scientific and technical achievements that created these social illnesses as their by-products would also have the power to cure them. The modern world had created the conditions under which the visionary promises of Christian love are now real possibilities. All that is required is that Christians begin truly to practice what they have always preached.

The optimism of the Social Gospel was quickly contradicted by the realities of total war and the modern totalitarian state, so that at the end of Rauschenbusch's century, we look back on his time as a last flowering of civility and hope before the real barbarians showed up at the gates. (We recently have made the *Titanic* into a metaphor for that whole era.) For Reinhold Niebuhr, who began his career as a pastor in Detroit in 1915, the urgent task of his generation would be to respond to the horrors of World War I, the racial conflicts and labor unrest of the 1920s, and the economic collapse of the 1930s with a version of Christian ethics that rested on a more "realistic" assessment of the depth of human problems and the power of the forces resisting justice and change.[3]

As the movement for racial equality gathered steam in the 1950s, American Protestant theologians who had lived through the earlier disappointment were not about to let it be repeated. Nor did they intend to let their pupils, including the young Martin Luther King, Jr., forget what had happened to the idealism of an earlier generation that lacked sufficient political realism. The political strategies of the civil rights movement in the 1950s and 1960s, as well as the movement's understanding of the legal and political order it meant to change, reflected what Protestant theology had learned about civil society and social change during the first half of the twentieth century.

Niebuhr's realism began with the recognition that Christian love is not something that people just suddenly decide to live out on the stage of history. Inspired exhortations by the privileged to love our neighbors usually become mere sentimentality, masking a more basic commitment—often unacknowledged—to prevent change and hold on to power. The political realist knows that those who hold power will not surrender it voluntarily out of concern for others. The only way to effect change is to acquire power, even though that process itself is often corrupting, and runs the risk of turning the newly empowered into the next generation of oppressors.

Niebuhr applied this realistic assessment of the struggle for justice explicitly to race relations in the United States. In a brief passage that is especially notable because Martin Luther King, Jr., would recall that it influenced him when he read it many years later, Niebuhr recommends Gandhi's techniques of nonviolent resistance as a response to racial injustice in America, but he also cautions against mistaking the strategic decision to eschew violence for an idealistic reliance on the power of love. Nonviolent resistance is a form of power and, used effectively, it is a way to acquire more power. Those who seek racial equality must remember this, because people who hold power do not surrender it by appeals to moral persuasion alone. They surrender it when they are confronted by greater power. "However large the number of individual white men who do and who will identify themselves completely with the Negro cause, the white race in America will not admit the Negro to equal rights if it is not forced to do so. Upon that point one may speak with a dogmatism which all history justifies."[4]

Over time, Niebuhr became increasingly interested in the ways that historical systems of justice could incorporate and manage these tensions between powers and interests, creating relatively stable systems in which self-interest could be held in check, though not eliminated, and claims to justice could be supported, albeit imperfectly, by the power of government. Niebuhr's classic defense of democracy, *The Children of Light and the Children of Darkness,* maintains this realistic skepticism toward all systems of justice.[5] The book points out that a democratic polity, because it recognizes the tendency of all parties to hold power in service of their own limited interests, provides the best defense against both the cynical children of darkness who want to exploit power and the foolish children of light who think that they do not need power if they have justice on their side.

Despite Niebuhr's early involvement with race conflicts as a pastor in Detroit and his strategic suggestions for the use of nonviolent resistance in *Moral Man and Immoral Society,* he was not a pioneer in the civil rights movement. His attentions during the 1940s were focused on the conflict with Nazi Germany, and after the war, he spent much time redefining the Western democratic tradition against its new Soviet rival.

His Christian Realism, nevertheless, prepared him to respond to the early stirrings of the movement. When Supreme Court decisions began to articulate the constitutional case against segregation, and sit-ins, marches, and protests began to dismantle its practice, Niebuhr was prepared to take these developments seriously. His response to the school desegregation decisions strikes us, in retrospect, as perhaps too cautious. Because he knew that people do not readily give up power in response to moral and religious arguments, he cautioned the advocates of equality to go slowly, regardless of the strength of their constitutional case, lest they provoke resistance and endanger the order on which any approximation of racial justice must rest. When the movement hit full stride, however, Niebuhr was with it fully in spirit, despite illnesses that kept him from playing as active a public role in the struggle as he might have had it come a decade or two earlier.

Christian Realism took the civil rights movement seriously, but it was also conditioned not to claim too much for it. Those who had learned from the failure of the Social Gospel not to identify social movements with the Kingdom of God could not, in the 1960s, simply abandon that caution and transform racial equality into a divine imperative.

Instead, they emphasized the constitutional imperative by which the case for equality was made in the courts. The aim of the movement was understood to be equal rights, or equal opportunity. Persons were to be made as equal as they could be by "equal protection of the laws," the Fourteenth Amendment guarantee that was the foundation of the constitutional case against segregation.

Niebuhr saw the conflict here in very secular terms, though he described it in ways that seemed to assure the triumph of equality through a kind of historical inevitability. In an important essay titled "Liberty and Equality," Niebuhr traces the history of the tension between liberty and equality in Western political life, especially in the Anglo-American tradition. The case for equality has not always been theoretically coherent, and progress has not been consistent, but in the long run of history, the direction is clear: People are to be treated as equals before the law. Niebuhr concludes the essay with the confident assertion that this deep, prevailing current in political history is now being applied to the question of racial equality in the United States:

> The "American dilemma" is on the way of being resolved, and one of the instruments of its resolution has proved to be the constitutional insistence on equality as a criterion of justice, an insistence which the Supreme Court has recently implemented after generations of hesitation in regard to the application of the principle to our relation with a minority group, which has the advantage of diverging obviously from the dominant type in our nation and which still bears the onus of former subjugation in slavery. At last the seeming sentimentality of the preamble of

our Declaration of Independence—the declaration that "all men are created equal"—has assumed political reality and relevance. It is not true that all men are created equal, but the statement is a symbol for the fact that all men are to be treated equally, with the terms of the gradations of function which every healthy society uses for its organization.[6]

This, too, is a form of realism, though it is more subtle than the appeal to preponderant power in *Moral Man and Immoral Society*. Historical developments have their own momentum, and that in itself lends a kind of power to one side or another in history's epic conflicts. Familiar local custom must give way to the generalities and regularities of national law, especially where the law rests on principles that have stood the test of history. Niebuhr contributes little to the theoretical formulation of the requirements of racial justice. Perhaps he did not feel the need to do so. He accepted the framing of the problem as it was presented to him, because in those terms he could demonstrate that the movement for equality has the power it needs to sustain itself in history.

Niebuhr's political realism thus contrasts sharply with the idealism of the Social Gospel, which saw its efforts at social amelioration as a straightforward expression of divine love, continuous with a process of gradual transformation by which God would use the possibilities of history to bring in the Kingdom. For Niebuhr, the Kingdom of God always remains beyond history.

This distance between the Kingdom of God, which is the end of history, and the working out of justice within history is not, however, a reason for religious indifference to questions of justice or for religious withdrawal from historical conflicts. Our human nature expresses itself in the justice that we seek for ourselves, not because the struggle is God's struggle, but because it is ours, part of the creative process by which we live. More important, for the Christian, we cannot ignore the claims to justice that other persons make against us, not because the claims are God's, but precisely because the claims are their own, a product of their own historical struggle, which includes their experience of the limits and burdens that we have placed upon them.

We cannot claim to love our neighbors as God loves them, as though we could determine what God's justice demands and then gladly give it to them. That was the mistake of the Social Gospel, the mistake made by the foolish children of light. But we cannot claim to love our neighbors at all if we refuse to hear what their idea of justice seems to require of us. That is the mistake made by the children of darkness.

Thus, Niebuhr's Christian Realism, by sharply differentiating between human history and divine justice, provides reasons to pay attention to the nuances of the struggle for justice in history. Having ruled out a historical choice for absolute good or absolute evil, the choice between relative goods and evils becomes proportionately more important. There was little doubt in Niebuhr's mind or in the minds of his many followers that the movement for civil rights represented just such an important historical choice.

THE CONSENSUS VANISHES

In 1964, one might have thought that this commitment to racial equality, based on the constitutional imperative of equal protection of the laws and supported by the moral authority of the nation's major religious traditions, would become the benchmark from which future developments in American politics and society would be measured. Today, we find ourselves in a very different situation. While the basic principles of civil rights laid down from 1954 to 1964 have not been abandoned, at least not by any significant mainstream political voice, so many of the remedies by which those principles were supposed to be effected have been challenged or repudiated that the question arises whether the principles themselves still provide any guidance for policy.

If we ask why Protestant churches, outside of the African-American denominations and congregations, have not sustained the commitment to civil rights that was a defining goal for many in the early 1960s, divisions arising from these political and legal arguments about the implementation of civil rights provide a partial explanation. As the impact of a theoretical commitment to equal rights on real political and economic interests becomes more clear, a Christian Realist would expect the enthusiasm of the initial commitment to cool and the unanimity of the consensus to fray. What seems to have happened, however, is something more than the maturing of the movement that a Realist might predict. What seems to have happened is a quite unexpected questioning of the connection between faith and civil society on which the Christian Realists' commitment to civil rights was built in the first place.

The questions come from two developments, located at opposite ends of the political spectrum. First, on the political "left," there is liberation theology. Second, and far more important in American religion today, there is a conservative challenge posed by the rapid expansion of evangelical Protestantism, and by the contemporary reformulation of a Reformation-era critique of Christian involvement in politics.

By the time Reinhold Niebuhr died in 1971, many were pronouncing his Christian Realism hopelessly compromised. What had seemed dangerous radicalism in the 1930s appeared altogether too cautious after the changes of the 1960s. The effort to gain and hold power within the existing political order, which the Realists saw as the basis for turning moral ideas into effective politics, now seemed to be a collaboration with a system of domination and exploitation that had to be demolished, not reformed. Power could not be wrested from the white establishment by generating some countervailing power. Freedom had to have a base in a power all its own.

The call for "Black Power" was already familiar from the latter days of King's leadership of the civil rights movement. James Cone made it the basis for a new Protestant social theology that rejected the compromises of Christian Realism and provided the basis for a more radical approach to social change. Cone soon linked his theology of Black Power to a theology emerging among Catholics in Latin America, a "theology of liberation" that rejected the economic domination of privileged elites and called for an empowerment of the people.[7]

Cone's African-American liberation theology has retained its commitment to radical political action, but the liberation theology adopted most widely in North America owes more to the Latin American theologians, including Gustavo Gutiérrez, Juan Luís Segundo, and Leonardo Boff. All rejected attempts to gain a share in the prevailing systems of power and authority. Christians were to free themselves through participation in "base communities," where study of the Bible provided an alternative to ideological rationalizations for their suffering and powerlessness, and where they could gain control of their own lives through economic self-sufficiency.[8]

Liberation theology could hardly be said to have become popular among North American Protestants, but it has received attention in many of the academic centers where Christian Realism previously dominated social theology. The ideal of Christian base communities that free themselves through Bible study, and the articulation of their own experience, from the values of a consumerist, exploitative, and ecologically destructive society has now influenced several generations of theological students who have introduced their own, milder versions of liberation theology's methods into their ministries. In these contexts, the internal tasks of creating community and sustaining Christian identity sometimes replace the reform and gradual transformation of political systems as the goal of Christian action.

Far more prominent than liberation theology on the contemporary American religious landscape, however, is the rapid growth of evangelical Protestantism. While the mainstream denominations from which Niebuhr and his Christian Realist contemporaries came have lost membership and influence over the last three decades, evangelical congregations and denominations have grown steadily.

Evangelical Protestants are too large and diverse a group to be easily categorized. Their theology tends to center on biblical doctrine, personal conversion, and strict standards of personal morality. Their social and political beliefs range from the radicalism of the Sojourners community in Washington, D.C., to the political conservatism and commitment to free market economics found among the New Christian Right. Some of these new evangelicals reject prevailing American political and economic values with as much vigor as any liberation theologian, while others uncritically identify those values with the core of Christian faith.

Attitudes among evangelicals toward civil rights are similarly diverse. Many African-American congregations, of course, would characterize themselves as part of this evangelical Protestant growth, and they are likely to regard the civil rights movement as an important part of their history and their religious heritage. Others, however, have moved to the new evangelical churches precisely because they were alienated by the emphasis on civil rights and social action that they found in the mainstream denominations to which they once belonged. In general, the emphasis on personal conversion takes precedence over the call for social transformation, and where the latter does not entirely disappear, it is often argued or assumed that any hope for real social change depends on changing individual lives.

In recent years, evangelical Protestants have rediscovered some of the political strategies that the mainstream denominations deployed so effectively during the civil rights movement. While this has made evangelical Protestantism a force to be reckoned with in contemporary politics, evangelicals have not in general produced a political theology that would allow them to take secular movements for justice and the values of constitutional law as seriously as Niebuhr's Christian Realism took the historic quest for racial equality and the constitutional principle of equal protection. The distinction between secular values and Christian values remains quite sharp in much evangelical thinking, and the use of the political process tends to be instrumental, rather than moral.

Contemporary writers who adopt the perspective of the Protestant

Reformation, when Luther sharply distinguished the power of the church from the power of the state, include Glenn Tinder, whose book, *The Political Meaning of Christianity,* is quite possibly the best work of Christian political thought since Niebuhr, although I disagree with it fundamentally in ways that will soon become clear. Tinder argues that the appropriate political role of Christians is to keep everyone mindful of the limits of politics. Those who forget those limits may drift off into sentimental idealism when their moral aspirations are disappointed, but they are perhaps even more likely to resort to totalitarianism. And because it is inevitable that their moral aspirations will be disappointed— politics just isn't that kind of venture—those who aspire to achieve moral good through politics are the most dangerous kind of politician. Politics can sometimes prevent evil, or keep it from getting worse. It cannot do good.[9]

There is in Tinder's rigorous rejection of political idealism more than a trace of Reinhold Niebuhr's Realism, though Niebuhr would insist that we balance the rejection of naïve political idealism with an equally firm refusal to set prior limits on what the political struggle for justice can achieve.[10] Niebuhr and Tinder would nonetheless agree that Christians can participate in politics if they can keep their expectations appropriately limited.

There is another tradition from the Reformation era that holds that Christians must avoid altogether participation in the coercive use of force, which inevitably accompanies political authority. This is the historic stance of Christian pacifism and the churches of the "Radical Reformation." It has been ably represented in recent years by John Howard Yoder.[11] Yoder understood the difference between a modern democratic polity and the authoritarian monarchies in which the radical Reformation tradition first was formulated, and he was by no means so complete in his rejection of politics as the churches in his tradition have sometimes been. Inevitably, however, a theology that limits participation in political community focuses attention on the Christian community, seeing it as the place for nurturing virtues that cannot be brought to birth in other environments and that are, indeed, radically at risk in the realm of politics and power that lies outside.

Stanley Hauerwas has a post-modern version of this Christian rejection of politics that stresses the role of the Christian community of discourse in creating and sustaining Christian virtues.[12] What lies outside of the Christian community is not merely a realm of force and power in which the Christian values are radically threatened. Outside the Christian community Christian values are simply incomprehensible. Without the Christian narrative to make sense of the ethics of nonviolence and care for all life, its imperatives are drained of meaning and motivating power. Attempts to translate an ethics formed by love of God and love of neighbor through Jesus Christ into general principles of justice are doomed to failure, and an attempt at Christian politics, which invests historical movements and constitutional principles with religious import in the way that Niebuhr's Christian Realism did, trivializes the Christian commitment and compromises its radical critique by accepting the rationalization of dominance that prevails in the realms of politics and economics.

Readers who know this literature will recognize how cursory and over-generalized my summary of it necessarily has been. My purpose, however, is not to analyze recent Protestant ethics, but to connect them to the loss of religious passion and commitment toward civil rights issues that we are attempting to understand in this essay. Even this brief account of liberation theology and the neo-Reformation skepticism about politics reveals the enormous changes that have taken place in American Protestantism since the days of the civil rights movement, when Niebuhrian realism built a solid connection between the biblical image of justice that flows down like waters and the practical commitment to reform that worked itself out in the courts. Protestant thought today is more diverse than it was thirty years ago, but what it shares across the theological and political spectrum is an increased suspicion that the public realm of law, politics, and policy is not susceptible to moral transformation, and may not even be capable of understanding a moral argument. The attention of the ethicist therefore shifts to the Christian community, where alone the values and virtues that make it possible for people to live truthfully and faithfully can be nurtured. Diminished attention in the churches to issues of civil rights is not the result of failure of nerve or a failure of memory. It reflects, at best, the shared conviction of these more recent theologians that social equality is a poor substitute for the genuine acceptance found in Christian love and, at worst, the suggestion by some of them that the whole concept of civil justice is a bad idea in the first place.[13]

CHRISTIANITY AND CIVIC COMMUNITY

Liberation theology and the new versions of Reformation political thought, different as they are, have both exerted strong influences on contemporary Protestantism. They have challenged a key point of connection between Christian Realism and the civil rights movement that went unnoticed at the time precisely because no one would have thought to challenge it. Christian Realists understood participation in civil community as an integral part of Christian life. The terms a society sets for participation in its elections, for living in its communities, and for access to education and public services are not matters to which Christians, as Christians, can be indifferent.

Niebuhr seldom stated this understanding explicitly in his arguments for civil rights and racial justice. His thinking was rooted in a long Christian tradition that included Augustine and Luther, but also Thomas Aquinas' theological interpretation of Aristotle and John Calvin's affirmation of the importance of political society. Civil justice, as Calvin noted, may be "superfluous" in the Kingdom of God, "but if it is the will of God that while we are aspiring toward our true country, we be pilgrims on the earth, and if such aids are necessary to our pilgrimage, they who take them from man deprive him of his human nature."[14] Participation in civil society and in the search for justice and peace on its terms is not something separate and distinct from the Christian life. It is an integral part of it.

Reinhold Niebuhr clearly lived as though politics were an essential part of the Christian life. He also thought about it that way. Central to his understanding of human nature is an idea of human freedom that is able both to envision alternatives to the present state of affairs and to join with others to realize those new possibilities. Martin Luther King's ability, which he expressed in his "I Have a Dream" speech, to imagine a future of freedom and equality is, for Niebuhr, the most characteristic power of human nature. But King and Niebuhr both realized that such dreams, to be worth anything, have to be realized in civic communities. Otherwise, they remain mere fantasies. For Niebuhr, it was also important to understand that the realization of our visions depends as much on those who oppose us in this civic community as it does on those who join us. We need the collaboration of those who share our vision if it is to be made real and lasting, but precisely because our vision is always partial, and partly self-interested, we also need those who question our aims and counter them with their own claims to justice.[15] A political community that limits the participation of some of its members by law or silences them by threat of violence does damage not only to the humanity of those who are thus excluded, but also to the humanity of the excluders.

Because every ideal of justice and community is both a creation of the human freedom by which we share in the image of God, and a reflection of our human finitude that overlooks its own limitations, we cannot easily distinguish between Christian virtues and secular ethics. Our identity is formed both in Christian community and civil community, and it takes real discernment to identify just which formation is the source of any particular moral commitment. Nor is it clear that there is much to be gained by the attempt to sort out the influences, since our moral lives must always be lived in a particular civic context anyway. We want to avoid the casual identification of cultural values with Christian virtues, but vigilance against most obvious confusions does not imply that all of our moral commitments can be neatly sorted into sacred and secular categories. In Niebuhr's Christian ethics, the bright line is the one that separates all moral ideals, religious and secular, from the ultimate resolution of human conflicts in the Kingdom of God, which lies beyond history. That is the line he learned to draw in his early efforts to distinguish Christian Realism from the Social Gospel, and it remains far clearer and more important in all of his thought than the line that later voices, seeking to revive the Reformation traditions, have drawn between the Christian community organized around the virtues of faith, hope, and love, and the civil community organized around power and the threat of violence.

Niebuhr perhaps devotes too little attention in his writings to the Christian community, its distinctive opportunities for moral formation, and its capacity for resistance to the corruption and self-deception that sometimes—dare we say often?—pervade civic morality. The civic community should not be confused with the Christian community, and it certainly cannot replace the Christian community, no matter how engaging its moral struggles become. But neither can the Christian community replace the civic order or render it irrelevant to the moral life. It is not the case that once we have found the truthful community and been formed by its virtues we can safely dispense with the requirements of civility and politics. Politics may be superfluous to the Kingdom of God, but while we remain within the limits of history, whether we attempt to dispense with it for ourselves or we are excluded from it by others, we are, as Calvin would put it, deprived of our human nature.

This reading of Niebuhr's Christian Realism, with its positive evaluation of the moral opportunities in civic community, is necessarily more than just a report of what Reinhold Niebuhr said. Apart from a few arguments during World War II with Christian pacifists who defended their rejection of military participation against his realist case for the use of force, Niebuhr did not directly address the sharp distinction in that tradition between Christian community and civil community. He was realistic about the moral pretensions of all political systems, including his own, but he could hardly have imagined a time when dominant voices in Protestant social ethics would treat the civil community as a sort of moral void.

A restrospective look at Niebuhr's Christian Realism from the standpoint of contemporary Protestant social ethics thus makes more clear the essential connection between a religious commitment to civil rights and a positive religious valuation of civil society. Niebuhr's thinking about the relationship between nonviolent resistance and a realistic strategy of power is historically important for its influence on King, and his speculations on the historical origins and meaning of the American commitment to racial equality are often insightful, but it is his underlying assumption about the religious and moral importance of civic community that provides the starting point for thinking about the future of religion and civil rights.

THE FUTURE OF CIVIL RIGHTS

Many changes since the 1960s have made the future of civil rights uncertain in law, in politics, and in our society at large. What once seemed a unified movement has fragmented into those who back familiar strategies of affirmative action and equal opportunity, those who follow a politics of racial and ethnic identity, those who see the underlying problem as class, not race, and yet others with yet other positions that do not come together in any plausible, unified national agenda.

Among these many changes, however, the changes in Protestant ethics draw our attention to a social and cultural transformation that is connected to the future of civil rights in ways that we might otherwise overlook. The civil rights movement, like the Protestant theology that supported it, presupposed the importance and value of civic community, and the loss of momentum and direction in that movement may reflect confusion about this important underlying presupposition.

The goals that the civil rights movement sought, from voting rights to public accommodations to equal opportunities in employment and education, all presumed that there is a society in which it is worthwhile to be accepted as a full participant. We want to go about our business secure in our dignity as people who belong in this shop, on this sidewalk, at this lunch counter, in this classroom, because we live our lives more completely and more truly in the image of God when we step out in public with confidence than when we closet ourselves in segregated communities where rituals of exaggerated civility assuage the doubts that exclusion has raised in our own minds about our own worth.

King and other leaders of the movement, like Niebuhr and the theologians from whom they learned, rarely articulated this premise because no one challenged it. But this is what equal protection of the laws is all about. If there is no civic community in which to be accepted, or if it is morally unimportant whether we are part of it or not, then there is little meaning to the struggle to obtain a place in that community on equal terms. And there is little future in asking people to run risks and bear burdens to continue that struggle. The most serious challenges to civil rights today are not the legal and legislative challenges to busing, affirmative action, and other means that have been employed to achieve equal opportunity. The most serious challenges are the ideological changes that lower the value of participation in civic community and the social and cultural changes that reduce the possibility for it.

Much has been written in recent years about the loss of community in American life and the erosion of our "social capital."[16] The focus of this literature has been a middle-class, suburban culture in which mass entertainment, consumer values, and a pace of life required to keep up with expectations, have undercut the human relationships and shared activities that keep people engaged with one another in their local communities. Because this literature on the loss of community is focused on the middle-class, it does not usually occur to us to connect it with the problems of civil rights. The loss of community may be lamentable, but it is in some sense a choice, and middle-class citizens who no longer care to make civic commitments to one another in a general community have ample resources to create alternative, elective communities in their chosen corners of private space.

Shift the scene to the rural poor or the urban underclass, however, and the case changes. For large numbers of people, especially African Americans who have not benefited economically from the possibilities that equal opportunity opened three decades ago, anything that approximates civic community is at risk and rapidly disappearing, not because of their own choices, but because of the inexorable economic pressures that drain their communities of services, leadership, and opportunity. The urban "underclass" is segregated by race and class in ways more isolating than a Jim Crow society ever conceived, and the communities to which the underclass are confined lack effective education, basic public services, access to employment and consumer goods, and even a minimal sense of security on the streets.

The important achievement of the civil rights movement—equal opportunity to participate in a broad civic community—means little here. Rights to participate in elections, to enjoy public services, and to receive effective schooling are mere abstractions in places where none of these things are available in quantity or quality sufficient to make a difference in people's lives. Faced with the apparent meaninglessness in this environment of everything that the civil rights movement fought for, we begin to see clearly what thirty years ago we simply assumed: The most basic civil right is the right to a civic community in which all the other rights can make a difference. Without a place in which to become a person with an identity among other people, equality of opportunity is an abstraction, not a goal worth struggling to obtain. Seen in this light, the future of civil rights may depend on a more general renewal of civic community, not one that merely addresses the alienation and isolation of the middle class, but one that restores the civic infrastructure in communities of the poor.

We will learn little that is useful for this task if we confine ourselves to the political and legal strategies of the Christian Realists and other mainstream Protestant participants in the civil rights movement that began after World War II. From the time of Gunnar Myrdal's *An American Dilemma,* they believed that advancing civil rights meant taking an American ideal of equality and applying it to the realities of race relations on a local and regional level.[17] Niebuhr himself suggests as much in his assertion that with the Supreme Court's desegregation decisions, ". . . the seeming sentimentality of the preamble of our Declaration of Independence—the declaration that 'all men are created equal'—has assumed political reality and relevance."[18] Civil rights at mid-century required the persistent, courageous application of a well-formed national ideal in local settings, especially in those places where the ideal had been contradicted by the practice of segregation. The civil rights movement was a national movement. It tried to use the same strategies in the small towns of the South and in the big cities of the North because the results wanted were the same. The national media became an effective ally against local resistance because what civil rights required was consistency—the same rights for all citizens in all places.

If civil rights at the end of the century requires a rediscovery of the importance of civic community, that mid-century strategy of national ideals with local applications will not be of much help. There is little on the national scene to inspire confidence in the practice of civic community, and that ideal itself, as I have been at pains to show in this essay, has been abandoned by some of the religious communities that once gave it great moral importance. There is no general principle that we can bring to bear on every local reality, and no one strategy that will create civic community wherever it is applied. In the absence of a plausible national ideal that could provide the norm for local practice, local practice will have to generate strategies and models that may then find more general affirmation in our national life.

Here, as in the earlier civil rights movement, religion will have an important role to play, but it will also be a role that begins on the local level. In destroyed urban neighborhoods and deserted rural ones, the churches are often the survivor institutions, the only remnants of what once was a rich fabric of shops, businesses, community organizations, clubs, clinics, schools, and charities. Such a church is not a community of believers gathered to form the character of its members and unmask the moral pretensions of the surrounding secular community. For churches that minister among the poor, the community of faith is not even a safe place to be unless it reaches out to the violent, alienated, and dispossessed people who surround it. It is not so much a matter of unmasking the pretensions of this surrounding secular community, as it is coming to grips with the harsh reality that there is nothing there about which we might any longer have illusions.

What these churches do when they are most effective is to recreate some of the conditions for civic community on the most basic level. They work in partnership with government agencies, local entrepreneurs, neighborhood mothers, suburban do-gooders, earnest seminarians, volunteer lawyers, and handymen with barely operable pickup trucks. When they are successful, they create a fragile semblance of civic community where people can learn the satisfactions of effectiveness, acceptance, and competence, even though they may be obliged to create for themselves the circumstances under which those satisfactions can be experienced. Despite the theological critique of civic community by neo-Reformation Protestant ethics, it appears that the urban church is discovering about the world something like what Voltaire said about God: If the world does not exist, it will be necessary for the church to create it.

Judging from the energy and dedication that some of these ministries evoke, it might just be possible for Protestant Christians to rekindle the passion that once linked their faith to the civil rights movement around this more elemental civil rights agenda. The new goal would not be access to a set of opportunities that are already in existence, and need only to be made available to all. The goal would be the new creation in a local setting of a civic community that can sustain a basic set of opportunities for and relationships between the people who live there.

Civil rights presuppose a civic community. Where that community does not exist, it must be created in order for our constitutionally protected civil rights to mean anything at all. Because civic community has moral and religious importance, faithful Christians and civil rights activists have a common stake in its creation and preservation that recalls the partnership they once created around equal opportunity and equal protection of the laws.

Their cooperation on this new agenda will not, however, be based on the enactment of national legislation and the application of general norms of equality to recalcitrant local situations. This time the local situations will provide a network of experiments in which the requirements of civic community will eventually become more clear. When we know what is required to create and sustain civic community in a local setting, then we will once again have an agenda for civil rights at the national level.

The coalition of religious commitment and social activism that came together in the civil rights movement drew its energy and wisdom from many sources, including Christian Realism, which warned an idealistic generation of civil rights activists not to expect much justice from love, unless they could also acquire power. Justice still needs power, and a renewal of the civil rights agenda will require legal acumen and strategic thinking as well. But in the making of this new agenda, the contribution of Christian Realism may be to warn a cynical generation not to expect much justice from power and intellect unless they are also informed by love and creative of community.

PART II

BROADENING THE BASE: NEW INSIGHTS FROM DIVERSE TRADITIONS

A long the border of Texas, there are areas called "colonias." These are rural communities whose land was sold by developers to families in search of affordable housing. These lands were "developed" and sold without water, a waste system, or even streets. The communities have been in existence for thirty to forty years. The people who live in them are poor, so poor that the median income level is below $13,000.

Elizabeth Valdez, lead organizer with the El Paso Interreligious Sponsoring Organization (EPISO), has helped in efforts to make the colonias' condition a public issue. Under the umbrella of the Industrial Areas Foundation (IAF), she has been engaged in organizing work for over twelve years. The IAF draws on democratic principles as well as from the traditions of many faiths. Valdez was raised a Roman Catholic, but only after working with the IAF was she able to translate religion, and more specifically Scripture, into the work she was doing in communities. Raised in the lower Rio Grande valley at the southern tip of Texas, Elizabeth Valdez believes that faith has to be taken to the streets. The challenge to become a faithful community has to be coupled with faith based on action. Valdez explains, "When we are baptized, we are basically saying that we will be responsible for being the agents of change in making God's kingdom here on earth."

Valdez believes that church-based organizing can serve as one vehicle for people to use in doing good for their communities and society. In her words, "It is the first step to putting the Gospel into action; churches and schools are the primary institutions that families have." She continues, "They teach us that we have a responsibility to respond to the needs of those around us; and as we become clearer about what is happening in our communities, our clergy is making religion more real for people, connecting Scripture to what is happening in people's lives."

One of the biggest challenges Valdez sees in her work is the need for more organizers. Valdez describes the work of organizing as "establishing relationships with people, and this takes time—it's a process." In describing her work with the IAF, she explains that "IAF is about developing the person. It serves as a mini-university for the organizers and leaders it trains because it recognizes the kind of intellectual capital necessary to do this kind of work." The issues themselves are secondary to the primary purpose of developing leaders. As Valdez puts it, "People on the whole know what needs to be done in their communities, but they may not have the vehicle to do it. IAF organizations are the vehicle for change."

When the Industrial Areas Foundation organization, Valley Interfaith, decided to organize people in McAllen and other colonias along the Texas border, state officials became defensive. They feared embarrassment, worrying that companies would not want to come to Texas because they would see families crying out for water. Valley Interfaith's response was, "If you can't provide water for families, what makes you think you can provide water for corporations?"

EPISO and Valley Interfaith succeeded in making the colonias story heard not only in Texas, but also across the nation. Legislation was passed aimed at halting the uncontrolled development of colonias along the border. The Texas IAF network organizations were ultimately able to secure $1 billion in local, state, and federal funding to bring water, sewers, and roads to over 1,400 colonia communities. Valdez recalls: "An ecumenically and racially diverse community came together and said, we are going to put a stop to this. Today in the twentieth and twenty-first century it is not just for anyone in our society to be living under these conditions."

Valdez reflects on a poignant story that summarizes the process of faith-based organizing:

> When EPISO first started working on this issue, the people said, "Don't bother, nothing is going to change." Mrs. Ledesma, a woman in her seventies, was told she was wasting her time. The other day this same woman came to our office with some grapes; she said, "I have a grapevine in the backyard of my house and the grapevine would not give grapes year after year because I did not have any water. Today I have water, and now my grapevine is giving me grapes."

The story of the grapes is symbolic of what has happened in these communities.

About a year ago at an elementary school on the east side of predominantly Hispanic- and African-American Austin, Texas, there was a rat problem. Willie Bennett, lead organizer for Austin Interfaith, said he was told this was a school where there was "no parental involvement—parents didn't care." When Bennett met with the teachers, they said, "Parents don't really care about their kids in school." Bennett asked them, "Have you ever asked the parents about the rat problem?" and they replied, "Well no, but they must know." Then Bennett answered, "No, they don't know if you haven't told them." Two days later Bennett, along with Reneé Barrios of Austin Interfaith organized a meeting of twenty-two parents, the principal, and the head of maintenance for the district. Parents at the meeting demanded that the rat problem be taken care of and by the end of the meeting the maintenance department was already patching up holes.

This did not solve the problem; rats were nesting in ventilators and needed to be removed. Schoool officials said this would be done in 1999 as part of the school bond. According to Bennett, at one organizing meeting "a Hispanic mother of three, who had never gone past the eighth grade, chaired the meeting and said, 'No—1999 is not good enough for our kids'; she was surrounded, and supported by, the African-American parents, the other Hispanic parents, and members of congregations from all around the neighborhood. That weekend those ventilators were removed."

Willie Bennett was raised National Baptist and trained as a minister at a Southern Baptist seminary. His work in communities began when he was still a seminary student working part time at an organization called Urban Allies, where he helped coordinate work on an adult literacy program, a food voucher program, and an after-school tutoring program for elementary school kids. When he moved to Fort Worth, Texas, he worked as the director of a Methodist community center, an experience that Bennett believes prepared him for his future work with people of various religious denominations and of many different faiths.

Bennett was introduced to the Industrial Areas Foundation (IAF) during his work at the community center. He explains, "After seeing a lot of unsuccessful organizing practices in the social services arena, I saw IAF's efforts, working with existing institutions, as so effective and was intrigued." After joining IAF, Bennett was placed in Dallas for three years after which he became the lead organizer for Austin Interfaith. Austin Interfaith is a mediating organization made up of thirty member organizations. The congregations are Jewish, Catholic, Protestant; African-American, Hispanic, and Anglo; and they are from all over Austin. The purpose is to enable people from these diverse constituencies to work together on public issues that affect the well being of families and neighborhoods in Austin.

Bennett believes that the religious traditions of all faiths compel us to do more. In his daily work Bennett often returns to the Gospel—the call to Moses, God's concern for the oppressed, and Luke 4:18, describing how Jesus defined his ministry, teaching how God works through people and how, if something has to be done, we have to be prepared to do it. Speaking about his own religious background and beliefs, Bennett says, "I consider myself very conservative, almost fundamentalist theologically speaking, but in my politics and my work I am a liberal, working for change." His religiosity and his work as an organizer have been connected from the beginning. He explains, "When you are an African-American minister, it is a given that you are involved in your community; it is expected of you to work with the NAACP or the Urban League—it just comes with the territory."

Working as a full-time organizer was not a big jump for Bennett, who feels that this is what he was called to do. He has turned down pastoral jobs because he felt that it was not what God was calling him to do. In his work, Bennett relies on religious institutions to assist him in his organizing efforts. He finds that religions are the crucial mirrors to show one how things are versus how things should be or how people should be treated; they point people to where they should be.

About his work with the Industrial Areas Foundation, Bennett states, "Organizing does not revolve around one person, the idea is not to be another King or Malcolm or Jesse, rather to train people how to do the work. As organizers we are not going to be in the front, the key is for this to outlive us, for the organizations to still be here when we move on." He defines IAF's work as counter-culture in that it works against a culture that teaches us that we are only individuals, and in which developments such as the Internet have increased our isolation. All of IAF's organizing is done face-to-face.

Bennett believes that the story of ridding rats at the inner-city Austin elementary school could not have been possible if the parents and teachers had seen it only as a rat problem. In fact, when this same group of parents and teachers came together to celebrate the end to the rats, they also discussed a new health program at the school, a new playground facility, and a new academic agenda. Bennett reflects on the efforts of Austin Interfaith, "This is about developing leaders and developing people; not looking for another charismatic leader. I got the ball rolling and Reneé Barios did over one hundred individual meetings and house meetings to find and train the leaders. This was just one issue, the group now deals with much more than just a rat problem—it now addresses nursing, education, playgrounds, and other issues affecting the community. You know you have done something right when you help people to reach their potential."

CHAPTER FIVE

Buddhism and Civil Rights

DAVID W. CHAPPELL

To the surprise of many, Martin Luther King, Jr., held a news conference in 1966 with a Buddhist monk, Thich Nhat Hanh, and publicly criticized American involvement in the war in Vietnam. He went
on to compare the Vietnamese Buddhist peace movement with American civil rights activities and later would nominate Thich Nhat Hanh
for the Nobel Peace Prize. Martin Luther King, Jr., was a citizen not
just of Atlanta or the United States but also of the world, and civil
rights were not just about local or federal laws, but about justice and
human well-being everywhere. Similarly, American Buddhists are concerned not only with the treatment of Asian immigrants and minorities
in the United States who happen to be Buddhist. Rather, Buddhist social
activists share with Martin Luther King, Jr., the same concern, namely,
that injustice is wrong and should be corrected wherever it arises.

While there is a growing literature on human rights and Buddhism,[1]
less attention has been given to the local application of these principles
in the United States. Buddhist groups have been in America for over a
century,[2] and for the first sixty years the vast majority were Japanese-
Americans. Although Buddhist clergy were active in support of striking
plantation workers in the 1920s and of Japanese language schools in the
1930s, the first issue to erupt on a national scale was the suspension of
the civil rights of Americans of Japanese ancestry who were imprisoned
in 1942 after the attack on Pearl Harbor. The fact that most Buddhists
accepted this massive denial of their civil rights without protest needs explanation. Buddhist ideas of karma and the traditional subservience of
Buddhism to political authority in Japan encouraged passivity. Much
more important factors, however, were the blatant discrimination that

Asians were forced to accept from European-Americans in the nineteenth and early twentieth century, plus the shame that Buddhists of Japanese background felt for Japanese military aggression.

Most Americans who think of themselves as Buddhist, or proto-Buddhist, have never joined a group, so that the recorded membership of Buddhist groups in America is well under two million—less than a third the size of the American Muslim population. However, the Buddhist influence on individual lives in America is enormous, as reflected in positive movie and television coverage, the popularity of the Dalai Lama, book sales, and numerous college courses.

Theravada Buddhists have been active on behalf of civil rights in Sri Lanka and Southeast Asia, but most American Buddhists follow the Mahayana form of Buddhism, which arose in India and flourished in East Asia, where it was banned from social activism by strong Confucian rulers. As a result, contemporary Mahayana Buddhist leaders in exile like Thich Nhat Hanh and the Dalai Lama have become the principal models for American Buddhist social activists.

After examining the wartime experience of Buddhists in Part One, Part Two will analyze the Mahayana threefold ethics—to avoid evil, to cultivate good, and to save all beings—in relation to American Buddhist social activism on behalf of civil rights.

PART ONE: JAPANESE AMERICAN BUDDHISTS AND CIVIL RIGHTS

Labor disputes between white American bosses and Asian contract workers in Hawaii—Chinese, Filipino, but mostly Japanese—erupted in many strikes after annexation of Hawaii on July 7, 1898, when American labor laws were applied to the new territory. During the first two decades of this century, Buddhist priests worked to calm these labor protests, urging Japanese workers to serve their employers with loyalty and honesty as was their duty (*ando shugi*). By 1920 conditions had become so bad that six Buddhist leaders jointly sent a letter of protest to the Hawaii Sugar Plantation Association.[3] On January 24, 1920, a newspaper headline blared "Buddhist Priests Interfere to Aid Strikers." The strike did not end until June 30, 1920, but the Buddhist priests remained firm in their support and some temples held fund-raisers to help the strikers. White Americans saw these actions as anti-Christian and anti-American, and began a campaign against Buddhism that later shifted to a legal battle to close down Japanese language schools.

Over the following decades as children and grandchildren of Asian immigrants were born as American Buddhists, they too inherited the anti-Asian "yellow peril" stigma, especially in the mainland United States, and today cultural lines still separate American Buddhists. The major surveys of Buddhism in America are often presented as a European American story—such as by Rick Fields, *How the Swans Came to the Lake*, or by Don Morreale, *A Complete Guide to Buddhist America*[4]—but until the 1960s, Buddhism in America consisted largely of Asian immigrants. In 1998 Morreale listed over one thousand Buddhist centers, but omitted two of the largest Buddhist groups with roughly two hundred centers: namely, the Buddhist Churches of America (BCA), a Jōdo Shinshū (Pure Land) group, and Soka Gakkai International-USA (SGI-USA), a Nichiren lay Buddhist movement. Although both groups originate in Japan, the vast majority of members are American citizens. This neglect of BCA and SGI-USA is unfortunate since the story of how Buddhism relates to civil rights in America is especially connected to BCA and SGI-USA.

In spite of Fields and Morreale, the fact remains that until 30 years ago, most American Buddhists were of Asian ancestry and most of these were ethnically Japanese.[5] As mentioned earlier, the first national civil rights issue to confront American Buddhists was the wartime relocation and internment of Japanese Americans living in the western region of the United States. Following the Japanese attack on Pearl Harbor on December 7, 1941, most Buddhist priests of Japanese descent were immediately imprisoned because of their leadership roles in the Japanese community. Then on February 19, 1942, President Roosevelt, citing national security, signed Executive Order 9066, which authorized General John DeWitt to designate the western region near the Pacific coast a military area from which all Germans, Italians, and Americans of Japanese ancestry were to be evacuated. The civil rights of Japanese American citizens living in this area were suspended, and 76,650 were relocated and imprisoned (along with 38,520 Japanese who were foreign born). Of the American citizens, 35,327 were Buddhist.[6]

How did Buddhists respond? The majority of Japanese Buddhists in America belong to Mahayana Jōdo Shinshū (True Sect of Pure Land Buddhism),[7] so the record of the sect's experience can be taken as representative. Priests of Jōdo Shinshū began arriving in the United States in 1899 and organized their temples in 1914 as the North American Buddhist Mission (NABM). Immediately after Pearl Harbor, the NABM issued a statement condemning the attack. Then, after the evacuation order, Rev. Kumata of the NABM sent the following directive to the Buddhist churches:

1. Respect the Government of the United States and its laws and regulations; to hold fast to your religious faith in Buddhism, and to be calm and collected at all times.

2. Cooperate with the Defense of the United States of America and as loyal citizens and residents understand the vital necessity of and conform with the regulations pertaining to evacuation. . . .

   May we remind you to complete the survey of your community as has been suggested to you . . . and be ready to evacuate in a quiet and orderly manner.[8]

No protest nor resistance was offered by the Buddhist establishment nor by individual Buddhists. On the contrary, the NABM urged its members to respect the government, to be loyal citizens, and to evacuate in a quiet and orderly manner. If anything, Japanese Americans tried to identify themselves more closely as American, even if it meant denial of their civil rights. For example, in signing its letter, the NABM renamed itself the Buddhist Churches of America (BCA). It used English in its services rather than Japanese during internment, and in 1944 the ministers formally adopted a new set of bylaws that gave preference to American-born priests (called second generation, or *nisei*).[9]

Ironically, it was not Buddhists or any Americans of Japanese ancestry who initiated the first legal protests against the internment; it was two Irishmen from San Francisco, Wayne Collins and James Purcell.[10] Collins filed an action on behalf of Toyosaburo Korematsu, who was arrested for disobeying a military order by staying home in San Leandro to get married. The Supreme Court upheld his conviction over the dissent of Associate Justice Owen Roberts, who argued that such an action violated Korematsu's constitutional rights by "convicting a citizen as a punishment for not submitting to imprisonment in a concentration camp, based on his ancestry, and solely because of his ancestry, without evidence or inquiry concerning his loyalty and good disposition towards the United States."[11] Furthermore, recently declassified government documents reveal that Korematsu had not acted wrongly, and that the military and Justice Department had misrepresented the situation to the Supreme Court:

> government intelligence services unequivocally informed the highest officials of the military and of the War and Justice Departments that the West Coast Japanese as a group posed no serious danger to the war effort and that no need for mass

evacuation existed; and second . . . the Supreme Court was deliberately misled about the "military necessity" which formed the basis of the Korematsu decision.[12]

The loyalty of *nisei* and the misrepresentation by the military and Justice Department before the Supreme Court exposed a problem in U.S. government policy in wartime. In order to prevent such injustices in the future, Eric Yamamoto is attempting to develop "a clear and simple principle of judicial review for government restrictions of civil liberties for reasons of military necessity or national security."[13] Since the issue of civil rights in wartime is a legal matter beyond the scope of this chapter, this inquiry will be limited to an examination of why American Buddhists did not protest such a serious violation of their rights as Americans.

WILLING ACCEPTANCE OF SUFFERING

Four factors contributed to the lack of Buddhist protest: Mahayana Buddhist values, Japanese political culture, longstanding discrimination against Asian immigrants in the United States, and shame over Japanese aggression. Buddhists have a two-thousand-year heritage that discourages expressing resentment and any protests against injustices that one may personally experience. Underlying this attitude are the doctrines of karma and rebirth that argue that misfortune, persecution, or suffering are consequences of misdeeds performed in previous lifetimes.[14] Instead of expressing resentment, outrage, or protest against abuse, Buddhist monks teach acceptance, and even gratitude, for being able to dispose of the bad karma that they had accumulated in past lifetimes. An often-reported contemporary example is the acceptance of suffering by many Tibetan monks imprisoned and tortured by the Chinese government in the 1950s and 1960s who expressed gratitude to the Chinese for removing their bad karma from previous lifetimes.[15] The classic Zen text by its legendary founder, Bodhidharma, focuses two of its four practices on accepting any suffering that arises:

When the practitioner of Buddhist spiritual training experiences suffering, he should think to himself: "For innumerable eons I have wandered through the various states of existence, forsaking the primary for the secondary, generating in myself a great deal of hatred and distaste and bringing an unlimited amount of injury and discord upon others. Although I have not committed any offense in this [lifetime, my present suffering constitutes] the fruition of my past crimes and bad karma, rather than anything bequeathed to me by any heavenly or nonhuman being. I shall accept it patiently and contentedly, completely without hatred or complaint."

The second is the practice of the acceptance of circumstances.

Living beings have no [unchanging] self and are entirely subject to the impact of their circumstances. Whether one experiences suffering or pleasure, both are generated from one's circumstances. . . . Since success and failure depend on circumstances, the mind should remain unchanged.[16]

This Zen attitude of avoiding resentment and cultivating oneness with all circumstances was reflected in the response of Zen teachers to internment. Nyogen Senzaki was sent to Heart Mountain, Wyoming, and interned with another man, his wife, and child in a small cabin, which he regularly used for meditation with a dozen followers. "They are the happiest and most contented evacuees in this center," he once wrote.[17] This attitude of joyful acceptance of all circumstances is not exclusive to Zen but is fundamental to the practice of Mahayana Buddhists: The third of the six primary values of Mahayana is the willing acceptance of suffering with patience and endurance.[18]

Unlike the early European immigrants, most Japanese came to America not to escape religious persecution but to earn money so they could return to Japan to help their families. As a result, they did not expect to practice religion free from government interference. Instead, they were primarily concerned with providing food for their families in Japan and later in America. They also maintained a low profile to avoid trouble. All East Asians had long experienced government control over religion. Conformity to the state was a requirement for a religion to survive.[19]

Third, it is important to remember the racial persecution that Asian immigrants experienced from their first arrival in the United States.[20] In a sense, the wartime internment of Americans of Japanese ancestry was only the last in a series of social and legal restrictions they had to endure.[21] Moreover, the shock and shame that most Japanese-Americans felt as a result of the Japanese attack against America made them feel obligated to atone for the wrongs of the land of their roots. Not only did this attitude result in compliance to imprisonment, but it also contributed to exceptional bravery on the field of battle.

The concept of civil rights was not something that Buddhists knew from their past in Asia, nor even from their experience in America. Only with the return of *nisei* veterans from Europe, strengthened and sharpened by their participation in a war for freedom and justice, were they able to claim civil rights for themselves as Americans. Nevertheless, old attitudes persisted. On February 19, 1992, a motion was placed before the annual National Council of the BCA to support human rights. Even after the bitter wartime experience and the increasing influence of American-born *nisei* and *sansei* (third generation) ministers in BCA, the motion was defeated as not fitting with Buddhist doctrine. Alfred Bloom, one of the few European American Jōdo Shinshū ministers and dean of the only Jōdo Shinshū seminary outside Japan, reminded the Council that the rejection came fifty years to the day after President Roosevelt signed Executive Order 9066, which led to the wartime internment and loss of civil rights of their parents and grandparents.[22]

PART TWO: BUDDHIST APPROACHES TO CIVIL RIGHTS

No Buddhist organization had an explicit concern for civil rights until the Buddhist Peace Fellowship (BPF) was formed after the Vietnam War in 1978, even though individual Buddhists were involved in the civil rights movement of the 1960s (such as Susan Moon, the present editor of *Turning Wheel,* the quarterly journal of BPF).[23] Today civil rights are still not a major concern of most American Buddhists. Nevertheless, projects in the 1980s and 1990s, such as the Greyston Mandala in New York and the Engaged Buddhism Master of Arts program at the Naropa Institute in Boulder, Colorado, are concerned with social development and justice, including civil rights, based on Buddhist principles and practice. Although the most racially diverse Buddhist group in the United States is SGI-USA,[24] as an organization, it has not entered court battles for civil rights.[25] Nevertheless, SGI-USA has emphasized multiculturalism and peacemaking in its policies and programs. Accordingly, these groups will be used to illustrate Buddhist approaches to civil rights in the United States.

BUDDHISM, RACISM, AND HUMAN RIGHTS

Historically, Buddhism arose as a movement to free people from being victimized by a false sense of self (an eternal soul caught in an endless cycle of rebirth based on karma). As a result it helped to liberate people from being victimized by social discrimination based on the assumption of an unchanging individual nature (e.g., the Hindu caste system). Early Buddhism summarized its understanding as the "three marks" of existence: (1) inevitably people will experience misery (*dukkha*) because they get attached to things as if they were permanent; (2) but everything is impermanent (*anicca*); (3) including ourselves (*anattā*). The solution to human misery involved cultivating nonattachment to false ideas of permanency about ourselves (egotism or individualism) and about our relationships with others (social discrimination). The Buddhist movement may thus be seen as a practice that frees people from being trapped both by caste systems and by the American cult of the individual.

It is common to divide the Universal Declaration of Human Rights into three levels ("generations"), namely, articles 2–21 condemn government abuse of the individual, articles 22–27 affirm social responsibility for human development, and articles 28–30 propose a global political order. Buddhists claim that nothing is absolute, including human rights, because everything and everyone arises and exists within a web of changing conditions. But it is precisely this web of interdependency and kinship that facilitates universal sympathy and social responsibility. As a result, Buddhism provides a way to bridge the gap between the first generation of human rights principles (articles 2–21 dealing with protecting the individual from those who claim more absolute authority than is justified) and the second generation of human rights principles (articles 22–27, dealing with developing supportive social relationships). Currently, American civil rights advocacy is caught in the tension between these first- and second-generation human rights principles: on the one hand, trying to ensure the equal protection of individuals under the law, while, on the other, legislating social programs for human development that acknowledge special human needs. Because American doctrine emphasizes the protection of the individual against state interference, it has difficulty nurturing a supportive social fabric and state responsibility for the less fortunate.[26] American society reflects this dilemma as people increasingly sue each other to protect their individual rights, thereby creating a hostile environment for the expression of human compassion, so much so that medical professionals who stop to help accident victims have to be protected from being sued for malpractice by so-called Good Samaritan laws.

Buddhism has no concept of human rights at the level of metaphysics, but its criticism of ideological absolutes can play a positive role in protecting individuals from discrimination based on the false view of racial or gender superiority.[27] At the practical level Buddhism cultivates compassion for individuals, and this serves as a basis for social action. Too often the Buddhist rejection of the idea of an eternal, unchanging soul (*anattā*) at the ideological level is falsely interpreted as a rejection of human rights at a practical level. Fortunately, there are famous Buddhist champions of human rights who reject this interpretation, such as the Dalai Lama of Tibet, Aung San Suu Kyi of Myanmar (Burma), and Sulak Sivaraksa of Thailand. These champions cherish the preciousness of human life and believe the concept of human rights can be a powerful tool to check governments that imprison, torture, and kill those who hold dissenting views.[28]

Most Buddhists are not as familiar with the concept of civil rights as they are with that of human rights. Civil rights require an elected, representative government and a stable, independent legal structure so that laws can evolve to promote the welfare of all citizens. But in my lifetime, all major Buddhist countries (nations in which most citizens are Buddhist) have experienced the collapse of law as a result of conquest (Tibet, Korea, and Japan), or revolution (China and Vietnam), or military coups (Burma and Thailand), or civil war (Sri Lanka, Laos, and Cambodia). Only Mongolia and Bhutan have remained semiautonomous and peaceful, but their combined populations total only about three million (and Mongolia recovered religious freedom only in 1990, after several generations of communist rule). The discussion of civil rights has been a luxury available only to those countries like England and the United States that have had the good fortune to have stable, elected governments and an independent judiciary.

THREE LEVELS OF BUDDHIST ETHICS, HUMAN RIGHTS, AND CIVIL RIGHTS

The vast majority of American Buddhists are Mahayana, as are all East Asian Buddhists. The great scholar of Buddhist law, Gyōnen (A.D. 1240–1321), summarized Mahayana ethics in his *Risshū Kōyō* as threefold: to prevent all evil; to cultivate all good; and to save all beings.

1. Preventing evil includes: (a) dissolving false views and attitudes that lead to discrimination and racism; and (b) maintaining the basic five precepts, namely, not to kill, steal, lie, commit sexual misconduct, or become intoxicated.

2. Cultivating good includes nurturing inner understanding and attitudes of kinship, compassion, and joy toward others.

3. The goal of saving all beings is affirmed by Mahayana as its distinctive contribution to the Buddhist heritage and arises from the union
   of wisdom and compassion in the life of a bodhisattva (a person
   dedicated to attaining enlightenment, a future Buddha). Everyone is
   called to be a bodhisattva.

Mahayana Buddhism has various bodhisattva guidebooks that
begin with regulations and restrictions, but then move to universal
ideals and vows. These precepts are discussed in two popular Buddhist
texts: the *Brahma Net Scripture* (used both by monastics and laity)[29]
and the *Upāsaka Scripture* (used only by the laity).[30]

Just as human rights and Mahayana ethics have various levels, so
civil rights function in the same way, beginning in regulations and
law, but needing social values and ideals for support, guidance, and
fulfillment.

In contrast to Asian Buddhism, in America the Buddhist monastic
life (designed to prevent evil, as in the first ethic) is very weak. Instead,
the laity tend to emphasize relationships (cultivating good, ethic 2). In
the classic Mahayana tradition, the bodhisattva is said to postpone final
enlightenment until even the blades of grass are liberated (saving all beings, ethic 3).[31] Or as it is expressed in the Four Bodhisattva Vows first
set forth by Tiantai Zhiyi (A.D. 538–597) and still recited by contemporary Mahayana Buddhists:

Beings are infinite in number, I vow to save them all.
Obstacles are endless, I vow to end them all.
The teachings are innumerable, I vow to learn them all.
Buddhahood is supreme, I vow to embody it fully.

Although committed to saving all beings, Mahayana Buddhism does
not have a social vision similar to the Kingdom of God in the West. Instead, Buddhism places value on each individual as the locus of freedom
and the embodiment of Buddha nature: Everyone has the inherent potential to become a Buddha. Accordingly, everyone is to be treated with
respect, even those who abuse you. According to legend, when the Buddhist saint Sadāparibhūta was criticized and attacked by others "with
sticks or stones, he fled from them yet still proclaimed loudly at a distance, 'I dare not belittle you. You will all become Buddhas.'"[32] The vision of Mahayana, and the justification for civil rights, is that no one
should be demeaned, that everyone should be nurtured and respected,
since everyone will become a Buddha.

Unlike medieval religion, human responsibility today cannot be confined to individual thought and action, but is extended through space and time by numerous forms of technology and institutions. Since all Americans participate in a multitude of institutions, it is impossible to avoid doing evil (harming others or the environment) either through the government or our financial and corporate institutions. On the other hand, we have many new techniques to save beings and a much clearer idea of how many varieties of beings there are to be saved. As a result, new kinds of social and ecological engagement are required to fulfill Buddhist vows that must involve fresh analysis and application of Buddhist ethics in various social realms, including politics and economics. Some examples of how Mahayana social ethics might apply to civil rights are organized below in terms of the three levels of Buddhist ethics: (1) preventing evil, (2) cultivating good, and (3) saving all beings.

1. Preventing Evil   Specific guidelines for modern social action can be drawn from the five lay precepts shared by all Buddhists (don't kill, lie, steal, sexually misbehave, or become intoxicated). Underlying these rules is a basic respect for all life that does not discriminate against people based on their birth. Sakyamuni Buddha lived in ancient India where caste and clan divisions were common. Buddhists and their Jain contemporaries were the first to develop counterculture religious communities based on the idea of equality. In the foundational bylaws (*vinaya*) of Buddhism, caste restrictions are rejected in the Buddhist community (*sangha*), all decisions are to be made by consensus, and preferential seating arrangements are made only in terms of seniority. The only area of separation was gender—monks and nuns lived in separate communities—but otherwise family background or social status had no bearing on spiritual attainment or social arrangement within the *sangha*. An early version of one of the oldest and most popular Buddhist texts, the Prakrit version of the *Dhammapada*, states this position in its opening lines, namely, that a religious leader (*brāhmana*) is defined not by circumstances of birth or outer appearance, but by inner character:

Not by matted hair [of an ascetic guru], nor by family, nor by birth does one become a brāhmana;
but in whom there exist both truth and righteousness, pure is he, a brāhmana is he.
What is the use of your matted hair? O witless man! What is the use of your antelope garment?
Within you are full (of passions), without you embellish.[33]

Buddhists were among the first in history to develop not only a community based on equality, but also core arguments to support communitarian values. The concept of *anattā* (no permanent self; *anātman* in Sanskrit) asserted that the meaning of oneself was not defined by, nor limited to, one's birth. Karma was not unchanging, enlightenment (waking up) was the way to become free from the limits of karma, and everyone had the opportunity to become enlightened. The various Buddhist critiques of the caste system of four classes (priests, warriors, merchants, and serfs) have been carefully analyzed by Jayatilleke under seven points, which are summarized by Unno:

> *biological*—plants and animals have many different species but humans make up one species; *anthropological*—the caste system arose from divisions of labor and occupational distinctions and has nothing to do with race or color; *sociological*—the four-class system is not universal, not found among neighboring kingdoms; *legal*—punishment for crimes crossed class lines (not necessarily true in Hindu law as it is known today); *moral*—we are all subject to the karmic law; *ethical*—we are all equally capable of good and evil; *religious*—we are all endowed with the potential for enlightenment.[34]

Early Buddhism rejected the caste system and racism. Buddhism arose as a message of freedom and peace in reaction to a society dominated by discrimination that divided people into different castes and to an ideology that trapped people in an endless series of rebirths based upon the doctrine of karma.

The earliest writings of Buddhism reject both social discrimination and all ideologies as constructs that were not worth arguing over since doctrines are subject to so many changing conditions (such as language, social structure, and culture).[35] Instead, the foundational principles of Buddhism affirm that there can be peace only when we let go of our false discriminations and recognize that everything and everyone changes because they arise and exist in a web of evolving conditions.

Economic injustice can be considered another form of stealing, or another form of killing if people starve, or another form of sexual misconduct when daughters try to save their families by earning money as prostitutes. Today American Buddhist social activists are struggling for civil rights protections in many countries. As an expression of their Buddhist social responsibility, BPF writers in *Turning Wheel,* for example, regularly protest the denial of the civil rights of workers in factories outside America that are American-owned, or that make products under contract with American companies.

2. Cultivating Good The phrase "engaged Buddhism" was coined in the 1950s by Thich Nhat Hanh and meant "social as well as personal liberation."[36] In the midst of war, the task was to bring peace to society, but Buddhists felt that peace would not be lasting without inner peace. One of the gifts that Thich Nhat Hanh gives to social activists is to remind them of the need for balance in their lives. When the Vietnam war had become unbearable for him in 1966, he recalled an incident when his friend, Sister Chan Khong, asked him to identify the herbs she had prepared to serve with rice noodles:

> Looking at her displaying the herbs with care and beauty on a large plate, I became enlightened. She had the ability to keep her attention on the herbs, and I realized I had to stop dwelling on the war and learn to concentrate on the fine herbs also.[37]

The practice of being mindful of the present moment has been a constant lesson throughout engaged Buddhism and is summarized in Ken Kraft's book on *Inner Peace and World Peace*.[38] Buddhist inner peace depends upon seeing the interconnectedness and the preciousness of all things, and being mindful of our own physical reactions by watching our breathing.[39]

In September 1965 Nhat Hanh opened the School of Youth for Social Service (SYSS) with 300 students as a way to help those suffering from the war.[40] In a deeper Buddhist response to the war, Nhat Hanh founded a new Buddhist order in February 1965, the Order of Interbeing, which set forth fourteen rules based on several principles: (1) nonattachment to doctrines, "even Buddhist ones," in order to be open to the views of others, because truth is "found in life and not merely in intellectual knowledge"; (2) constant mindfulness of the suffering in the world, of our breathing, and of the wondrous details of each moment; (3) skillful methods to help people in all possible ways while avoiding doing harm in our livelihood, our words, and our relationships; and (4) mindfulness of our consumption, both its effect on the well-being of our bodies and the needs of others.[41] The SYSS no longer exists in Vietnam, but the Order of Interbeing continues to promote peace, wisdom, and kindness in the West, and to urge that inner peace is a prerequisite for world peace.[42]

BPF sponsored U.S. tours by Thich Nhat Hanh in 1985, 1987, and

1989, which helped to build a diverse coalition of social activists. Judith Simmer-Brown writes that "The most striking 'engaged' contribution he made on these tours was his compassionate embrace of American Vietnam veterans, whom he called 'the light at the tip of the candle,' the bearers of the guilt of a nation for a brutal war on the other side of the world. He sought reconciliation with them, and with the entire nation, for the destruction of his country."[43] Using the example of Thich Nhat Hanh and the Dalai Lama of Tibet, many American Buddhists claim that this search for inner peace and reconciliation with former enemies is needed to bring about civil society. Not only does "social work entail inner work," but Buddhists like Ken Tanaka and Ken Kraft also claim that a particular gift of Buddhism is its capacity to enable people to deal more constructively with conflict through Buddhist inner transformation.[44]

Mahayana Buddhism expanded the East Asian emphasis on the biological family by affirming that our relatives are universal since, based on karma and rebirth, we are related to every being. For example, Shinran (A.D. 1173–1263), the Japanese founder of Jōdo Shinshū, urged people to pray for all beings, not just their immediate family, since "all living beings have been my parents and brothers and sisters in the course of countless lives in the many states of existences."[45] East Asian Buddhism extended Confucian social ethics beyond the immediate family to include all people, and beyond the human realm to include all animals, insects, ghosts, and hell-dwellers. As a result, the modern environmental movement has found a ready ally in the Buddhist tradition.[46]

Compassion is often considered an emotion in the West, but in Buddhist tradition it is presented as an insight: once we have seen that we are related to others, that we are the same kind, we develop a sense of kinship, and kindness becomes an expression of this insight in action. Compassion is not based primarily on our emotions, but on our understanding. The Buddha urged his disciples to teach others by appealing not to a special virtue possessed only by the enlightened, but by calling upon their common human sympathy to help others who are less fortunate. As Buddhists become free from attachment to things, themselves, and ideologies, they are free to allow their natural sympathy for others to emerge.

This conviction that people share a common bond of sympathy when they are freed from discrimination and attachment permeates Buddhism. Harvey Aronson explains that in the four earliest collections of Buddhist teachings (*nikāya*), the Buddha Gotama refers to his own practice only five times by using special terms for goodwill (Pali *mettā*) and kindness (Pali *karunā*), but uses the common word "sympathy"

(Pali *anukampā*) more than twenty times. Whereas *mettā* and *karunā* had to be cultivated, *anukampā* is universally available: "Sympathy is the fraternal concern that is present in an individual and does not require cultivation or meditative development."[47] Accordingly, the early texts describe the Buddha's dedication to helping others as based not on some rarefied motive, but on the most common and universal sympathy, as an "individual who arose and came to be for the welfare of the multitudes, for the happiness of the multitudes, out of sympathy [*anukampā*] for the world; for the benefit, welfare, and happiness of gods and humans."[48] Similarly, the Dalai Lama repeatedly says that he is convinced that all people are good at heart.[49]

3. Saving All Beings   Early Buddhism emphasized character development and personal responsibility: hatred was to be avoided at all costs,[50] and actions were to be motivated by kindness and sympathy. But when Mahayana added the vow to save all beings, Buddhists embraced an ethic of social responsibility and accountability. The *Upāsaka Sūtra* assigns special priority to helping those who are sick and to treating your enemies as kin.[51] Other Mahayana scriptures reinforce this vision, such as the vow of the bodhisattva in the *Śrīmālādevī Buddhist* scripture:

> If I see lonely people, people who have been jailed unjustly and have lost their freedom, people who are suffering from illness, disaster or poverty, I will not abandon them. I will bring them spiritual and material comfort.[52]

Having compassion for others has always been a Buddhist value based on an individual, person-to-person ethic, but the problem for Mahayana in society has been developing legal and institutional structures free from political control.[53] However, encouraged by the freedom of religion permitted in America, Buddhists are again trying to apply their principles to society. For example, a concern with "right livelihood," one step on the Buddhist eightfold noble path that is as old as Buddhism, relates to Article 23 of the Declaration of Human Rights.[54] When Zen master Bernard Glassman started a Zen community in New York in 1979 with his family and students, they searched for a means of livelihood, but not just for themselves. Glassman explains in *Instructions to the Cook:*

> We wanted to develop a way to make a living, a livelihood, that would help others as well as ourselves. And we wanted to become

involved in our community—in the world of social action—in a way that would transform the lives of the people we were helping. . . . I wanted to start a business that could also provide jobs and job training outside our community. But more than that, I was looking for a way for business itself to become a force for social change and a way of spiritual transformation.[55]

When Glassman, now the abbot of the Zen Community of New York and the Zen Center of Los Angeles, writes about organizing a bakery for the homeless and unemployed, he likens it to cooking a Zen meal: Cleaning the kitchen is like cleaning the mind. Work must be not only socially useful, but also have a spiritual base to be satisfying. "The spiritual aspect of right livelihood is that it helps us attain a transformation of consciousness from an ego-centered attachment to a recognition of interdependency, with each other and with the earth." Glassman goes on to write:

> For example, many of the people who come to work at the bakery start out thinking only of themselves. To help them get a glimpse of the interdependence of life, we created teams that were paid according to how well each team produced. So if someone on the team didn't know the job very well, it behooved the rest of the team members to teach that person how to do the job better, because then they would all make more money. Working in teams helped to shift consciousness a little bit away from thinking just of how they were going to improve themselves. The focus was still connected with making more money, but now it functioned in terms of the whole group. This moved workers another step toward seeing their interdependence, which then allowed the next step to unfold, and the next, and the next.[56]

As a second-generation human right, gainful employment requires not just job creation, but also training and building personal skills of responsibility and confidence. The social service provided by religiously committed communities is conducted outside the roles of government and business, but is important to the functioning of both. Jeremy Rifkin argues that our society has overemphasized government and business to the neglect of the social community. His hope is that in the high-tech global economy a new social contract will emerge that reemphasizes the value of social and community service.[57]

The universal responsibility expressed in the third level of Mahayana ethics requires active Buddhist participation in global decision-making. Today American financial interests are dominating the global market, but forms of global governance to inform and channel the global market toward a fair and just world order for all beings are lacking. Today, the global market favors the few at great cost to the well-being of the many; it is a vehicle for the expression of American power but often denies democratic and Buddhist principles.[58]

The U.S. Congress is properly concerned about linking trade agreements with human rights issues in other countries. We can limit our concern to civil rights in the fifty states only if we ignore that our companies and government invest U.S. dollars in foreign governments and overseas markets, only if we ignore that American prosperity is fed by workers for American companies around the world, only if we forget that Nike footwear is made by underpaid women and children in Haiti and Indonesia, and only if we turn a blind eye to Disney Mickey Mouse toys made in Burma by child labor in army-owned factories.

From a Buddhist view, the twentieth-century idea of a "free global market" is destructive when it violates local communities and is used by the industrialized countries to bully smaller nations into surrendering their autonomy to foreign influence and ownership.[59] Not only Muslims criticize this destructive economic imperialism; a Muslim-Buddhist-Christian coalition seeking "Alternatives to Consumerism" has been formed by the Buddhist layman, Sulak Sivaraksa, and includes American Buddhists.[60] David Loy sees consumerism as a modern religion,[61] and other Buddhists condemn it as an addiction that stimulates greed and violates Buddhist principles, a cancer that devours inner peace, natural resources, and social justice.

AMERICAN BUDDHISM AND CIVIL RIGHTS

Standing with Martin Luther King, Jr., before the American press in 1966, Thich Nhat Hanh appealed to the American people to live up to their democratic values and vision. For many Buddhist Americans, Thich Nhat Hanh still inspires and guides them in a struggle against civil injustice. When BPF was founded in 1978 in Hawaii by Zen master Robert Aitken, it began as a protest against the Vietnam war.[62] When BPF expanded to its present site on the West Coast, it sponsored Thich Nhat Hanh's first U.S. tour in 1983. Also in 1983 a Buddhist affinity group of BPF committed civil disobedience while demonstrating at the nuclear weapons laboratory in Livermore, California. No longer passive nor concerned only with local issues, Buddhists began challenging American policies in an effort to protect the life and civil rights of all occupents of the planet.

Today BPF has four thousand members internationally with headquarters in Berkeley and is the American representative of the International Network of Engaged Buddhists (INEB), established in 1989 by Sulak Sivaraksa in Bangkok (on the inspiration of Thich Nhat Hanh). INEB publishes a quarterly journal called *Seeds of Peace,* while in the United States BPF publishes the quarterly *Turning Wheel.* Other journals that treat civil rights issues are the nondenominational *Tricycle* (with a circulation of fifty thousand and focused on Tibetan Buddhism, Zen, and the Vipassanā-meditation movement),[63] the *SGI Quarterly* (a journal of Soka Gakkai International), and *Sakyadhita* (a journal of the international Buddhist women's movement). Also, in the 1990s the Naropa Institute of Boulder, Colorado, began offering a certified master of arts program entitled "Socially Engaged Buddhism" that integrates teachings of INEB, BPF, Thich Nhat Hanh, and the Buddhist Sarvodaya movement of Sri Lanka[64] into its curriculum.

In 1983, the BPF Board included not only Zen Buddhists like Robert Aitken and Gary Snyder, but also an American woman from the Theravadan tradition, Joanna Macy, and a third-generation (*sansei*) Jōdo Shinshū minister, Ryo Imamura. Recently Macy recalled that it "was extremely arrogant of us—BPF people—to think that we represented Buddhism in America, when both in terms of time and numbers, we were overshadowed by the Pure Land and Nichiren Buddhists. And we were from different cultures. Our social concerns were different."[65] Ryo Imamura was an important bridge. The grandson of Bishop Yemyo Imamura who had publicly supported the labor strike by sugar plantation workers in Hawaii in 1920, and the son of Bishop Kanmo Imamura who was an early teacher of Snyder, Ryo was one of a handful of Jōdo Shinshū ministers who were antiwar activists in Hawaii in the early 1970s along with Alfred Bloom. Later Bloom became dean of the Jōdo Shinshū (BCA) seminary in Berkeley, and his work has been distributed in a book entitled *Engaged Pure Land Buddhism* (1998),[66] which raises issues about how Jōdo Shinshū can better relate to social needs. A recent service activity of American Buddhists is Project Dana, an organization of volunteer caregivers who respond to the needs of those who are homebound. Having begun in Jōdo Shinshū temples in Hawaii in the early 1990s, the project has already spread to other denominations and to California, and is the only Buddhist group among the more than 700 members of the National Federation of Interfaith Volunteer Caregivers (NFIVC).[67]

The largest American Buddhist group is SGI-USA[68] with about one hundred thousand members. Whereas the Jōdo Shinshū membership remains at least 90 percent Japanese-American after more than a century in America,[69] by contrast local leaders of SGI-USA are less than 20 percent Japanese and more than 30 percent African American or Hispanic.[70] Also, it is the only Buddhist group with a weekly newspaper, *World Tribune,* the only sectarian Buddhist publication that regularly highlights social issues and civil rights.[71] The social activism of SGI-USA is based on the teachings of Nichiren (A.D. 1222–1282), who was arrested and condemned to exile on several occasions for challenging the government.[72] In the 1930s, a school teacher, Tsunesaburo Makiguchi, founded an educational reform movement called Soka Gakkai based on Nichiren's teachings. In 1944 Makiguchi died while in a Japanese jail for protesting against the military government. The second president, Josei Toda, also was imprisoned, but after the war he fought against other religions, which had collaborated with the government during the war, and against nuclear weapons. Accordingly, SGI-USA has inherited a tradition of social protest both from Nichiren and from its own twentieth-century lay leaders.

SGI-USA members believe that all people in the world are bodhisattvas and that this world can be transformed into a Buddhaland through chanting together and through support for each other, one's family, one's neighborhood, as well as by advocating democracy, nonviolence, human rights, and the work of the United Nations. Challenging the concept of race as an artificial social construct,[73] SGI-USA formed a committee at the national level in 1996 to promote greater sensitivity to ethnic and gender diversity.[74] The Youth Peace Conference (YPC) formed in 1991 by the president of SGI, Daisaku Ikeda, actively collaborates with the United Nations in New York and has held seminars on "Human Rights, Human Responsibilities" (New York, 1991), "Environmental Security, a Basic Human Right" (New York, 1992), and "Treasuring the Future: Children's Rights and Realities" (traveling exhibit, 1995-present).[75] SGI-USA also celebrates numerous cultures with annual festivals in New York, San Francisco, and Chicago. While cultivating civil rights concerns among its members and reorganizing its local districts nationwide to be more responsive to the needs of their neighborhoods, SGI-USA does not become embroiled in politics as it did in Japan. As an organization, it believes in the separation of church and state.[76]

CONCLUSION

Buddhism and Jainism began as part of a cultural movement of ascetics (*śramaṇa*) who left their families searching for alternatives to conventional society in order to find a more satisfying and lasting way of life. As a community founded by a former prince who was committed to nonviolence and detachment from worldly concerns, Buddhists rarely challenged local governments. As a result, the Buddhist community has been easily manipulated by dictatorial governments, and rarely been involved in reforming society. But Buddhism also has a long history of rejecting ideas of discrimination.

The three Buddhist disciplines of morality, meditation, and wisdom cultivate an awareness of the interdependence of all things in order to avoid false attachment and injury to others and oneself. Mahayana Buddhists added the idea that because of our interdependence, peace and wisdom could not be complete until all other beings were saved. Although Buddhist practices have emphasized the application of the three disciplines to individuals, now Buddhists are applying these practices to society at large.[77] Just as individuals need to be freed from suffering that comes from delusion, hatred, and greed (the three poisons), so do institutions.[78] In the social sphere, Buddhists traditionally have applied the three disciplines by advocating regular consultation and public dialogue on issues.

Even though these principles are fundamental to Buddhism, they have not always been followed historically. American Buddhists interned during the war did not protest the violation of their civil rights, nor did they demand consultation or sue the government. On the contrary, after the war they tried to resume their normal lives. A scar has remained on that generation, however. Very few Japanese American Buddhists protested the Vietnam war, and they have not been actively engaged in the civil rights struggle. It seems clear that their imprisonment in American camps, plus their religious and cultural heritage, have shaped them and their children to cultivate a low profile, to work hard, and to obey the authorities in order to be accepted as good citizens.

Buddhists have been most active in civil rights, protesting violations against others—in Tibet, Thailand, Burma, and elsewhere. But recently, the nonsectarian Buddhist Peace Fellowship (BPF), and several Buddhist sectarian groups (such as the Zen Community of New York and SGI-USA), have become active in America on issues of social development and civil rights. Although he now lives in exile in France, Thich Nhat Hanh's Order of Interbeing has become active in America,[79] but the effort is still small. Buddhist beliefs in the lack of permanancy of all things and the need to be constantly mindful of each moment remain the basis for their compassionate involvement in society. Accordingly, the engaged Buddhism of SGI-USA, of the Zen Community of New York, and of Thich Nhat Hanh has much in common with the faith-based beliefs of the Christian activists who led the civil rights movement of the 1960s.

All the Buddhist social activist groups have encouraged interfaith collaboration. The Naropa Institute,[80] Robert Aitken,[81] Sulak Sivaraksa,[82] the Dalai Lama,[83] and Thich Nhat Hanh[84] have all participated in numerous, longstanding interfaith activities.[85] Glassman has ordained Christian clergy into his order,[86] and after its break with the Nichiren Shoshu priesthood, SGI-USA dropped its exclusivism to become a supporter of interfaith cooperation in the 1990s.[87] Given its concern to save all beings, SGI-USA has committed itself to the work of the United Nations as a necessary part of its mission, under the assumption that global well-being requires global dialogue, the extension of international law, and the support of relief organizations. Although SGI-USA and BPF have not yet collaborated in a united Buddhist social project, in 1996 they jointly participated in the "Socially-Engaged Buddhist-Christian International Conference" held in Chicago.

Few American Buddhists have been active in the courts, in voting registration efforts, or in developing civil rights legislation. Just as the declaration of human rights has three levels—protecting the individual, developing the social, and establishing the global—so Mahayana Buddhist ethics has three levels: to prevent evil, to cultivate good, and to save all beings. While the law can be effective at the first level in defending the individual and preventing evil, in the end it cannot legislate personal character, supportive relationships, responsibility, and the values that are nurtured at the second level. As Jeremy Rifkin has argued, neither government nor business can adequately promote social development, which relies more on human relationships nurtured by the home, school, community, and religious observance. Most American Buddhists and religious people of all traditions make their strongest contributions in promoting these relationships, and it has been a special concern of BPF and SGI in America.[88]

Equally significant but more far-reaching is the third level, the salvation of all beings, the global objective proclaimed by Mahayana rhetoric. Even though these third-level values are supported by all American Buddhists, global responsibility has become the active agenda of only three American organizations: BPF, the Naropa Institute, and

SGI-USA. The work for local and global responsibility is inspired by a new style of Buddhist leadership represented by Sulak Sivaraksa, Thich Nhat Hanh, Daisaku Ikeda, A.T. Ariyaratne, and the Dalai Lama. Local Buddhist activists remain alert to tackle injustice whenever it appears, cultivating spiritual resources to give depth to their struggle, and mobilizing efforts through sharing information in journals and over the Internet. For the long haul, new educational programs are going forward to equip young people with a global vision, such as the Naropa Institute's M.A. in Socially Engaged Buddhism and SGI's Soka University of America in Los Angeles. It is hoped that Martin Luther King, Jr., would be pleased.

CHAPTER SIX

Evangelical Cooperation in the Cause of Racial Justice

JAMES W. SKILLEN

What was the American public's understanding of the civil rights movement in the 1960s? On what terms did the majority, including Christians of various stripes, promote or at least acquiesce in the rejection of legal discrimination—legalized racism—against African Americans? What were their expectations of the consequences?

While it would be impossible to know for sure the answers to these questions, I want to hazard a generalization in response, with two aims in mind. The first aim is to contrast the opinion of the broader public with that of most African Americans and civil rights leaders, both black and white, whether religiously motivated or not. The second is to use this contrast to shed light on the current climate of opinion regarding further attempts to end racial discrimination, in order to set the stage for an evangelical Christian argument on behalf of broad public cooperation to advance equal treatment of all citizens.[1]

When I speak of "racism," I will be referring to attitudes, habits, and practices that manifest a deep bias against people of another race because of their race. I mean by racism a bias deep enough to constitute a considered view or enduring feeling that people of the other race are of a lesser human value or quality and deserve discriminatory treatment. By "legalized racism" I mean public laws that represent and uphold racism as defined above. Legalized racism amounts to legally approved discrimination against citizens of one or more races. When laws have been changed to uphold equal treatment of all citizens, then companies, organizations, or persons that violate those civil rights laws may be challenged in the courts in accord with the nonracist standards of the law. Many racist attitudes and practices, however, cannot or should not be fought by legislative or legal means. And not every act by which people distinguish or separate themselves from people of other races is an act of racism. While legalized racism has, for the most part, been eliminated in the United States, many illegal practices continue to be contested in the courts and many private attitudes, habits, and practices of a racist character remain.

Let me begin now to try to answer the questions above. With regard to the difference of outlook and expectations between the broader public and those who vigorously led or welcomed the civil rights revolution of the 1960s, I would suggest that Americans in general accepted civil rights advances in the 1960s and 1970s for a variety of reasons. First, against the backdrop of the constitutional amendments that followed the Civil War and in the face of post-World War II court rulings and federal legislation, even most of those who did not applaud the civil rights movement were inclined to abide by the law once the reforms were in place. Second, many were moved by the nonviolent protests under the leadership of Martin Luther King, Jr., which made manifest to a national public the unjust, unconstitutional treatment of African Americans: Thus, people were moved to accept changes in the law that overcame legalized racial discrimination. Finally, most Americans came to accept for blacks what they believed immigration or hard work had offered them, namely, an opportunity to make their way in American society on the same terms as everyone else.

In stating the generality this way, two qualifications are important. First, I believe that a large percentage of Americans, and not only Southerners, remained uncomfortable about the fact that the courts and the federal government had to impose changes of this magnitude. Their discomfort represented not simply a "states' rights" mindset, and not, in most cases, a deep-seated or abiding racism. Instead, their discomfort was due to the fact that social life and social policy outside the South before World War II had, for the most part, changed under conditions of local and state governance and gradual social and economic adaptation rather than by federal mandate. Similar reservations about federally imposed change had been expressed in opposition to the national income tax, for example, and would be expressed again by opponents of *Roe v. Wade* and other Supreme Court decisions and federal government actions perceived to be acts of "social engineering."[2]

The second qualification is that, regardless of people's attitudes toward federal action, a large percentage of, perhaps even most, Americans understood their "freedom to be American" as something to be expressed through local communities, ethnic enclaves, small towns, and culturally distinct or class-based churches, clubs, and other organizations. The civil rights successes, whether welcomed or acceded to, were not expected to change this picture radically. In other words, the majority could recognize as legitimate the legal right of African Americans, like that of Italian Americans or Scandinavian Americans or Chinese Americans, to vote, own property, seek employment, form their own clubs, and organize religious institutions. However, in the view of most Americans this did not imply or require a radical reordering of society by judicial or legislative fiat from Washington. In fact, most Northern whites felt that the American social, economic, and political order was legitimate in a way that they did not think the Southern slave society had been legitimate. Once African Americans had the right to participate in society without legal discrimination, the majority of Americans expected they would desire the kind of society that the majority already knew and accepted—a racially as well as institutionally differentiated society. This was the bias of both conservatives and most liberals.[3]

The point here is simply that many Americans supportive of "equal opportunity" or "civil rights for all" did not envision further, legally enforced, social and economic "special treatment" for African Americans of a kind not given to them when they or their ancestors immigrated or when they suffered similar deprivations. Whites, in this regard, failed to grasp the weight of the debt that African Americans felt was owed them, a debt that had mounted up over hundreds of years. Blacks, on the other hand, underestimated the ethnically diversified, unintegrated, often insecure and class-divided character of "white" society.

In contrast to this broad generalization about "most Americans," another sketch must be drawn to represent the outlook and expectations of most civil rights leaders and African Americans. Overcoming the legal discrimination that African Americans had endured since the Civil War carried for this minority the hope of full inclusion in American society, a society they thought of, perhaps too naively, as a solid, relatively homogeneous, socioeconomic enclave from which only blacks were excluded. America, after all, had been home to African Americans for hundreds of years. They were not new immigrants from another world or culture. Yet for all their contribution to the development of the United States, they had known only a marginal existence and wanted full access to and benefit from society. This is what the civil rights reforms were supposed to achieve. Once the laws changed, all doors should be opened. The hope of integration was a hope for full entry, for full "brotherhood" in one family under God in which whites and blacks together would share in the fulfillment of the dream of a just and fully integrated kingdom of God in America. Black as well as white preachers and many civil rights leaders encouraged these expectations by their visionary rhetoric of a new human community.[4]

This second generalization may be no more accurate than the first as an oversimplified picture of a complex reality. Certainly there were significant differences among civil rights leaders and African Americans, just as there were among Americans generally. Those who broke away to form the Black Power movement, for example, had a different idea of pluralism and inclusion from those who adhered to King's ideals. Nevertheless, if these two generalizations are warranted, then they may help explain why the civil rights movement, led largely by black Christians with support from some white church leaders and people of other faiths, did not keep expanding or even hold together as a religious-civil rights movement after the initial successes of the 1960s.

To put it in its simplest terms: On the one hand, a majority of Americans, including Christians, accepted the achievement of civil rights for blacks (meaning that blacks would no longer be singled out by the law for discriminatory treatment), but they did not expect racial harmony to be produced by means of legal interference in every institution of society. They believed in a political order that protected individual freedom and social diversity, not in a natural community that homogenizes all diversity and trumps all other authorities. They came to believe, or at least to accept, that African Americans should be allowed to enjoy the same constitutional rights they enjoyed, but not that government and the courts had authority to force change everywhere in society. On the other hand, those—including Christians—who had the grandest expectations about civil rights reform, which was supposed to lead to full inclusion and integration, would not be satisfied until racial inequality was completely eliminated. And the chief institutions to which they continued to look to bring about change were the federal government and the courts.

From a Christian point of view, it seems to me, there are truths on each side of the contrast drawn above, truths that were not, and have not yet been, brought together into a single reform movement. The truth on one side is that a constitutionally limited government and legal system should protect and support a highly differentiated society of diverse institutions, diverse ethnic communities, diverse churches, and diverse convictions about the task and limits of government itself. The health and well-being of most nongovernmental organizations and relationships have to be worked out within them, on their own terms, in relative independence. The United States is, and should be, a pluralistic society. To say this is not to advocate a laissez-faire attitude on the part of government. Rather, it is to argue as a matter of principle that a just government is one that upholds the rights and respects the independent responsibilities of nongovernment institutions and relationships. The United States also is and should be a political order, a constitutional polity, governing a complex society, not an undifferentiated community in which government and the courts serve as all-pervasive, omni-competent authorities.

The truth on the other side is that racial discrimination of the kind that demeans people violates the integrity of creatures made in the image of God and is wrong everywhere, in every institution and relationship. The challenge in seeking to overcome racism, then, is to avoid the error of disregarding the first truth, a disregard that is evident when citizens try to use legal and political means to achieve racial respect, integration, and equality everywhere and in every institution of society.

Christians who cling to the first truth about limited government and the relative freedom of independent institutions may resist the force of the second truth. They may be slow to challenge racism with appropriate nongovernmental means and slow to accept rightful government action simply because it is taken by government. However, those compelled by the second truth to seek the end of all racism by political and legal means may be slow to see the violation of the independent responsibilities of nongovernmental institutions when government acts inappropriately. Each side produces a reaction on the other, pushing each toward error rather than the truth that it harbors. Those resisting too much government intrusion and social engineering end up resisting even legitimate efforts by government to redress racial grievances. Those seeking to overcome racism everywhere become convinced that any resistance to their efforts is evidence of racism.

If, in looking back on the last thirty-five years, contemporary antidiscrimination leaders, including Christians, focus on the second truth and judge that all resistance to legal/political reform efforts is due to deep-seated racism, their judgment will likely be to continue to fight by political and legal means to eliminate every inequality between blacks and other Americans. Christians who share this conviction will probably continue to seek better, clearer theological/moral arguments for just such a legal/political campaign. Given the importance of the first truth, however, I would question such theological/moral arguments to see if they err because of too undifferentiated an idea of society.

If, on the other hand, those, including Christians, who believe that racism everywhere is wrong can also recognize that some of the resistance to certain racial reform efforts has been due not to deep-seated racism but to the feeling or conviction that some of those reform efforts have actually caused other injustices, then the reformers may conclude that a different assessment of the situation and a different approach to ongoing reform may be necessary. In this case, the aim, which I advocate, is not to go soft on racism but to recognize that racism must be opposed by many different means appropriate to, and built on respect for, the diversity of institutions and responsibilities in our society.

In what follows I will try to show how the two truths hang together in a Christian public philosophy and argue that antidiscrimination efforts should be incorporated into a larger quest for social justice in a complex, differentiated society.[5]

ANTIDISCRIMINATION AND SOCIETAL COMPLEXITY

What do I mean by suggesting that there may be reasons other than racism for resisting some of the political and legal efforts made in the name of seeking racial equality? Is it possible that the legal fight against racial discrimination could unintentionally cause injustice? Let me illustrate by turning to one of the most important arenas of social life—education—where the struggle for racial justice continues to this day.[6]

Since the 1970s, one of the means chosen to seek racial integration in society has been school integration, with heavy dependence on busing. As long as attention is focused only or chiefly on the legal requirement of equal treatment of all child-aged citizens within a publicly owned enterprise, the attempt to integrate public schools by means of busing appears to be an entirely rational reform effort. If every citizen should be treated equally before the law, if all children are citizens and must attend school, and if schools are part of the civic commons controlled by government, then what could be more rational than to try to overcome racial separateness and unequal treatment by proportionately mixing differently colored children throughout publicly controlled schools? If the variables to be considered are simply school-aged citizens of all colors, on the one hand, and all available public school buildings, on the other, then a rational answer is for the public authorities to find technical means (buses) to disperse the children in a manner that achieves integration.

But what if additional variables ought to be considered in order for government to do justice to the education of children? What if justice also, at the same time, needs to be done to families, neighborhoods, social networks, and religious communities that are not directly owned or controlled by public authorities? What if busing, despite its intent to remedy racial injustice, creates or aggravates other injustices?

These questions are only partially rhetorical, because many integrationist busing attempts have failed to achieve their aim and many have provoked angry reactions from parents, including African-American parents. Why? Because schooling does, in fact, have to do with several different institutions and responsibilities. It has to do with parental child-rearing responsibilities and family well-being, including the close connection between families and neighborhoods, among families, and among parents and teachers. Busing has often done damage to these other relationships, separating families from the schools their children attend, dividing neighborhoods, and weakening the connection between teachers and the families of students as well as the connection between parents and children.[7]

One might of course argue that all the negative reactions to busing have arisen solely or chiefly because of racism on the part of whites. And there is no doubt that legally enforced unequal education for different racial groups is unjust. However, what if the negative reactions to busing have arisen not because of racism and not because most whites object to blacks receiving an equal education, but because, for example, parents, regardless of race and ethnic background, do not want their children bused far from home or to a school serving a community foreign to them?[8] And what if there are other ways to achieve a more equal educational opportunity for all children of all races, ways that can also do justice to more, if not all, of the social, economic, religious, and other human variables?

By raising this last question in the context of a series of "what ifs" I am intentionally opening the door to a different approach to civil rights reform. I agree completely that legalized racism going back to slavery has been a universal blight that traumatically affected every sphere of life for African Americans. But once legalized racism was overturned, subsequent legislation aiming to overcome educational, economic, and other disadvantages of African Americans had to deal justly with the educational, economic, and social institutions involved. Once racial discrimination was no longer legal, the multi-dimensional character of social, economic, cultural, and political advancement for African Americans could no longer be addressed by the means used earlier.[9] Each of the diverse social, economic, cultural, and political spheres of life must be considered on its own terms, in its own integrity, with its own evaluative criteria. Not every inequality or injustice in every sphere of life can be judged racist in origin, even though the long shadow of slavery and racial discrimination will remain a factor for years to come. Other inequities, such as income disparity, and other injustices, such as government's failure to provide adequate services and protection, on the one hand, or government's improper interference in non-political spheres of life, on the other, must be addressed.[10]

An analogy might be helpful. Worldwide anticolonialist movements that arose during and after World War II showed considerable unity in different colonial contexts. Large majorities rallied around those who led the fight against the single evil that affected all of colonial life. Once independence came, however, the focus on reconstruction and governance of society had to be complex and many-sided. Decisions about economic development, education, trade, mutual accommodation of diverse racial, religious, and cultural groups all required different types of judgment appropriate to each sphere of life. At this stage, society-wide unity became next to impossible because different groups, different professions, and different economic interests disagreed about the terms and the outcomes. Cooperation could no longer be reduced to the agreement to fight colonialism, even though the shadow of colonialism would remain for a long, long time.

Once the civil rights movement had succeeded, by and large, in changing the law so that it no longer discriminated against blacks because of their skin color, the positive construction and reconstruction of society required widely diverse judgments and strategies about economic, educational, cultural, and political reforms. Christians and non-Christians alike, both black and white, moved off along different paths to reform. It is not surprising that a coalition of many groups, religious and non-religious, organized to oppose one great evil, would have difficulty hanging together to promote five or ten great goods, each requiring different criteria of judgment about how to advance, and most of them not realizable by means of direct government mandates against racial inequalities. While it is true that all blacks suffered in many areas of life under legalized racism, just as all former colonials suffered in many areas of life under colonial rule, the achievement of civil rights reform, like the overthrow of colonialism, presented the liberated ones with the possibility of exercising full, complex, diversified personhood in many human relationships and institutions. In other words, the basis of their communally organized identities could no longer be reduced to "black" or "colonial" as had been the case under oppression, but now could become—had to become—as fully differentiated as human identity allows.

RUDIMENTS OF A CHRISTIAN PUBLIC WORLDVIEW

What can be said, then, from an evangelical Christian point of view about the demands of justice in a complex, differentiated society where the influence of centuries of legalized racism still exists but where constitutional and statutory law is now on the side of nondiscrimination? What does biblical faith have to offer as a basis for bringing together the two truths of racial equality and of doing justice to the full range of differentiated human responsibilities?[11]

The argument I am making[12] grows from my wholehearted commitment to Jesus Christ and thus to the encompassing vision of biblical Christianity. I do not see Christian theology as an ingredient simply to be added to supposedly secular knowledge about politics, economics, and culture. Rather, I approach all the arenas of human responsibility, including the political, as arenas of created life that require a biblical framework of understanding to comprehend their true meaning and normative obligations. Because of the biblical teaching about creation and human responsibility, my argument takes for granted the legitimacy of a complex society, differentiated into multiple institutions, organizations, and relationships, each with a distinct responsibility before God and deserving of just treatment under public law. It also starts from the conviction that people of all races have been created in the image of God and therefore deserve equal treatment.

Biblically speaking, the gospel of Jesus Christ encompasses creation in its entirety, revealing not only that in and through the pre-incarnate Word of God all things were created (John 1, Colossians 1, and Hebrews 1), but also that in and through the incarnate Son of God all things hold together and find their true meaning and ultimate destiny. Christianity, like Judaism, is not simply a salvation religion; it is a creation-restoration religion, a creation-fulfillment religion, a way of life that interprets the meaning of all things in their relation to the purposes and actions of the Creator-Redeemer. In order to understand the Christian salvation story, therefore, it is necessary to understand what and who is being saved, and that means understanding the original meaning and purpose of the creatures God has made. This has everything to do with the way we interpret diverse human responsibilities and the way we address injustice and seek reconciliation, restoration, and reform.

What is creation? Biblically speaking, this world in its entirety is the result of God's seven days of creation (Genesis 1:1–2:4; Hebrews 4). The unfolding of the human generations (including all races) in the context of the complex environment of air, water, heavenly bodies, plants, sea creatures, fowl, and animals takes place beneath, and on the way to, God's Sabbath rest. The grand Sabbath of all creation is God's culminating celebration of the completion, the fulfillment of the divine labors.[13]

One of the fruits of God's labors is the image of God—human creatures, male and female—who constitute part of God's sixth creation day and the climax of what God makes. The Creator has appointed human creatures to labor as stewards of one another and of the rest of creation. The work, the fellowship, the communication of human beings throughout their generations all come from God's hand and anticipate fulfillment and peace in God's Sabbath rest. God's labor thus inaugurates, encompasses, and incorporates human labors, and God's climactic seventh day stands as the ultimate goal and hope for the creation's blessing, including the anticipated eschatological blessing to human stewards— "Well done good and faithful servant." Humans live in a God-centered world; God does not revolve around a human-centered world.

God's covenant with Israel is structured from start to finish by this Sabbath framework: six days of labor and a seventh day of rest; rest every seven years for land and people; and a jubilee celebration every fiftieth year as a climax to the seven sets of seven years (Leviticus 23–25). All of this is loaded with political and economic conditions and consequences. God's covenant in Christ is then revealed as the ultimate, eschatological fulfillment (not yet complete) of Israel's Sabbath hopes, of God's promise of peace to the nations through Israel.

For the purpose of this paper two points need emphasis. First, God's Sabbath celebration (the climax of creation) is not something realized within the unfolding of the creation's sixth-day human generations; the fulfillment of God's creation-encompassing purposes, the kingdom of God, is, in that sense, not a human achievement within history by political or any other means. The Creator creates the seventh day; the Lord completes and finalizes the divine Sabbath; the divine Judge and Redeemer settles all scores and carries the chosen people into eschatological fulfillment. Consequently, all human desire to reach the end-time within this age is an outgrowth of human pride, lust, or greed.

Humans have been called to labor with a view to honoring God and receiving the divine blessing. They pray as Moses did for God to establish the work of their hands (Psalms 90). Yet the final blessing, the ultimate establishment and fulfillment of human labors is God's gift. Human labors are not in vain if done in accordance with God's will, but God is the one who finally gathers all the fruits of human labors into the kingdom and reveals it when the time is right. And that fulfillment is beyond history; it is the seventh-day blessing of the first six days in their entirety, not simply the last part of history at the end of the sixth day. From this point of view, God's Sabbath celebration in peace is what Christians anticipate as the new heaven and new earth, the day of resurrection joy when every knee is bowed and every tongue confesses Christ as Lord.[14]

Second, the shaping of history through the work of the human generations has led, by creation's design, to ever-increasing societal complexity. By their very nature human beings—the image of God—are creative, history-making creatures, manifesting ever more diversified accomplishments in organization, the sciences, the arts, economic productivity and commerce, education, media, government, and dozens of other areas. Humans in culturally diversified communities are similarly complex. In all of these activities together, humans image God; all of this diversity is required for the full meaning of humanity to be expressed.

Human disobedience to God, sin, comes from and goes to the root of all that is human and of all that is involved in the relationship between humans and God. Sin distorts everything good, and not simply in a general way or in the disposition of the heart. The distortions become manifest in every dimension of life as degradations peculiar to each sphere of creaturely responsibility, including institutional structures and conduct. Sin means hateful marriages, child abuse, environmental destruction, cheating on exams, political corruption, violated business contracts, murder, racism, and much more. Racism is an expression of human sinfulness and its formal entrenchment in public law as legalized racism corrupts the entire political/legal order. An injustice anywhere, in any sector of life, will have negative consequences everywhere. At the same time, however, the attempt to overcome one form of injustice, in politics or economic life, for example, or in the family, or schooling, will not be sufficient to overcome the same injustice in every sphere of life. Each sphere requires its own reforming. Nor will the reversal of an injustice like racism be sufficient to overcome other kinds of injustice. Each sin must be met on its own terms. Injustice is as manifold as human nature and expresses itself with as much complexity as society exhibits.

The good news of God's grace, demonstrated in God's release of Israel from Egypt and later through the birth, crucifixion, and resurrection of Jesus Christ, proclaims God at work overcoming sin and renewing creation—the full, seven-day creation. The death, resurrection, and ascension of Christ have thus reopened the way to creation's fulfillment, to the Sabbath rest of God, to the promised land anticipated by Abraham from the beginning (Hebrews 11:10). Humans, through God's redeeming grace, may once again have hope for eschatological peace, or "shalom," which is more than simply gaining an infusion of moral energy to seek the renewal and reform of life in this age (I Corinthians, 15; Hebrews 12:22–29). Consequently, the earthly quest for justice, whether in the political or other spheres, grows from God's creation-restoring grace and anticipates God's final gift of Sabbath rest, which is not designed or built by human hands but rather has been the creation's goal from the beginning. Nevertheless, the work of human hands, including our struggle for justice, finds its way into the kingdom insofar as the good work of God through us in our daily labors is part of what God gathers into the storehouse of the fulfilled kingdom (Philippians 2:12–18; Revelations 21:1–4, 22–27).

The calling to pursue public justice is the Creator's call to citizens and governments just as the call to parents to love their children and the call to agriculturists to steward land and animals is the Creator's call. Within our earthly generations, justice requires giving what is due to each creature and to each unique sphere of differentiated human responsibility. Family life, schooling, business, journalism, government and politics, church life, and everything else must receive its due. Every attempted reductionism does injustice to human beings, whether it be a reduction of people to their racial identity and then discriminating against them, whether it be a political reduction of human society by means of totalitarian government, or whether it be a reduction of society to economics and the market. Human life in all of its grand, constantly unfolding complexity may not be reduced to a single dimension or sphere. Nor can the reform of injustice be achieved by a single means or through the agency of a single institution, even if it is the most powerful institution (state) or one with transcendent aspirations (church).

Given this emphasis on creation, it is legitimate to ask what, if anything, is significant about the church when it comes to facing questions of racism and social reform. And with the emphasis I have placed on societal differentiation, what if anything does the church have to do with the state? How does my argument help address the question of how Christians should cooperate with people of all faiths and of no apparent faith to work for racial justice?

In the New Testament the church is identified as the community or body of people called to turn over their entire lives, in all areas of creaturely existence—heart, soul, strength, and mind—to the disciplined following of a new way, the way of truth and life in Jesus Christ. Christians are variously called the people of God (I Peter 1:1), the bride of Christ (Revelation 21:9), brothers and sisters of Christ (Hebrews

3:1), a kingdom of priests (I Peter 2:9), and more. This new people, called by Christ's name, may not be identified simply as one socially differentiated institution among others (distinct from state, family, enterprise, etc.) or as something that stands over and against various aspects of creational life in this world.

The people of God, according to biblical revelation, are those who, in the entirety of their lives, embracing all of creation, are being restored in Christ to the true meaning of their creaturely purpose and identity. When Paul addresses the church (the body of believers) in a particular city, he almost always addresses them in multiple capacities, including their families, marriages, employments, and "citizenship" (Romans 13; Ephesians 5:21–6:9; Philemon). The distinction between the "people of God" and "the world" is not between one organization and others, not between the religious and the secular, but between the people in Christ who have accepted the call to obey God in all areas of life (the city marked by the love of God) and the people who place their faith in someone or something else and, within the same creational reality, are moving in a different direction, following other loves and dedicating their lives to a different ultimate lord or purpose.

If religiously deep ways of life divide people in fundamental ways across all spheres of life, then how in the world is it possible for them to find common ground? From a Christian point of view, Christian believers and non-Christians hold in common (or are held in common by) the same Creator, the same creaturely identity as the image of God, the same sinful disobedience that distorts the life of all humans, and the same grace of God that restrains sin and upholds creation. Of course, to make this statement is to demonstrate the inescapability of starting from some kind of religious or religiously equivalent standpoint, because many people do not believe there is a Creator, nor do they believe that their identity is that of God's image, or that they are sinners defying God's will, or that Jesus Christ is the hope of the world. Thus, what I profess that all people hold in common will not be admitted by others, and that which they believe everyone has in common I may not agree with. This brings us back to the fundamental significance of the competing or contrasting worldviews and religious commitments by which people live in the same creation.

To claim that biblical Christianity has something distinctive to say to every sphere of life, including civil rights in America today, does not mean that Christians have biblical grounds for claiming a privileged position for themselves. That to which Christians bear testimony is the lordship of Jesus Christ, who has commissioned them for service by calling them back to standards of truth, justice, stewardship, and love that bind all human creatures. Through allegiance to Christ by faith, Christians accept God's forgiveness of their sins and God's invitation to seek paths of repentance from evil in every sphere of life. Inspired by the hope of God's promise of Sabbath fulfillment, Christians are supposed to learn the habits of service to others. Through the disciplines involved in the Christian way of life, they are obligated to discover more and more of the true meaning of being human, of being the image of God. Allegiance to God through Christ should come to expression chiefly through the way Christians live and work together and in the ways they relate to non-Christian neighbors in all spheres of life. And that witness includes the aim of urging others to turn in faith to Christ to find renewal of their lives both in this age and in the age to come.

To love God and one's neighbors so much that one wants the neighbor to find restored communion and eternal life with God through Christ should go hand in hand with wanting to work with those same neighbors in every way possible to cooperate in restraining evil and promoting good among all human beings (Romans 12:18; Hebrews 12:14; I Peter 2:12–17). By such love Christians bear witness to God's love in Christ. Christians hold no monopoly on God's grace or favor. God is not willing that any should perish and sends rain and sunshine on the just and unjust alike (Matthew 5:38–48; Romans 12:9–21). Christians simply bear witness to the God who is gracious in Christ, and they ought to radiate that grace by loving and seeking justice for all their neighbors.

Christians should see no contradiction between, on the one hand, urging others to turn to Christ in faith in order to find redeeming paths of truth along which to walk in all areas of life and, on the other hand, working cooperatively with non-Christians in various spheres of life where agreement can be found to walk those paths together. In certain areas of life, such as politics and the market, everyone shares the same citizenship and the same market even if they disagree about how those arenas of life should be shaped. From an evangelical Christian point of view, Christians are those among the unrighteous who believe that Christ's love is restoring them and the whole creation to a righteousness acceptable to God. And faith in God's restoring work has everything to do with the pursuit of justice and peace and stewardship in this world because all humans belong to God, and Christ now claims authority over all creation (Matthew 28:18–20).[15]

From this point of view, one may not approach political and cultural issues with the assumption that religion and the church function

on one side of an equation that puts the state and "secular" political organizations on the other side. Although organized churches are differentiated social institutions, religions are all-encompassing ways of life.
Differentiated organizations called churches can be distinguished from
business enterprises, professional organizations, families, and states. But
Christianity and the Christian way of life cannot be confined to church
life and theology. Nor is religion reducible to one function among many.
Rather, church institutions and their leadership serve as a central, but by
no means exclusive, way of organizing Christian communities that are
always more extensive than those church organizations themselves. The
Christian way of life is as broad and as diversified as creation, and
Christian leadership will also have to be as diversified as creation. Thus,
in addition to ecclesiastical organizations and leadership, there need to
be educational, scientific, artistic, economic, political, medical, and
other kinds of Christian organization and leadership. And this drives us
back again to questions about the proper identity and healthy meaning
of various relationships and organizations in a differentiated society.

One of the weaknesses of Christian ethics as practiced by many
ethicists is that much of Christian ethics tries to move from redemptive
love, or from general norms of justice, stewardship, love, etc., to specific, individual behavioral outcomes or practices, without distinguishing the unique character and responsibilities of different kinds of
institutions. At the same time, in order to extend Christian ethical considerations widely enough, the attempt is often made to seek a standard
that is accepted by enough people and enough religious traditions to
demonstrate that standard's universality.

The mode of reasoning I am adopting can be called a creation-
redemption mode. Its claim of universality comes by way of God's redemption of the entire cosmos in Christ. The creation includes everyone,
and the Creator's standards and mandates for human life hold for everyone. The standards and mandates are no less binding on human beings at
this point in the unfolding of history with its complex, differentiated societies than they were at an earlier stage of historical development. The
fact that everyone on Earth does not agree with a biblical perspective on
life does not contradict its universality, because on its own terms the biblical story gives an account of the reasons for just such disagreement
among God's creatures. The antithesis between truth and error is constituted, therefore, by human obedience and disobedience to creation-order
standards that hold everyone accountable to God and neighbor. This antithesis does not always correspond to the difference between self-identi-
fied Christians and non-Christians, for all are sinners. Nor does it

correspond to the distinction between majority and minority. The majority is often wrong. People standing even within the biblical tradition may disagree in interpreting God's will and in making judgments about what is right and best for families, corporations, friendships, and politics. Yet the judgments people must make about which agreements to accept as correct and which side of a disagreement to affirm depend on the normative standards being acknowledged. And the nature of one's response to creational standards depends on the fundamental worldview or faith commitment orienting one's life.

Unlike those, on the one hand, who contend that a universal rationality or ethical reasoning can transcend fundamental religious/worldview differences,[16] and unlike those, on the other hand, who contend that worldview differences are so fundamental that they are largely unbridgeable,[17] I would contend that God's will and normative standards for creation, judged and redeemed in Christ, call into question (for blessing or condemnation) every human judgment and action. At the same time it is precisely that common reality of a dynamically differentiating creation under divine standards that is disagreed about among people who hold contending views of the meaning of the universe and of human responsibility in the world. The final settlement of what is true and loving and just will not occur short of God's final judgment and celebration of the eschatological Sabbath, but in the meantime, contention occurs among groups that live in the same universe. What binds humans together is God and creation, including our very humanity, and our humanity is fundamentally religious (tied to and dependent on the Creator) such that when people dedicate their hearts to false gods and mistaken ambitions, they will in certain respects stand fundamentally at odds with one another in their views of reality, in the ways they try to shape history and society, and in the ways they choose to live in diverse spheres of life.

In the face of these divisions, the gospel of Jesus Christ explains not only why Christians should be committed completely to Christ, but also why they should be committed to an open, pluralistic, and democratic political order. As I will outline more fully in the next section, the basis for this is that God alone through Christ assumes authority to carry out final judgment. God has not given Christians authority to separate wheat from chaff, sheep from goats. In this age, Christians and non-Christians both live by God's grace in the same world. The Christian community is not a separate political entity; it is a community of faith that extends across all national and political borders. Thus, the quest for truth and justice must be an open quest. Every human should enjoy the same rain and sunshine in the field of this world, the same right to participate and exercise voice in public. Until Christ returns in glory, Christians have been called to act like their Lord in seeking to bless every neighbor. Thus, in seeking to live at peace with everyone, Christians, as a matter of principle, must seek to build political community with all neighbors, not allowing divisions to stand as if they are final or ultimate. Working to end racial discrimination, to promote religious freedom, and to uphold a constitutionally limited government that protects the rights and freedoms of nonpolitical institutions is a direct expression of evangelical Christian obedience and witness.

AN EVANGELICAL CHRISTIAN CONTRIBUTION TO RACIAL JUSTICE

Let us return now to the questions and concerns about civil rights and the splintering of religious cooperation in the ongoing fight for racial equality and harmony. What contribution should evangelical Christians be making to the achievement of racial justice in American society?

Cooperation in the civil rights movement of the 1960s among black and white Christians and people of other persuasions contributed little toward the development of a Christian public philosophy sufficient for life in a religiously diverse and institutionally differentiated society. The movement and its impact reaffirmed the normative standards of the Bill of Rights for individual citizens, insisting that African Americans be treated as full citizens. Beyond that, however, it left largely intact the idea that politics is essentially a means to the interest-group ends pursued by diverse groups of citizens, including ends that are sometimes quite utopian and morally undifferentiated in character. Consequently, the particular identity, quality, and limits of the political order as a public community of citizens distinct from and yet related to non-political spheres of life, each with its own integrity, was not sufficiently understood and thus failed to unify even those who locked arms in the civil rights struggle. When the goal of a fully integrated and equal American society did not materialize, the movement that had successfully united opponents of legalized racism was not strong enough to maintain a movement for justice in a complex society.

One of the most important contributions that evangelical Christians should be making to American politics today, especially for the purpose of encouraging cooperation to advance reconciliation among diverse races, is to develop a public philosophy adequate for a complex and religiously/philosophically diverse society. Unfortunately, this aim does not occupy the attention of enough Christians. Most continue to approach politics as other citizens do, with a rather simplistic conservative or liberal bias oriented by an interest-group mentality rather than by a public-interest mentality.

Far too many evangelical Christians, for example, are most visibly at work to recover the simpler, largely WASPish moral order of an earlier America in which the majority was loosely united in an American civil religion rather than by a biblically reforming vision of public life.[18] Most evangelicals are not racists in the sense that they believe African Americans are less than the image of God or should not have equal access to public life. Most evangelicals simply want people of all races to enter into what they believe is the agreement held by the moral majority about what constitutes a good American society—the America still thought of by many Christians as God's specially chosen nation. Christians of other stripes may hold a more conservative or a more liberal view of what the national community should be, but few if any are clamoring for a Christian political philosophy that can make a substantial contribution to resolving issues of complex justice in a pluralistic society where people of all races and religions should have equal legal standing and receive equal treatment.

In contrast to the various denominations of American civil religion, with their competing but largely undifferentiated national moralities and political pragmatics, biblical Christianity calls believers to a political responsibility rooted in whole-life allegiance to Jesus Christ. Christianity is a way of life that is incompatible with any version of civil-religious nationalism and any mode of politics that does not answer the demands of justice for a highly diverse society.[19] Christians ought to be working for a political order that does justice to all citizens in all of the differentiated relationships and institutions in which they bear responsibility before God. On the one hand, this means relinquishing utopian dreams of an undifferentiated national community, particularly of an America as God's new Israel or as the Kingdom of God on earth. The society of the United States is not a faith community; it is structurally differentiated and religiously diverse, and as a national political community it can be just and do justice only as an institution of citizens under public law. At the same time, a just political community is more than simply an enforcer of market contracts, as if all that exists beside the state are individuals and the market. Individuals are always more than citizens and consumers. A just polity is one that upholds equal and fair treatment under law for families, churches, schools, businesses, and other organizations that have become differentiated with their own distinct meaning in the historical course of creation's unfolding. A just polity is also one that recognizes and gives equal treatment to people of all faiths. Public laws do equal justice to all citizens in their social-cultural diversity.

Consider, for example, the large consensus Americans of all colors and faiths share about the non-establishment of religion. We may hold different philosophical and theological convictions about why this is good, but the political agreement or unifying consensus is that religious practices should not be forced by government and that all faiths should share the same right of religious freedom under the law. Our constitutional political agreement is to support religious pluralism. We do not insist that citizens hold a unified religious agreement in support of the political agreement.

The evangelical Christian basis for this political principle, I would argue, is the biblical teaching that God sends rain and sunshine on the just and unjust alike, that Christians are supposed to be like their Father in heaven, and that until Christ returns to complete the earth's judgment and redemption, his followers have no authority to try to separate wheat and tares or to try to enact any form of final judgment within the field of this world (Matthew 5:43–48; 13:24–30, 36–43; Romans 12:11–21). Even while being convinced on biblical grounds that atheists and nature-religionists, for example, are fundamentally mistaken in faith, Christians should work as a matter of biblical political principle for equal legal treatment of atheists and nature-religionists, as an expression of God's grace and providence. As an evangelical Christian I want to be free as a citizen to work publicly on behalf of the equal treatment of people of all faiths and worldviews as an expression of my Christian faith. This will mean arguing against Christians who do not share this public philosophy while also standing politically with those who support this political position even if they do so on different religious or philosophical grounds. In both cases, however, I am seeking political cooperation for the support of freedom for diverse faiths, the consequences of which may include the flourishing of religious practices that I believe are mistaken and ungodly.

Taking into consideration the diversity of faiths, the diversity of races, and the diversity of institutions and organizations in our complex society, how can justice be done to all at the same time? In what respect can a pluralist perspective offer more hope for equal justice for all than can other viewpoints?[20]

Without due attention by government to diverse nongovernmental institutions and responsibilities, justice cannot be done to citizens. Race cannot be abstracted from the complex and diversified institutional reality in which different races exist. A clear and extensive injustice existed under slavery and during the era of the exclusion of blacks from basic civil rights protections. But once the civil rights reforms put an end to legalized racism, the means by which justice had to be done to African Americans had to become as complex and diversified as necessary for the just treatment of all citizens and people of any race in all of the institutional responsibilities they bear.

In making the case for religious freedom, I argued that the American political consensus has been in favor of pluralism, recognizing the importance not only of equal public treatment of all faiths but also of the church's independence from public government. What if the same were now instituted for education, combining the same two principles of pluralism?

Institutionally speaking, government can do justice to the educational needs of all citizens only by recognizing that families and schools are differentiated institutions with their own identities and needs, different from the political order of citizens under law. Government cannot do justice to them by treating either family or school as an instrumentality of the state.

In addition to recognizing the institutional diversity of society, government should also do justice to the diverse range of religious/philosophical views of its citizens. Whether or not citizens are traditionally and explicitly religious, their faiths or philosophies should not be used as the basis for discriminatory public treatment of the educational needs of children. Public justice must be done to all families with their diverse views of life, and any inequity (for example, in educational funding) will be unjust to those families who are excluded from, or compelled against their will to conform to, the majority's uniform schooling option.

One reason why some parents, whether black or white, might choose one school over another is for religious or other conscientious reasons. A poor African-American family that wants to educate its children in a thoroughly Muslim or a thoroughly Christian way should not be discriminated against because the family is black or because it is poor or because it is Muslim or Christian. And each of these qualifications requires a different level of consideration. Government does not do justice to this family if it excludes it from public benefit or legal protection because it is black. Justice is not served if the family is ignored or left without educational choice because it is poor. Justice fails if the family suffers educational discrimination because it is Muslim or Christian. The attempt to secure racial equality in a way that violates the family's values or educational choices or religious freedom is not just.

CONCLUSIONS

A Christian public philosophy is needed to deal with the complex, differentiated society in which racism is still alive even though legalized racism has been almost entirely dismantled. Evangelical Christians should be locking political arms with other Christians and people of diverse faiths and convictions for the sake of advancing justice for all citizens. Many of the needs of African Americans and other racial minorities cannot be addressed by direct legal and political means that pre-select race as the qualifier and then use economic, educational, or other institutions as means to overcome racial inequalities. The reason is that in a differentiated society, educational, ecclesiastical, familial, and economic institutions cannot be treated simply as means to a political end. They have their own ends and qualifications, and justice must be done to them on their own terms.

Once citizens of color are not singled out for publicly enforced exclusion or negative discrimination because of their color, the manner and means of their inclusion must come about in ways that do justice to the responsibilities and standards appropriate to institutions and relationships that are not racially or politically qualified.

Evangelical Christians need to repent of their racism and, among other things, recognize that even within their own ranks there are all kinds of people, red and yellow, black and white. Beyond that, evangelicals should seek, in cooperation with other citizens, to reform educational, economic, and family policies that do injustice to people within those spheres either because government is overstepping its bounds or because government is failing to address injustice entrenched in public law itself.

What is needed in all of this is not simply more preaching about racial equality, or an appeal for greater moral willpower on the part of those who want the "brotherhood of all people." What is needed is a movement that can draw together people of all races and faiths for the cause of public justice in a pluralistic society, justice that begins with equal civil rights for all and continues with the just treatment of people in their diverse non-political roles—in the differentiated institutions and relationships free from government interference—without discriminatory treatment because of faith.

CHAPTER SEVEN

Latino Popular Religion and the Struggle for Justice

ALLAN FIGUEROA DECK, S.J., AND CHRISTOPHER TIRRES

In the late 1970s, I realized that although I was a strong critic of institutionalized Catholicism, whether I liked it or not I was culturally and ethnically a Catholic, and that my (ex-Catholic) agnosticism was merely the other side of the same coin. In other words, five hundred years of Mexican Catholicism couldn't simply be erased with political awareness. . . . Despite a conscious rejection of formalized religion, my sensibility and my symbolic languages were soaked in the pathos, the high drama, and the excessive aesthetics of Mexican Catholicism.

—*Guillermo Gomez-Peña*[1]

This chapter deals with the relation between two defining character-istics of Latino[2] culture today: (1) a thriving religious tradition and (2) a set of very severe civil rights problems. In many ways, the contrast could not be starker. Though Latinos are projected to become the na-tion's largest minority group in the first decade of the twenty-first cen-tury, the majority of Latinos at present experience substandard education, limited political representation, discrimination in the hous-ing and job markets, schools more segregated than those attended by blacks, and political and legal attacks that have curtailed, among other things, the rights of legal immigrants in this country.[3] What are we to make of this present crisis, and how, if at all, can Latino religion be a resource?

This essay will seek to explore one fundamental, if not defining, aspect of Latino culture—Latino popular religion. For over five hundred years, popular religion has served as a locus of meaning out of which people of Latin American descent have conceptualized justice. In light of the economic, social, and spiritual crises of our day, we will seek to show that Latino popular religion continues to be both a symbolic resource of meaning as well as a potential agent for change, especially as it is connected to broader, concrete social and political concerns.[4]

In this chapter, after first briefly situating Latino popular religion within a historical context, we shall consider how popular religion, seen as a syncretism of indigenous, Spanish, and African roots, espouses inclusivism, performance, and community—three necessary criteria for any vibrant model of justice. Then, using the example of César Chávez as our guide, we will consider the transformative political possibilities of Latino popular religion by situating it within a critical-theological framework. What we hope to illustrate to the general reader and religious specialist alike is that U.S. Latino religion evinces a real potentiality for engaging structures of injustice, discrimination, and oppression, and thus has much to offer to any discussion on civil rights.

Latino Popular Religion
within a Historical Framework

U.S. Latino popular religion is an amalgam of three distinctive strains of religion: the pre-Columbian, the medieval/baroque Spanish, and the African. Today, this mixture of religious currents often takes on a more popular than official religious character. In Latino popular religious practice, special attention is given to the felt quality of the sacred. Often emotive and tactile, Latino religious expression is epitomized not only by established rituals, such as Holy Week Passion plays that highlight the suffering drama of Christ's crucifixion, but also in daily interaction, through everyday verbal expressions like *"¡Válgame Dios!"* ("Bless me!" or "Oh, my God!") or *"con el favor de Dios"* ("God willing"). Latino popular religious practice also inscribes marginal religious rituals with new meaning. To take a well known example, *Día de los Muertos* ("Day of the Dead"), originally an Aztec practice, is given new Christian significance. Finally, in Latino popular religion, official church creeds are recontextualized locally. The *posada,* for example, is a culturally specific, communal reenactment of Mary and Joseph's search for a birthplace for the coming Christ. The meaning of religion in this popular context is less about what the official church says than what the people practice. As an affective, marginal, and recontextualized religious expression, Latino popular religion has often been considered by clerics to be at odds with official church practice, even though official church practice may itself espouse affectivity, was at one time itself marginal, and is situated within its own contextualized cultural context.

Though one can make numerous other interpretive distinctions between official and popular religion, as we will note later, these two tracks need not be construed as mutually opposed. In many ways, it was precisely the marriage between the symbolic valence of popular practice and the critical sway of official institution that propelled the United Farm Workers' movement into this nation's political and religious consciousness. As this case shows, a symbiotic existence between popular and official religion can indeed lead to new actualizations of greater justice. In order to better understand this, one must first examine Latino religious practice as a mixture of three distinct historical traditions.

Before Christianity arrived in the Americas, it is estimated that a vast population of over twenty-five million native peoples, representing well over a thousand indigenous cultures, flourished in the New World, particularly in Mesoamerica, the Caribbean Islands, and the Andean region of South America. Although the variation among indigenous groups is dazzling, the diverse Amerindians tended to share one common orientation to the world: religious life (as we now call it) was an integral part of everyday living. There was not, for all intents and purposes, a steadfast distinction between the realm of the sacred and the realm of the profane.

The indigenous peoples of the Americas constructed their cosmovisions around their revered gods. Myths, symbols, and poetic expression endowed their lives, and their everyday actions were filled with drama, sounds, ritual, and sacrifice. The Amerindian relationship with the divine was a sacramental one, that is, a relationship that was materially and symbolically mediated. A deeply aesthetic approach to the sacred grounded their sense of reality.

Spanish Catholicism arrived in the New World in the late fifteenth century, brought by Franciscans, Dominicans, Augustinians, and Jesuits. This distinctive form of Christianity was not *Roman* Catholicism but Western Christianity in its *Iberian* form.[5] It blended in a distinct way elements of medieval and baroque culture. Like the already existing indigenous practices, this Iberian form of Christianity thrived on sacraments and symbols and was highly ritualistic, graphic, and dramatic.[6] The question of how Amerindians interpreted these new symbols is, of course, an important one. Though some Amerindians may have indeed made a wholesale substitution of their native symbols for newer Christian ones,[7] it is probable that a great many appropriated the Christian symbols provisionally and subversively. New symbols, at least initially, were conduits for the worshipping of familiar, native gods. Though uniquely Christian doctrine and symbols (especially after the Council of Trent, 1545–63) were to gain more and more prominence among the natives, especially among successive generations, one should note that to this day Latino religious practice retains, at least in its style, an affinity with an earlier *Iberian* Catholicism.

Beginning in the sixteenth century and extending to the 1800s, hundreds of thousands of African slaves were brought to the Americas by the Spanish, Portuguese, and English. The religion of the Yoruba and other West Africans was suppressed but continued to find expression in Afro-Latin styles of religion. Like Iberian Catholicism, African religions shared common features with the pre-Columbian religions: rich mythologies, a dramatic sense of ritual, a plethora of symbols, and a highly developed sense of mediation. Again, syncretism between indigenous and Catholic symbols predominated. In the same way that the Aztec goddess, Tonantzin, became *la morenita* (the brown-skinned Virgin of Guadalupe in Mexico), the African goddess of the sea, Yemayá, became Our Lady of Regla (patroness of sailors in Cuba). The Africans, like the Amerindians and the newly arrived Iberian Christians, imbued their rituals, symbols, and polyrhythmic music with sensuality and power as well as with a sense of freedom and autonomy.[8]

With its rich 500-year history of religious syncretism, Latino popular religion continues to manifest itself throughout the Americas. To speak of U.S. Latino religion as being completely different from Latin American religion would be a mistake, given that large parts of the United States today have a "Latin American" history that predates the birth of this nation. Half of Mexico's land and all of Puerto Rico, for example, were annexed by the United States in 1848 and 1898, respectively, owing largely to the seductive appeal of manifest destiny. In both of these cases, the United States not only acquired new lands, but also inherited centuries-old cultural-religious practices.

Moreover, one cannot so easily delineate a clear line between U.S. Latino and Latin American religious practice today given the enormous influence of emigration from Latin America to the United States, which continues to infuse the U.S.-Latino context with Latin American religious practices. With the arrival (and, oftentimes, return) of Mexicans, Dominicans, Salvadorans, and others to and from this country, U.S.-Latino religious expression continues to encompass a strong Latin American component (and vice versa). The infusion from Latin America has occasioned, among other things, a sharp rise in U.S.-Latino Pentecostalism. As is now evident, the dramatic growth of Pentecostalism within Latin America has had profound effects on the growth of Latino Pentecostal communities in the United States.

Of course, one must avoid any facile conflation of "Latino U.S.A." and Latin America, especially given their varying historical, economic, political, and linguistic contexts. To cite a few examples, not all U.S. Latinos speak Spanish; "assimilation" tends to be a North American, not Latin American, concern; and poverty and repression have very different histories, responses, and effects in the two regions. In terms of a common religious imagination, however, U.S. Latinos and Latin Americans share much in common.

FEATURES OF LATINO POPULAR RELIGION THAT INFORM A CONCEPTION OF JUSTICE

Having noted that U.S.-Latino and Latin American religious expression is an amalgamation of pre-Columbian, medieval/baroque Spanish, and African influences, we turn to the significance of Latino popular religion today. Popular religion, broadly speaking, may be defined as "the set of experiences, beliefs, and rituals which ecclesiastically and socially peripheral groups create and develop in their search for an access to God and salvation."[9] Theologian Ada María Isasi-Díaz outlines five characteristics of popular religion within the U.S.-Latino context: (1) it is a communal way of thinking and acting, which expresses the religiosity of Latinos; (2) it attends to certain ritual practices considered marginal, such as sacramentals; (3) it is syncretic, in that it incorporates meaning from other religious traditions into (largely Catholic) practices; (4) it reinterprets "official" religious practices and gives them different meaning; and (5) it transmits these understandings as part of the Latino culture, in contrast to their being mere personal options.[10] The symbolic markers of popular religion in U.S.-Hispanic culture are wide-ranging and varied, and, within the Catholic tradition alone, may include such things as *curanderas* (a type of healing that usually mixes spiritism and Catholicism), *hiervería* (herbal curing), *santos* (the appeal to saints for intercession), folk religious sayings (such as *"Con el favor de Díos"*),

Marianism (especially, the deep veneration of *la Virgen de Guadalupe,* Mother of the Americas), *promesas* (promises of action made to God for God's benevolent intercession, such as promising to walk on one's knees to church for the healing of one's child), *madrina/padrino* (the godmother/godfather who helps raise the child, spiritually and otherwise), *veladoras* (lighting candles for sacred intercession), *la bendición de la madre/abuelita* (the special blessing of the mother or grandmother, who, in most cases, is popular religion's stalwart upholder), praying the rosary, building home altars, scapular-wearing, processions, and reenactments of biblical stories and religious folk tales. Many of these elements are part of the lived experience of Latinos in the United States, whether or not they are practicing Catholics.

In a significant way, U.S.-Latino theologians have helped to uncover the immense spiritual and political resources that can be found in popular religion. Scholars Roberto S. Goizueta, Orlando Espín, and Alejandro García-Rivera have pursued the nature of U.S.-Latino religion with considerable depth and creativity. Sociologists Ana Maria Diaz-Stevens and Anthony M. Stevens-Arroyo have recently produced the most thorough analysis of Latino religion currently available.[11]

One of the more important contributions made by U.S.-Latino theologians has been to point to the aesthetic quality of Latino popular religiosity. Latino popular religion has to do not only with religious symbols themselves, but also with the way that symbols are interpreted within a community. In short, the aesthetic quality of popular religion can be described as the communal interaction of the faithful, the lived experience of the people. For the majority of Latinos, popular religion remains, whether explicitly or implicitly, the "birthplace of the self."

Theologian Roberto S. Goizueta offers us some of the most exciting work on the communal, aesthetic nature of popular religion. Goizueta contrasts American individualism with Latino *comunidad* and argues that *comunidad,* both the Latino community itself and the sense of community that it fosters, challenges the detached sense of individualism within U.S. culture.[12] For Goizueta, Jesus and Mary, the primordial images of Latino popular Catholicism, reflect the relational, not individualistic, approach to human existence.

In defending a sense of community, Goizueta implicitly maintains that ethical stances within the Hispanic community emerge out of a sense of solidarity and compassion, which are born out of a memory of suffering.[13] Latinos, Goizueta argues, are attentive to the fact that "The fundamental and indispensable ground of human freedom is the historical expression of otherness, difference, or particularity. . . ."[14] The very historical experience of Jesus' pain on the cross is important to U.S. Hispanics today because, by pointing out their own communal pain and suffering, Latinos thereby point to its inevitable end.

Popular religion rooted in a communal history of suffering—from the Spanish conquest of the Americas to the present-day civil rights crisis among Latinos—helps to reveal the deepest dimensions of Latino existence. It lays the groundwork for a conception of justice because it affirms through everyday practices and actions that community and love are indeed important criteria for justice. As we will see more specifically, Latino popular religion highlights three important criteria for justice: inclusivism, performance, and community. In what follows, we shall briefly consider each of these.

If syncretism is, in fact, an acceptable word for describing the underlying spirit of Latin American and Latino Catholicism, syncretism can be said to be driven by a religious imagination that gives pride of place to symbols rather than to formal concepts. In Latino culture, the syncretic religious imagination reconciles inconsistent elements. It does not limit, define, or exclude them. The problem of identity is a case in point. For many U.S. Latinos, to be Latino is to "live on the hyphen" between U.S. and Latin American identity. The Mexican American is neither one nor the other, but both.[15] The same is true for the majority of Latin Americans: To be Chilena, Salvadoreña, Guatemalteca, or any other Latin American nationality is to be part European, part indigenous, and part African, given the reality of European colonization in the Americas. The result is an acceptance of difference, even when difference may manifest itself internally. To be *mulato* or *mestizo* is not seen as an anomaly; to be Spanish, black, and Indian is simply "to be."

Because the Latino religious imagination tends to reconcile apparent differences rather than to lead to a sense of existential disconcertedness, it promotes a sense of inclusivism. No one, even the oppressor, can be excluded from God's banquet, given that the mestizo or mulato herself is both Spanish and indigenous, oppressor and oppressed. As Guillermo Gomez-Peña describes it, "border culture" is not merely the sum of social practices along geographical borders, but a way of thinking and responding to others, irrespective of one's location, that

> can help dismantle the mechanisms of fear. Border culture can guide us back to common ground and improve our negotiating skills. Border culture is a process of negotiation towards utopia, but in this case, utopia means peaceful coexistence and fruitful

cooperation. The border is all we share/*La frontera es lo único que compartimos.*[16]

A second key characteristic of Latino popular religion is performance: Latinos express their religion largely through affective exchange. Religious communication among Latinos, for example, is fundamentally oral rather than literate. Walter Ong, in *The Presence of the Word,*[17] holds that one of orality's most notable features is affectivity. He persuasively argues that when information is communicated orally it is imbued with the personality of the speaker. Indeed, performance tied to an idea of affectivity seems to be a definitive marker of Latino popular religiosity. If we recall the three religious currents that configure Latino popular religiosity—the pre-Columbian, the medieval/baroque Spanish, and the African—we will note that all are primarily communicated orally, not in books or catechisms. They are almost always expressed in rituals and in narrative, but almost never in abstract propositions.

A third salient feature of Latino popular religion, as Goizueta demonstrates, is its strong sense of community. All symbols are by their nature polyvalent and communal. Among Latino communities, popular religious symbols are controlled not by intellectuals who dispute the truth as experts, but rather by community leaders, especially the elders, who attain their status through their ability to reproduce the wisdom, the collective learning, of the community. Their status has little to do with their personal, intellectual endowments, but rather with their gift of sharing popular religious wisdom with others.

In short, in a world of xenophobia, homophobia, patriarchy, and racism, the ethic or ethos that pervades popular religion is one of inclusivism; in light of general inaction and ambivalence toward the poor, Latino popular religion remains attentive to the affective dimensions of human life; in response to individual feelings of isolation and loneliness, Latino popular religion remains communally-minded. As should be clear, these three characteristics are significant not only in religious terms, but also in political ones. Without overstating its importance, Latino popular religion can serve, in its own small way, as a prophetic marker of—and call to—greater justice.

In looking at popular religion as resource, we must always be cautious of romanticizing it. In short, we must never overlook the fact that Latino religion both in Latin America and in the United States continues to experience what Paul Ricouer refers to as the "acids of modernity." Popular religiosity has been and will continue to be influenced by urbanization, modernization, and secularization.[18] Along these lines, for example, Latino Catholics, particularly the second and third generations, have been subjected to mainstream American Catholicism's insistence on making the faith more reasonable and self-appropriated through more catechesis and theological study. Arguably, these second- and third-generation Catholics are more exposed to a thoroughly modern U.S. culture.[19]

We must also always be cognizant that religious symbols can be used in an oppressive way. Consider, for example, the central symbols of Latino popular Catholicism: Mary, the Mother of Jesus (who, in the Americas, is most generally conceived of as *la Virgen de Guadalupe*) and the suffering Christ of Holy Week. Powerful, life-giving narratives, rituals, and symbols combine to make Mary and the suffering Christ immensely influential in the lives and cultures of Latinos. But not everything communicated by these symbols, not every interpretation of them as emotionally experienced meaning, is liberating in the fullest human sense of the word. Latina feminists like Ada Maria Isasi-Díaz and Maria Pilar Aquino have insisted on the need for the ongoing criticism of popular religion. Too much of "the people's religion" reinforces cultural patterns that do violence to women, children, homosexuals, and, ultimately, men themselves in Latino cultures.[20]

Despite these problems, Latino religion proves to be a major source of symbolic and social capital that fortifies Latino identity, as Díaz-Stevens and Stevens-Arroyo point out.[21] Latino religious expression has remained, in the face of Western rationalism, detachment, and secularization, a non-totalizable and non-commodifiable source of life for Latinos. The ending of Rodolfo Gonzalez's galvanizing poem, "I Am Joaquín," a clarion call of the Chicano Movement of the 1960s, captures this spirit well:

> I am the masses of my people and
> I refuse to be absorbed.
> I am Joaquín
> The odds are great but
> My spirit is strong
> My faith unbreakable
> My blood is pure
> I am Aztec Prince and Christian Christ
> I SHALL ENDURE!
> I SHALL ENDURE![22]

Gonzalez rejects the dominant goal of assimilation by turning to indigenous and Christian religion. It is the syncretic self-identification with his own indigenous and Christian religious heritages, in light of the haunting memory of colonization, that gives Gonzalez the strength to "refuse to be absorbed." As he writes in the beginning of his poem, "My fathers/have lost the economic battle/and won/the struggle of cultural survival."[23] Latino popular religion, in many ways, is the lifesource out of which the culture and the struggle flourish and survive.

Latino Popular Religion within a Critical-Theological Context

Up to this point in the chapter, we have primarily described the contours of Latino popular religion in terms of its historical context and its inherent relation to justice, as expressed in its sense of inclusivism, affectivity, and community. In this final section, we would like to examine Latino popular religion in a more explicitly theological manner. Using our own Roman Catholic tradition as our point of departure, we will attempt to articulate some of the ways in which Latino popular religion can be more fully responsive to a community of faith that seeks justice in this world. To this end, we must first situate U.S.-Latino popular religion alongside its Latin American counterpart, liberation theology.

Latin American Liberation Theology

Theologically speaking, U.S.-Latino theology can be described as a younger cousin of Latin American liberation theology or, simply, liberation theology. In short, liberation theology critiques structures of oppression, both within society and within the church, from the perspective of the suffering, the struggle, and the hope of Latin American poor. It begs the question, "How is one's active presence in history connected to the transformation of this world?"[24] In its reified extreme, liberation theology has been criticized by some, including the current Pope, for reducing the Christian faith to the "goal" of worldly transformation. For the most part, liberation theologians have instead maintained that their intent is not at all to reduce the Gospel to wordly aims, but rather, to make it a more manifest and present reality in the lives of the Latin American poor. Using Catholic social teaching, the Bible, and the experience of the poor as their guides, liberation theologians claim that liberation theology is, in fact, entirely orthodox; the experience and struggle of the poor, they argue, are the very criteria that ground Catholic theology.

Though John Paul II has taken many strategic-political measures to diminish the influence of liberation theology, the irony remains that the "official" church in Rome agrees, in principle, with liberation theology's central premises: that Jesus held in his heart a special place for the poor and downtrodden, that the church must point to and be critical of institutional structures that oppress, and that the poor and oppressed have much to teach us all about faith. Though Latin American liberation theology has suffered some political setbacks, it continues to influence the Catholic and larger Christian horizon.

THE THEOLOGICAL DEBATE OVER POPULAR RELIGION

Especially in liberation theology's early years of development, Latin American theologians often held the position that popular religion can be and frequently is oppressive and ahistorical. Popular religion, they charged, favors a cosmic approach in which God solves all problems. As one of the documents from the 1968 International Week of Catechists concluded:

> [Popular religion] is conformist and incapable of being critical, it does not commit itself to the transformation of the prevailing social system. This type of religion is, in fact, conservative, and to a certain extent, caused by the dominant superstructures of those who form part of the current ecclesial organization: for example, the implantation of new forms of religiosity, the commercialization of the same in sanctuaries, tourist exploitation of religious folklore, and the forms of the celebration of Eucharist Congresses. Unfortunately, the foment of this type of religiosity functions as a brake to stop the change of social structures.[25]

At the same time, however, one should note that Latin American theologians claimed that popular religious practice may be the "stammerings of an authentic religious sense." "In our evaluation of popular religion," one document reads, "we may not take as our frame of reference the westernized cultural interpretation of the middle and upper classes; rather we must judge its meaning in the context of the sub-cultures of the rural and marginal urban groups."[26] Hence, though many Latin American liberation theologians may have initially expressed deep suspicion toward popular religion, there already existed some sympathies toward it.

In a general sense, one could say that, from its inception, U.S.-Latino theology has been unambiguously sympathetic to and mindful of popular religion. The publication of Virgil Elizondo's *Galilean Journey: The Mexican-American Promise* in 1983 (some twelve years after the publication of *A Theology of Liberation,* the classic Latin American liberationist work by Gustavo Gutierrez) marked the beginning of what is now a burgeoning U.S.-Latino theology. "Culture" rather than "economics" had become the key theological starting point for the first generation of U.S.-Latino theologians.

Nevertheless, and especially in light of the Latin American context, U.S.-Latino theology finds itself in a precarious position. In its reified extreme, U.S.-Latino theology can be charged with not paying enough attention to the transformation of the world insofar as it neglects critically to engage structures of oppression. Though U.S.-Latino theology has, in many ways, been a necessary corrective to early liberation theology's dismissal of popular religion, one can ask whether it may, at times, tend to forgo the critical analyses that Latin American liberation theology developed so well. One central question seems to be, "What does liberation mean within a U.S.-Latino theological context?"

In reality, one of the preeminent challenges today facing theology in the Americas, both North and South, is to better connect the inherent power of religious symbols (the "aesthetics" of religion) with more practical and liberative efforts toward justice. Whereas early Latin American liberation theology can benefit from a greater appreciation of popular religion, U.S.-Latino theology can benefit from a more critical analysis of structures of oppression. Fortunately, as we will see in the next section, Latino popular religion is rooted in a communal and preformative memory of suffering, and thus is able to "set the stage," so-to-speak, for a pragmatic engagement with liberation.

WORKING IT OUT: THE CASE OF CÉSAR CHÁVEZ

To say that much theological work needs to be done in the Americas connecting popular religion to the realization of greater justice is not to say that the two have not been engaged throughout history. Numerous poets, clerics, artists, and activists—from Bartolomé de las Casas and Sor Juana Inez de la Cruz to Culture Clash and Cherríe Moraga—have critiqued social injustices, using religion and spirituality as points of departure. Perhaps the most well-known case in which Latino popular religion has been used to confront questions of injustice was the United Farm Workers' movement of the 1960s, led by César Chávez.[27] A son of a migrant worker and a migrant worker himself, Chávez successfully led a nonviolent battle against grape growers in California's

San Joaquin Valley to redress problems of low wages and substandard working conditions. What began as a local coalition of 1,700 farm-working families in 1965 galvanized into a national grape boycott observed by some seventeen million Americans over five years.

The religious categories, symbols, and rituals of popular Mexican Catholicism energized in a profound way this national social movement.[28] Chávez, by all reports, was a rather traditional Catholic who lived his faith with considerable integrity and sincerity. The scope of his spirituality, however, cannot be understood merely in terms of his own individual piety. Chávez maintained that, collectively,

> We need a cultural revolution. And we need a cultural revolution among ourselves not only in art but also in the realm of the spirit. As poor people and immigrants, all of us [Americans and Mexicans] have brought to this country some very important things of the spirit. . . . We must never forget that the human element is the most important thing we have—if we get away from this, we are certain to fail.[29]

For Chávez, Latino Catholicism came to life through the rich faith journey of the community. But what, exactly, were the contours of this faith journey? To be sure, in the early years of the movement, the community's journey of faith entailed a critique of the Catholic Church for its lack of support. Initially, Catholic leaders in Delano, California, banned the UFW organizing from within its facilities. Significantly, it was the Protestant ministries, such as the California Migrant Ministry, that helped the UFW survive the early years of the movement.[30] With the help of Protestants, the United Farm Workers' movement was eventually able to enlist support from local, regional, and even national Catholic organizations.

The political struggles of this ecumenical farmworkers' movement were bolstered by religious symbols and practices. The popular symbol of the *Virgen de Guadalupe,* the patron saint of Mexico, situated the farmworkers' struggle in light of the larger historical drama of the Americas. Within the context of this larger drama, issues like indigenous religious practices, immigration, freedom from oppression, and strategic negotiations with those in power were inscribed with new meaning. The fight for better wages and working conditions was not simply a matter of zero-sum, no holds barred politics, but rather, it was a deep-rooted attempt to get at what all human creatures deserve—dignity. The *Virgen de Guadalupe* was, for many in the movement, a cornerstone of faith in the concrete service of dignity and justice.

To a large degree, the UFW's political actions cannot be understood apart from an underlying spiritual context. Marches were transformed into pilgrimages, popular theater (*El Teatro Campesino,* a true expression of performance and affectivity) defended workers' dignity, and the picket line became the prayer line. In May of 1967, farmworkers were served with an injunction prohibiting them from picketing the infamous DiGiorgio grape ranch. Three women approached Chávez privately and suggested that instead of picketing the activists could pray across the road from the ranch. The suggestion was announced by local Spanish-language radio stations and became a huge success. Chávez's brother Richard constructed a makeshift altar on the back of his station wagon, which the farmworkers adorned nightly with flickering candles, flowers, and images of the *Virgen de Guadalupe.* As Susan Ferris and Ricardo Sandoval write in *The Fight in the Fields: César Chávez and the Farmworkers Movement,* the shrine "was such an attraction that some migrant strike-breakers braved supervisors and came out from the DiGiorgio camps to look at it. More than a few knelt and prayed, and they were embraced by the strikers, whether they returned to work or not."[31] The picket line was, for Chávez, the place "where a man makes his commitment, and it is irrevocable; the longer he's on the picket line, the stronger the commitment. . . ."[32] No doubt for Chávez and a majority of farmworkers, commitment was understood as a religious fight for justice.

Without a doubt, the farmworkers' struggle represents the most influential and far-reaching sociopolitical movement that has emerged from within the Latino community to date. Paradigmatically, it points us to a future of civic engagement that creatively bridges religion and politics in the service of justice. As part of a larger civil rights movement, Chávez and the UFW employed strategies and approaches also used by black churches. In particular, the Rev. Martin Luther King, Jr.— with the help of a national network of churches and cross-cultural coalitions—helped move a black "popular" religious consciousness, which stressed Christian freedom, redemptive suffering, and faith-filled hope, into a national conversation on justice. Correlatively, César Chávez was able to challenge this country to rethink what is meant by dignity and justice. With priests, bishops, and even Pope Leo XIII on his side (Leo's 1891 encyclical *Rerum Novarum* criticized the violation of the rights of workers), Chávez tapped into one of the most organized and respected institutions in the world—the Catholic Church. He showed, firsthand, that popular Catholicism need not be inimical to some sort of official Catholicism. Without this partnership, it is very unlikely that the farmworkers' movement would have been able to impact the national imagination to the extent that it did.

As we have seen, Latino spirituality, manifested in communal expression of popular religion, presents us with politically redeeming possibilities. Five hundred years of subjugation on the part of repressive states as well as an often complicitous church could not silence the felt spirituality of the people. Whereas the official church in the sixteenth century intended to liberate the heathen Indian, today, one could say that the popular faith of the people—church in the largest sense—is instead liberating Catholicism.

LOOKING TOWARD THE FUTURE

Now, on the brink of the twenty-first century, the Latino faithful stand at another painful crossroads. The Latino population in the United States is booming. Estimates suggest that ninety-five million Latinos will be living in the United States by the year 2050, accounting for the fact that *one in four Americans will be of Latin American descent*. And yet, proportional to their numbers, Latinos continue to remain marginalized along educational, economic, health, and political lines.

The world we live in now is indeed a different one from that of King and Chávez. The DiGiorgios and Bull Conners of our day are arguably much more subtle in wielding power and in dismissing our collective problems. Serious issues like worsening poverty, deteriorating education, and an increasing sense of despair felt by citizens across social and economic lines are simply not yet part of our national dialogue in any significant way. Instead, we are constantly assured by politicians, media, and big business that progress is at hand—companies are making larger profits, the United States military has established itself globally, and (some) ethnic minorities are making it educationally and economically. What becomes clear, however, is that Latinos, along with so many other disenfranchised groups, have a lot to gain—or lose—from our country's current engagement with civil rights.

How are U.S. Latinos to draw upon popular religion as a resource in an age of technical reasoning, political apathy, and rampant individualism? For the MTV-watching, web-surfing postmodern person (especially youth) of today, how can the symbols and practices of the "faith expression of the people" reveal, in a truly meaningful and transformative way, the good news of Jesus Christ? No doubt, the challenge is a formidable one. For our part, not only do we face the pragmatic challenge of linking popular religious sensibilities to already existing institutions of change (such as churches, periodicals, and legal defense funds), but also we must continually be suspicious of forces that brand aesthetic religious expression as non-rational. Furthermore, we must have the courage both to point to the institutional injustices of our society, including those institutions closest to us, and to encourage human beings to become active agents in the shaping of their own history. Not an easy course, indeed.

But there are signs of hope. Latino popular religion has survived. Not only has it survived, it also continues to be a life-giving source of meaning for millions of Latinos and non-Latinos alike. The sense of the sacred in everyday action is present, even in our high-tech, scientific age. Popular religion invites us to imagine a reality that goes well beyond what we see on the six o'clock news. It encourages us to slow down, to re-think our place in the world relative to those who came before us and those who will come after. It tempers us with the knowledge that we cannot go at life's problems alone, that we must, in community, continue to be creative, to evolve and change as new problems arise. Latino popular religion reminds us that being "faithful" and "religious" is not merely a matter of sectarian affiliation: rather, it invites us to be ever sensitive to the lived and affective dimensions of human suffering and hope, as well as perennially engaged in the struggle for justice.

CHAPTER EIGHT

An Islamic Perspective on Civil Rights Issues

Amina Wadud

This chapter presents theological evidence from the Islamic tradition in support of the following statement attributed to Malcolm X: "America needs to understand Islam, because this is the one religion that erases from its society the race problem. . . . I have never before seen sincere and true brotherhood practiced by all colors together, irrespective of their color."[1] In addition, this chapter will demonstrate how certain spiritual and moral precepts in Islam with their symbolic manifestations in liturgy can affect social contexts. It was one such spiritual practice that led to the experience Malcolm described. The goal of this chapter is to address the Islamic view on race relations in the context of the current social and political climate in the United States. Most of my thinking for this chapter was conditioned by the theological principles as articulated in Islamic primary sources. The relationship between those principles and real circumstances in the contemporary political climate will be demonstrated throughout.

Nearly thirty years after his death, the statement about race and Islam by al-Hajj Malik al-Shabazz (Malcolm X) is still worthy of critical appraisal. Like all living religious communities, Muslim societies sometimes fall short of the level of social justice that I will outline here—especially with regard to gender. However, Islamic orthodoxy determines an intricate system of praxis or practice. The intersection between these two—orthodoxy and orthopraxis, doctrine and practice—yields a place where certain kinds of religious experiences can occur.

The experience that Malcolm describes occurred during his performance of one of the five fundamental pillars of Islam: the ritual pilgrimage, *al-Hajj*. After a lifetime of experiences with racial separatism and prejudice, Malcolm discovered during his pilgrimage to Mecca that orthodox Islam could help to heal racial divides rather than perpetuate them. The experience would change his outlook on race, as well as his legacy for the American civil rights conversation. From his hotel room in Mecca, he wrote that "in the Muslim world, I had seen that men with white complexions were more genuinely brotherly than anyone else had ever been. That morning was the start of a radical alteration in my whole outlook about 'white' men."[2]

THE FIVE PILLARS

Malcolm's transformative experience occurred during his completion of one of the five pillars, upon which Islam is said to be built. These form the basic foundation holding up the faith. They are the declaration of faith (*shahadah*), the five-time daily prayer (*salat*), giving to the poor in charity (*zakat*), fasting in the month of Ramadan (*sawm*), and the pilgrimage to Mecca at least once in a lifetime (*al-Hajj*).

Malcolm's experience was precipitated by his participation in a particular liturgical confirmation that has as its major symbol the unity of humankind. Millions of Muslims gather each year during the twelfth month of the Islamic lunar calendar to observe the Hajj, the rites of pilgrimage. The men leave aside their customary dress of nationality and class and don two huge, unhemmed cloths of white material, which are draped around the body. The overriding symbol of unity with the Hajj is reinforced throughout this rite in a variety of ways. Over a period of days, in the desert environment and in the places of worship constructed to accommodate millions of Muslims each year, the rites and ritual enactments help to remove the barriers that arise between people in their ordinary lives: race, class, gender, national origin, language, and culture.

In addition to the symbolization of unity in the Hajj, the principal form of worship or ritual prayer in Islam—which includes full body prostration—is observed five times a day, whether alone or in congregation. This is the *salat,* the second pillar of Islam. With its various body positions and the uniformity of its recitation, the *salat* confirms the dynamic relationship between the worshiper and God, the worshiped. The worshiper stands, as full agent in the service of God, and bows and prostrates, as obedient servant.

In congregation, worshipers stand in straight lines, shoulder to shoulder, with no space between them, and no means of giving preference or even acknowledging arbitrary divisions of race, rank, or class. A Muslim anywhere in the world can join with others in observing this ritual because of its uniformity. Imagine how this single obligation creates a bond between every Muslim, whether in Turkey, Nigeria, Indonesia, or New York. All can find solace, sanctity, and solidarity with others in the repetition of this ritual observance.

The third and fourth pillars are especially potent symbols for the eradication of class differences. The *zakat,* an obligatory giving of alms to the poor, prevents hoarding. It consists of giving 2½ percent of one's unused[3] wealth each year. The fourth pillar is the intense form of ritual fasting, *Ramadan,* observed throughout the ninth lunar month. The Islamic ritual fast requires every able-bodied man, woman, and older child to experience the physical reality of deprivation. Fasting from before dawn until sunset each day for a month is to experience an ongoing reality for much of the world's population—hunger.

I have saved the first pillar of Islam for last. It is the *shahadah,* or declaration of faith, in which a believer states: "I bear witness, that there is no god but Allah, and I bear witness that Muhammad is the messenger of Allah." This pillar emphasizes the most fundamental belief of Islam, that God is one. This is known as *tawhid,* a word that is derived from the triliteral root in Arabic, for "one." It is more than mere monotheism. It relates to a transcendent and yet eminent divinity or ultimate reality, and as an ethical term it relates to social and political development. *Tawhid* is the operating principle of cosmic harmony between the metaphysical and physical realities of the created universe.

In the social and political arena *tawhid* emphasizes the unity of all human creatures under one creator, God. In an Islamic context, to experience the reality of *tawhid* in everyday terms means that there are no distinctions of race, class, or gender. Reality is not perceived in terms of an evaluative distinction between "self" and "other." Islam affirms the irrefutable and unconditional notion of Allah's oneness. The concept of *tawhid* is so significant in Islamic cosmology that the Islamic holy book, the Qur'an, states quite unequivocally that all sins can be forgiven, except *shirk. Shirk* is the opposite of *tawhid.*[4]

That brings us to *Allah,* the Arabic word for God. Most words in Arabic, especially nouns, indicate gender and have a distinct plural form. The Arabic equivalent to the English word "god," *ilaaha,* can be used to form the plural and can carry grammatical gender. The word Allah is a composite. It contains the definite article (al-) and then the word *ilaaha* with an ellipsis of the initial letter. It creates a new term without operational declinations and grammatical derivations. The word itself indicates oneness. Hence, it is the word I shall use hereafter. In Islam Allah is not only one, Allah is also indivisible. That which emanates from Allah participates in Allah's unity, hence separateness between creature, self, and (Creator) Allah is an illusion.

This overarching concept of *tawhid,* the unicity of God, forms a matrix that organizes Islamic social, economic, moral, spiritual, and political systems. All are part of a single God. At the transcendent level Allah is the tension that holds opposites in juxtaposition. Opposites are the illusion of separation between self and other.

MARTIN BUBER AND THE GOLDEN RULE
OF RECIPROCITY IN ISLAM

The golden rule of reciprocity is one of the highest universal human ideals. Articulations of it are found in one form or another in most of the world's spiritual traditions. For example, in Christianity there is "In everything do to others as you would have them do to you."[5] In Confucianism, there is "Do not do to others what you do not want them to do to you."[6] The Islamic articulation of the golden rule of reciprocity is based on a statement by the Prophet Muhammad: "One of you does not believe until he loves for his brother what he loves for himself."[7] In his book *I and Thou,*[8] Martin Buber considers the meaning of these various articulations. I will reconstruct the basic principle of reciprocity from the perspective of Islamic cosmology and eschatology.

Regarding Allah, the Qur'an says, *"Laysa ka mithlihi shay'un"*— "there is no thing like It." By removing any similitude between created things and the divine, this statement expresses the idea of Allah's transcendence. However, this transcendence does not imply disconnection or distance between (the human) self and God, since in the Qur'an Allah also states, "Indeed, we created humankind and we know what his soul whispers to him and We are closer to him than the jugular vein" (50:16).

Hazrat Ali, the fourth caliph,[9] said "God is outside of things, but not in the sense of being alien to them; and He is inside things, but not in the sense of being identical with them."[10] This is not unlike Thomas Aquinas's claims that the human pursuit of an understanding of God often results in an inadequate knowledge of what God is *not,* rather than a genuine knowledge of a God who is in some ways beyond our understanding.

In the articulation of both Aquinas and Ali, using words prevents us from adequately articulating the true nature of God. We use language in an attempt to understand the full extent of the human relationship with the divine. It is not uncommon then that such articulations draw similarities between God and what we know as human beings. Yet the moment we attempt to make God into a thing, the thing itself can become the idol of our worship, causing us to commit *shirk* or idolatry. Hence the Qur'anic statement addresses this paradox and the limitations of language. The god of human knowledge and the formless God of transcendence are windows to look through with our limited vision in an effort to glimpse that which Taoists call the unnameable.

"*Laysa ka mithlihi*" is a statement that expands our thinking beyond the restrictions that our minds tend to place on God. Allah is not like any "thing" or *shay'*. In the Qur'an, all *shay'*,[11] or created things, are part of a system of dualism, divisible yet necessarily linked. Like male and female pairs in humankind, some of these pairs coexist as complementary equals. Other pairs, like night and day, are in opposition, yet are mutually connected. All of creation, according to the Qur'an, is interconnected in this way, except Allah, described as not like *shay'*. In this way, God is the tension that holds the pairs in juxtaposition for balance and harmony.

This Qur'anic system of correlated and contingent pairs at the metaphysical level is further emphasized at the social and moral level by a tradition that indicates that whenever two persons come together Allah is the third among them. This places human relationships within a supranatural triad. In this triad, the Ultimate, here known as Allah, is in a place of transcendence that supports and sustains the relationship between any two human beings on a horizontal plane. It is the presence of Allah that maintains the "I-Thou" relationship proposed by Buber. Buber indicates that "the primary word I-Thou can only be spoken with the whole being."[12] In other words this combination forms a unit that implies a relationship of reciprocity. Otherwise, "The primary word I-It can never be spoken with the whole being."[13] One aspect of this relationship is asymmetrical and reduced to a state of less than wholeness. Therefore, the Islamic triad would look like this:

Allah

I   Thou

Each person represented by the "I" and the "Thou" would be sustained in a reciprocal relationship of parity that is represented by the horizontal axis. The axis is maintained because the transcendent component in this relationship—Allah—always occupies the highest point. Only if that third transcendent element is missing can the vertical axis be constructed, such that "I" can be over "It." Metaphysically speaking, the presence of Allah continually creates parity among all people. Since Allah occupies the highest point, even that which appears as vertical must be understood as horizontal.

The continual awareness of Allah's presence—the metaphysical component of all human-to-human relations—creates an understanding that between any two persons there can be parity only on a horizontal basis. If a person seeks to place him or herself "above" another, it means the divine presence is being ignored or removed. Since Allah is present in all circumstances, then Allah must be acknowledged. This way of conceptualizing the Buberian formula creates a means for understanding how the sacred pact between I and Thou is sustained. Continual application of this transcendent component gives superiority only to God. To experience the reality of this three-dimensional relationship of wholeness, the two-dimensional relationship between humans must reflect an awareness of, remembrance of, and participation in the presence of Allah between them.

This conclusion, drawn from the *Laysa ka Mithlihi* statement in the Qur'an, is further enhanced by another principle in Islamic cosmology. Human beings are created for the purpose of serving as Allah's *khalifah* on the earth.[14] A *khalifah* is vice-regent, trustee, or moral agent. Each human being is a trustee for Allah on the *'ard* or earth, which is made subservient to us and which we are especially admonished to take care of in our vice-regency or trusteeship. In Islam, there is no implication of a "fall" from which humankind needs redemption. Instead, "earth" was always intended to be our dwelling place, and it is on the earth that we each serve as Allah's *khalifah*. What we do with this trust is the task of our humanity and that for which we will ultimately be called to account.

This moral agency brings us to a third principle in the Islamic conception of humanity, which affects race relations. That principle is exemplified in the term *taqwa*, which stands for piety or moral consciousness. When a person is mindful, or in remembrance of Allah, he or she has *taqwa*. We are created with the capacity to do many things, for good or for evil. What inspires us to act within constraints of honor and dignity is the awareness that we are always in the presence of Allah: "For even if you cannot see Him, He can see you."[15] So we perform all actions with sincerity and integrity because we are aware that our hearts and our deeds are transparent to Allah, who will ultimately call us to account for everything we do, even if it be an atom's weight of good or evil (99:7–8). In Islam, since the human agent has the capacity for free will, then it is *taqwa* that reminds us that we will be held accountable for our choices. *Taqwa* inspires us to use constraint by reflecting constantly on the presence of Allah.

The final consideration from Islamic cosmology affecting race relations is found in the creation story. In the Qur'anic stories of the garden of Eden, Satan entices the original parents into disobedience after he had refused to obey Allah's command to bow before the human creature. When he refused, he said "I am better than he" (38:76). The word for those who think they are better than others is *istakbar*. It was Satan's arrogance that created the schism between him and his Lord. For while Satan and the original parents were guilty of disobedience, the parents acknowledged their error and asked for forgiveness. They were not only forgiven but also promised the gift of guidance while here on earth. Satan persisted in his *istakbar* and would not seek forgiveness. The lesson drawn from this is whoever considers himself or herself better than another behaves like Satan, the most wicked.

MOVING BEYOND POWER PARADIGMS
TOWARD MULTICULTURALISM

I had a parallel experience with the one Malcolm described on the Hajj when I lived in Malaysia, where the differences between people are acknowledged and celebrated. My three youngest children experienced this environment for three years and then returned to the United States, where they were unprepared for the racism that is so common here. How can we integrate what happened in Malaysia into U.S. policy and practice? Like Malcolm X, I had taken racism so much for granted that I did not know how to describe its absence.

Here are some of the distinctions of multiculturalism that bear on the issue of race relations in America. In Malaysia, selective religious holidays, spiritual occasions, and cultural practices are acknowledged on the official level as well as on the cultural and communal level. The cultural imperialism of attributing Christian customs as belonging to everyone "is part of the broader phenomenon that shapes the experience of every oppressed group: the oppressed must know about the oppressor's culture, but the oppressor need know nothing about the oppressed."[16] In this way, oppressed people are made invisible. Those in a position of privilege do "not even know . . . that they don't know"[17] about these other cultures and traditions. Indeed, "those values, traditions, and customs that are intrinsic" to the very nature of various ethnic and religious peoples ". . . are not valued, are not remembered, are not celebrated."[18]

When "oppressed people need to know as much as possible about their oppressor in order to survive,"[19] they are forced to give up certain aspects of their own cultural experience and identity development because those aspects are disadvantageous for assimilation into the dominant culture.[20] What my children had not experienced in Malaysia was the power dynamics of American racism and exclusivism.

BEYOND THE POWER-BASED PARADIGM OF SECULAR MODERNITY

In what way does Islamic orthodoxy lead to a social praxis that eradicates racial discrimination and repudiates all forms of oppression? How might this be applied to civil rights concerns here in the United States, where, as Malcolm X noted, race is indisputably part of the power dynamic?

While living in Malaysia, I experienced the Islamic principle of reciprocity in a way that led to the insights on race relations that Malcom X referred to. In Malaysia, racial and ethnic differences are a natural aspect of the complexity of being human, like being short or tall. Race is not the basis for power and privilege and carries no political implications. I came to see that it is possible to transcend race if the basis for judging human dignity and worth is set upon principles like moral agency and *taqwa* (piety), as discussed above.

"Paulo Friere has argued that the true focus of revolutionary change is never merely the oppressive situation, but the piece of the oppressor, which is implanted within each person, and which knows only the oppressor's tactics and relationships," says Martha Minow in her recent book, *Not Only for Myself*.[21] I am indebted to her for its critique of the limitations of group-based identity politics. However, Minow's critique maintains an even more damaging assumption, that the goal of modern society is the maximization of power.

If power dynamics prevail, how can we avoid the choice between being oppressed and being an oppressor? One way to move away from power-based paradigms is offered in the very translation of the word Islam—"engaged surrender." As human beings, individuals and groups, we are free to choose whether or not to surrender to the over-arching harmony and synchronicity of the divine design in all of creation. Minow challenges the fixed nature of categories of group identity since people tend to be a composite of interlacing groups rather than a member of a single group. Ultimately, however, it is to the individual that she gives the highest value. She promotes a decrease in the power of group-based identity by increasing the power of the individual. Even when the individual power is achieved by deception, she considers it a merit. This emphasis of power, individual or collective, is problematic from the perspective of engaged surrender.

To break free of the vicious cycle of maximizing power, I argue that the articulation of Islam as engaged surrender operates on the premise that there is no separation between self and other, just as there is no separation between ourselves and the Creator of all harmony. Under this notion, people maintain various aspects of their cultural and ethnic identity, but none of these aspects is more important or more privileged than another. That which is deemed "most noble in the sight of Allah is *taqwa*" (49:13). Therefore, for us to operate with the moral consciousness of our continual relationship with Allah, we are encouraged to treat all other beings as we would want to be treated ourselves. To do this, we must remember that Allah is always present and that we are held accountable for all of our deeds—great and small. Our actions reflect our awareness of and agreement with these fundamental moral principles.

I accepted Islam more than a quarter of a century ago, after having been raised in a household made spiritually aware by my father, a Methodist minister. One of the things that I found most appealing about my initial experience in Islam was that all personal aspects integral to my wholeness as a person were also acknowledged by this worldview. I did not have to relinquish any of my personal diversity in a quest to transcend my very nature as a human being. I experienced this affirmation without the exclusion of others. I remember being inspired in an early reading of the Qur'an, "When a greeting is given to you, [you should] return a greeting equal to it—if not better. All things are noted by God" (4:86). I liked the idea of God taking notice of all things and I recognized that every aspect of my being and every action I perform is subject to a single evaluative criterion that transcends my race, class, or gender: Was that deed a part of my ultimate surrender to Allah?

In the context of the principle of reciprocity, I think the struggle for civil rights in America might benefit from Islam in several ways. Islam views race as one of many aspects of human diversity. In the Qur'an, Allah says, "We have made you into nations and tribes, to know one another, [not to despise one another] and, Verily the most noble of you in the sight of Allah is the one with the most *taqwa*" (40:13). As discussed above, this verse emphasizes personal and communal piety as the most distinguishing characteristic of humankind. In addition, the Qur'an exhorts us to "Hold fast to the rope of Allah altogether and be not divided among yourselves" (3:103).

In Islam, brotherhood is a bond that emerges from our choice to adhere to divine principles of honor, dignity, justice, and equality. Within Islamic orthodoxy, no distinctions are made on arbitrary facets of one's race, class, gender, or national origin. Race, a natural aspect of human diversity, is not a characteristic of intrinsic value, nor should it be a factor that determines access to resources, rights, freedom, or justice.

The United States government follows the modern secular construction of the nation-state, with a separation between church and state. This separation contrasts with the Islamic premise that all things fall under the sovereignty of Allah. In Islam, the government is responsible for carrying out the will of Allah, as articulated in the Qur'an and exemplified by the *sunnah* or normative practice of the Prophet. Anything less is considered contradictory to Islam. Hence it is not permissible in Islam for a government to promote or tolerate unequal treatment on the basis of race. Muslims in South Africa were divided into four separate racial groupings by the apartheid regime, provoking their resistance because the system violated the Islamic principle of a single brotherhood.[22] Political power should be determined on the basis of theological principles, which then inform public policy. Any call for justice in Islam is both theological and political, by definition.

CONCLUSION

Islam is the fastest growing religion in America (and in the world). The spread of Islam to the United States is fed by two major sources: conversion of indigenous Americans, mostly African Americans, and the emigration of Muslims from abroad. The problem of race in the United States is made more salient when the majority of the Muslims are either African American or immigrant.

With regard to immigration, negative media coverage has influenced significant policy changes in recent years aimed at curtailing Muslim immigration out of concern for national security and popular prejudice. Although Muslim nations also experience problems with immigration and construct policies to restrict immigrant flow, the situation is more complex for these countries. It is estimated that as much as one-third of the world's refugee population is Muslim. How many of these refugees can be absorbed within the borders of one or another Muslim country without aggravating the drain on resources? The situation is not nearly so critical for the United States, not even along the U.S.-Mexican border. Consider the situation of Palestinians, who do not have a recognized nation and are denied full citizenship by Israel. They often find refuge in one or another of the neighboring Muslim countries. Although Muslim nation-states continue to absorb refugees in large numbers, there is no official policy that would equal the common etiquette among Muslims that emphasizes the responsibility to act as a good host for visitors.

The other media and cultural focus on Islam in America relates to the national association led by Minister Louis Farrakhan, the Nation of Islam. Malcolm X had been a member of this organization prior to his transformative pilgrimage to Mecca. By then, he had disassociated himself from the group's policies of racial separation. Indeed, this was a direct result of his acceptance of the global Islamic movement and its policy of universal brotherhood under a single God. The vast majority of the Muslims of African-American origin are members of this global Islam, but as peaceful and law abiding citizens they are not the focus of media sensationalism. Many of them are especially disturbed that the Nation of Islam is even considered a part of Islam, since it espouses certain theological notions inconsistent with Islamic orthodoxy.

The reason that many of us dedicate ourselves to Islam in the United States is that we see in Islam a solution to the racial inequities we have experienced and that we do not wish to perpetuate in any way. Instead, we take our inspiration from the Qur'an and the *sunnah*. The Prophet has advised us, "Whosoever of you sees an evil action, let him change it with his hand, and if he is not able to do so, then with his tongue, and if he is not able to do so, then with his heart—and that is the weakest of faith."[23] The struggle for justice is a fundamental part of what it means to be Muslim, and Islam sees this struggle as simultaneously personal, political, and spiritual. Such a comprehensive agenda would help to eradicate racial inequality anywhere in the world.

PART III

LOOKING AHEAD: SPIRITUAL RESOURCES FOR A NEW MOVEMENT

Mary Gonzales, a Roman Catholic Mexican American, leads the Metropolitan Alliance of Congregations (MAC) in Chicago. MAC's mission, under the umbrella of the Gamaliel Foundation, is to bring change in public policy that contributes to the economic circumstances of many underserved communities and the people who live in them. The Gamaliel Foundation's goal is to promote democracy by building communities in which people can participate fully in the decisions that affect their lives. Mary Gonzales' role is to organize an urban constituency made up of mainly poor and working-class people of color. The organization she heads consists of 122 institutions, and is both congregation-based and congregation-focused. Gonzales describes the people who make up the Metropolitan Alliance of Congregations as: "African American, Hispanic—both Puerto Rican and Mexican—undocumented people, documented people, Chicago-born people, English-speakers and Spanish-speakers, poor people, middle-class people, working-class people, suburbanites, and urbanites."

Gonzales was raised in a Christian tradition that taught her that life was about being of service to others. She viewed the church and Scripture as a way of service, of healing the sick or feeding the hungry. "As a young person I was raised to see that side of Jesus Christ that was humble, loving, caring, in service to others, healing others, feeding others, and that's historically what our congregations have done—they set up food pantries, they set up housing programs, they set up rehabilitation services, legal aid services, and so on. And it wasn't until I entered this work that some powerful ministers and some powerful organizers introduced me to Jesus Christ as the agitator, and the confrontationalist, the nonconformist, as one who would in fact challenge authority. And so, it is that side of Christ that I am working very hard to introduce, and to reintroduce to the churches."

Recruited to be an organizer by her husband, Gary Galluzo, one of the founders of Gamaliel, Gonzales has witnessed tremendous change in the city of her birth. "Congregations are going through serious struggles and changes, pressures, funding crises. Neighborhoods, largely in urban centers, are very vulnerable to development changes, racially and economically, and the church carries a huge impact. If it is hard for the neighborhoods, then it is hard for the churches." Traveling from community to community, talking to African Americans, Mexican Americans, and many others, she often discovers that the forces and challenges facing the people she serves are the same. She believes that her organizing efforts rely on powerful ministers and powerful lay people who preach strength and struggle from the pulpit.

As a young woman, Gonzales strayed from the church, but her organizing work brought her back in a wholly different way. Today, as a practicing Catholic, she uses the church structure as a vehicle for building stronger communities. On a personal level, Gonzales' relationship to the church has changed. She explains, "It is much more than a warm place to meet or announce a meeting; it can play a much bigger role in shaping people and their communities." Gonzales often reflects on how courageous the church has been in confronting social injustices. Today Gonzales reads the stories in the Bible in a very different way: "The Bible is filled with powerful people and powerful actions, which they took to confront oppression, and of non-conformists who demanded justice." It has been exciting for her to reread Scripture in this way, and more importantly, to be able to act on what she has read.

Gonzales explains, "I do the work that I do because I am a person of faith, but this feeling has evolved. It was harder for me and it is harder still for people to see the pushy, demanding side of Jesus Christ, but that is the side that I see every day." She feels "blessed that I get the opportunity to live life this way."

Gonzales returns to the lessons found in Scripture regularly, remembering that "when Christ was crucified, the apostles, continuing to spread his teachings, were warned by authorities to stop. A wise, Jewish teacher at the time said to the authorities, 'leave these people alone, they are workers of God. If you fight them, then you fight God, if they are not doing the work of God, then it will die on its own.' Gonzales has always found that this teaching from the Acts of the Apostles can be applied to her organizing work. She explains, "if we are doing the work of God we will thrive, and when we stop doing the work of God, our work will die."

CHAPTER NINE

Civil Rights and the Common Good:
Some Possible Contributions of Religious Communities

DAVID HOLLENBACH, S.J.

The contributions of the black churches to the U.S. civil rights movement of the 1950s and 1960s are of course well known. In this brief essay, I will draw some generalizations from those contributions for the role of religious communities in the renewal of the civil rights movement today. I will offer three such generalizations, and then I will discuss them with the hope of orienting activists toward a future movement.

FIRST STATEMENT

Promotion of civil rights requires a lively appreciation that there is a universal human community that shares a common good—the good of being a community linked together by at least minimal bonds of solidarity.

Here, I want to suggest a diagnosis for why the civil rights movement in the United States has lost steam in recent years and what might be done to revitalize it. Studies of public opinion indicate that tolerance of the differences among people and groups is highly valued in America today.[1] Strong cases have been made that negative racial attitudes have declined in the decades since the civil rights movement was at its peak under the leadership of Dr. Martin Luther King, Jr.[2] It is also clear, however, that the plight of the poor, especially of poor minorities, has worsened during this same period and that the poor in core cities are economically more isolated from mainstream society than in the past.[3]

This raises serious questions about whether the problems faced by poor minorities today can be solved by increased tolerance.

The notion of "tolerance" of course can have a number of meanings.[4] For my purposes here let me stipulate that it means a "live-and-let-live" stance that rejects the imposition of beliefs and values upon other groups. It is a strategy of noninterference with the beliefs and lifestyles of those who are different. This is the prescription of John Rawls, who recommends that we deal with diverse values and lifestyles by what he calls "the method of avoidance." By this he means that in political life "we try, so far as we can, neither to assert nor to deny any religious, philosophical or moral views. . . ."[5] By recommending that we avoid voicing such views about the deeper meaning of the good life, Rawls hopes to neutralize potential conflicts and promote democratic social harmony. More strongly, this approach to tolerance suggests that we should abandon efforts to create bonds of community among persons who are different from each other in some significant way, lest these efforts perpetuate past injustices, deepen conflicts, or even precipitate war. Tolerance, understood this way, is a virtue for people who are suspicious of each other. It may lead to peace of a sort, but it does not have the power to transform differences into new bonds of solidarity.

Perhaps that is the best we can hope for. In my view, however, this kind of disengaged tolerance is inadequate to the task of reinvigorating the civil rights movement today. For tolerance of this sort can actually further entrench the divisions in society that most seriously threaten civil rights, namely the economic and class divisions between the middle class and the poor and between the suburbs and the inner city. Tolerance as a live-and-let-live attitude has little to say about how to overcome divisions of this sort. It can even strengthen the economic and class divisions in society by encouraging acquiescence in these divisions. As a strategy for dealing with the serious problems of urban poverty, it resembles that of an ostrich with its head in the sand, for it seeks to ignore serious differences rather than address them positively and actively.

In my view, this is just what the civil rights movement does not need. The basis of a functional democracy is not an agreement that citizens will leave each other alone and "avoid" the question of the good they share in common. The exercise of real freedom in society depends on the strength of the communal relationships that give persons a measure of real power to shape their environment, including their political environment.[6] Solitary individuals, especially solitary individuals motivated solely by self-interest and the protection of their rights to privacy, will be incapable of democratic self-government. Democracy requires more than this. It requires the virtues of mutual cooperation, mutual responsibility, and what Aristotle called civic friendship.[7] A more descriptive contemporary word for such civic friendship is solidarity. Pope John Paul II, in one of his more helpful observations, has defined the attitude of solidarity as "a firm and persevering determination to commit oneself to the common good."[8] Solidarity, in other words, is the attitude of mind and heart that motivates positive efforts to overcome social divisions. It goes beyond tolerance by energizing positive action to enhance the good shared by people who live together in a common world. It can encourage steps to take down the economic, class, educational, and other boundaries that divide city from suburb, poor from middle class. In doing so it can bring new energy to the civil rights movement today.

SECOND STATEMENT

Monotheistic religions possess important, perhaps unique, resources for promoting awareness of the common good of a community that reaches beyond divisions of class, race, ethnicity, and gender, and for generating the solidarity needed to sustain this community.

Judaism, Christianity, and Islam all affirm the existence of one God who is the creator, sustainer, and ultimate destiny of all that is, of all human beings, and all human groups. These religious traditions also affirm the dignity and sacredness of every human person, without regard to race, ethnicity, achievement, or status. Jews and Christians, for example, affirm the biblical belief that all human beings (not only Jews or Christians) are created in the "image and likeness of God" (Genesis 1:27) and are thus to be treated as sacred. The Qur'an tells Muslims that Allah made each human being worthy of reverence: "When I have shaped him, and breathed My spirit upon him, fall you down bowing before him!" (Qur'an, Sura XV, 29). Thus these monotheistic religions all hold that there is a universal community of which all human beings are members. Treating human beings as if they are not in some fundamental sense one's brothers or sisters is therefore to treat them as not fully human. There is a communal bond among humans that is deeper than all differences, and there is a human good that is more basic than the well-being of any of the subgroups constituted by race, ethnicity, nation, gender, or class. Thus it is technically idolatry to put the privileges of narrowly defined groups ahead of the most basic requirements of respect for God's creation.

In addition, the traditions of these monotheistic religious communities contain powerful resources that can address the fears that divide people of different races, ethnicities, and economic classes. Such fear is one of the most serious impediments to the promotion of civil rights today.[9] The fact that tolerance is often invoked as the solution to rights violations is evidence of the power of fear of those who are different. Recommendations of tolerance often take suspicion or hostility as the starting point for efforts to secure the dignity and rights of all persons. Achieving tolerance, however, calls for letting go of at least some of the fears that make tolerance necessary. Religious belief in a loving God can enable people to begin to let go of these fears. From there they can go on to use their influence to tackle the social problems and divisions that create the fears in the first place. This role of religion in countering inter-group fear was evident in King's contributions to the earlier civil rights movement. It can play a similar role today.

These religious perspectives have deep similarities with the more secular civic belief that "all persons are created equal" and the legal requirement of "equal justice under the law." The interconnection of the religious and secular roots of Dr. King's commitment to civil rights was consistently evident in his words. In King's addresses it is often difficult to determine where the language of the Bible ends and the language of the U.S. Constitution begins, as it is sometimes hard to know whether King's words are from a civic address to the larger public or from a sermon delivered in church.

Despite its partial overlap with the civic language of the Constitution, King's religious conviction that there is an encompassing "beloved community" under God added a dimension to his understanding of civil rights that is very much needed today. This religious vision implies that civil rights are linked to a vision of an inclusive common good. It implies that a vital civil rights movement requires an engaged solidarity with those whose basic dignity is denied, not simply a disengaged tolerance for those who are different. The religious communities of the United States possess unique resources for the development of such solidarity. In fact, these traditions, when functioning at their best, can contribute to reshaping the very notion of civil rights, as they suggest that guaranteeing people's rights means securing the minimum requirements for genuine and active participation in the human community. Attaining civil rights means sharing in the common good of that larger community to at least the minimum level required by basic human dignity.[10] Leaving people alone can fall far short of respect for rights understood this way.

THIRD STATEMENT

The most serious wounds on the body of an inclusive community today are the class boundaries between poor cities and middle-class suburbs. A revitalized civil rights movement today should take the overcoming of these class boundaries as its primary objective.

While it is true that racial, ethnic, and gender discrimination are alive and well in the United States, significant progress has been made on these fronts since the death of Dr. King. Unfortunately, the same cannot be said about the deep economic and class divisions that separate the urban poor from the suburban middle class. These economic divisions are also most serious threats to the well-being of women and children. These class divisions will not be healed by stronger appeals for tolerance of racial, ethnic, or gender differences. They require positive steps to rebuild the economic infrastructure of core cities, create genuine job opportunities for the unemployed, overcome deep educational disparities between city and suburb, and secure more adequate public safety in urban centers. All such initiatives will require positive political commitment by both the urban poor themselves and by those who see themselves in solidarity with the urban poor.

Churches and other religious communities can make important contributions to such political action through educational, advocacy, and empowerment initiatives. In fact, it has been shown empirically that churches are the single strongest counterweight to the class-based differences in political engagement by diverse groups in American society.[11] Underlying this political impact is a vision of a more inclusive community linked together by solidarity. This solidarity is rooted in the vision that can motivate religious communities when they are true to their most authentic insights.

Religious motivation requires strategic focus for it to be effective in revitalizing the civil rights movement today. Class divisions between city and suburb are the most likely location of such a focus. The precise issues around which such a focus can be developed will doubtless be different in different regions of the country. In my view, the glaring disparities in funding for education hold promise as a likely source of energy for religious participation in the renewal of the civil rights movement almost everywhere. These disparities call for new initiatives at the state house door, in state legislatures, and in state and federal courts. But any success in these venues over the medium and longer term will depend on conceiving civil rights as the justified claim to share in the common good of the larger community, not simply the right to be tolerated or left alone. Churches, synagogues, and mosques are potentially major contributors to re-envisioning civil rights this way. If they can realize this potential, they will be carrying on the legacy of Martin Luther King, Jr., and perhaps even advancing it.

CHAPTER TEN

From "Beloved Community" to "Beloved Communities": Inviting New Faith Partners to the Civil Rights Struggle

ANN CHIH LIN

As I read this volume, I can't help but be struck by the richness of the faith traditions presented, as well as the complementary nature of each tradition's critique of racism. Whether we are talking of the symbols, the ceremony, and the communitarianism of Latino Christianity; the Islamic principles of unicity, divine transcendence, and integrity; or the Jewish sense of racism as division and blasphemy, we find themes that are at once highly individual to each community and accessible to outsiders as well. This is particularly true now that our society is becoming more diverse and our contacts with those from other traditions are more numerous. In one sense, of course, the range of religious traditions in the United States today poses difficulties: We cannot assume that the biblical passages invoked by an African-American preacher will resonate with a multicultural, religiously diverse audience. But this diversity can also be a tremendous resource to a newly invigorated, newly configured civil rights movement.

I want to suggest some ways in which the diversity of faiths in the United States could become a political resource for the civil rights movement. I speak not only as a political scientist with an interest in political and organizational strategies, but also as a person fortunate enough to stand at the intersection of many faith traditions: the Roman Catholic faith of my baptism and practice, the Chinese religious beliefs of my culture, and the Islamic and Orthodox Christian traditions of the

Arab immigrants I study. This variety of experience leads me to a simple principle: Strong alliances and effective coalition work start from the particular strengths of each group within the coalition. The kind of partnership this principle implies will not be identical to the closely knit "beloved community" of the 1960s. But it has the potential to create a multidimensional civil rights movement, one that can call both our individual faith traditions and the country we share to a deeper understanding of justice.

What does it mean for strong coalitions to start from strong members? In the context of a faith-based civil rights movement, it means that the heart of faith-based organizing must be faith. The goal should not be the creation of a lowest-common-denominator civic religion to which all can assent, nor even a unified, interdenominational faith in which civil rights are at the core. Instead, the goal should be the development of authentic, distinctive justifications for civil rights struggles, justifications that are specific to each religious tradition. This rootedness in the language, the imagery, and the understanding of the sacred in each faith sustains activity by making it a religious commitment, not merely a secular ideal. It also provides an answer to detractors who accuse religious activists of becoming too political, reminding them that civil rights values are not intrusions of the secular culture, but integral to their belief.

The corollary to this is that people of faith need to do civil rights organizing "for themselves"—in other words, they must believe that the fight for justice is an imperative of their faith, not merely a nice thing that they do for other people. The difference is the difference between conviction and generosity, a subtle but important distinction. If civil rights organizing is something that is done for "those poor oppressed African Americans," because one's faith tells one to be good to others, then the commitment to civil rights will seem extraneous to the "real work" of prayer or seeking God's will. It will easily be abandoned when those poor oppressed people do not seem properly grateful, when political victories are hard to come by, when the faith community is preoccupied with internal divisions over doctrine and practice. By contrast, when civil rights is understood as essential to creed and spirituality, when it is prayer in active form, then the commitment to the struggle will be nourished by springs other than success, and it will persist even when other pressing issues claim attention.

This does not mean that the institutions of faith—the clerical conference or hierarchy—must first accept civil rights or the civil rights struggle as central to the religious community. It behooves us to remember the difficult relationship Dr. Martin Luther King, Jr., had with the National Baptist Convention; or the fact that the Catholic hierarchy has, in different places, supported entrenched power as often as it has supported social justice. But it does mean that a theological basis for civil rights in each tradition is essential. To take just one example, people must reach into their own faith traditions to create the songs, symbols, and practices that reinforce civil rights, rather than reflexively adopt those of the black Christian church, powerful and evocative though that tradition is. It also means that the dedication to civil rights in each religious community must not only draw on resources within that community, but also strengthen and reinvigorate that community itself. That strengthening can come from renewal or reaffirmation, from change or from celebration of tradition. But whatever form it takes, attention to how the faith community is made strong by the civil rights struggle is, in the end, the best guarantee that it will continue to lend its strength to the movement.

How can a faith community be "made strong" by participation in the civil rights struggle? One way is to pay attention to the kinds of actions it supports. Certainly activities that inspire individual members to act in the political system are important, as are activities in which the institutional weight of a religious tradition can be brought to bear on the political debate. Worshipers need to sign petitions and attend demonstrations, and synagogues, churches, and mosques need to be a voice for justice in secular political conversations. But in the long run, the activities that must strengthen a faith community are local, personal actions, which evolve as direct expressions of faith in immediate practice. The sanctuary movement, in which churches took responsibility for Central American political refugees whom the U.S. government would not accept, is one example; not only did it draw upon a longstanding tradition of the church as a place of sanctuary, it also challenged people directly to act upon their convictions.

But not all activities need be so dramatic or so risky. The authors have talked about incorporating civil rights beliefs and reinterpreting civil rights activism through rituals and reverences like the Passover seder, the Ramadan fast, or the recitation of the Rosary. Something as simple—and yet as profound—as the welcoming table at a Sunday church supper can be an important metaphor as well as an immediate personal action. The point is to involve the congregation as a community: to create activities that simultaneously teach and reinforce theological principles, that require members of the congregation to interact and cooperate instead of acting individually, and that make a concrete contribution to the civil rights struggle. (I should add that prayer and witness should definitely be considered concrete contributions.)

Another way to make the civil rights struggle a direct expression of faith is to challenge congregations to look at the problems in their own neighborhoods. The work done by the Industrial Areas Foundation (IAF) is a wonderful example of how religious communities can transform an abstract commitment to civil rights into concrete activities that bridge class, race, and ethnicity while encouraging greater justice at the local level. Not every community will have an IAF coalition, but organizers and leaders within the civil rights movement should give some thought to similar blueprints for local congregations who wish to engage in civil rights work. It is particularly important to create links at two levels: across local congregations with different religious traditions, ethnicities, and socioeconomic status; and among such coalitions in different localities, so that a group of congregations working together in Houston knows that it resembles a group of congregations in Philadelphia and another in Los Angeles. The first set of links allows real progress to be made at the local level; the second set creates a movement, with its resultant energy and optimism.

Such coordinating structures are not easy to create, especially if they are to provide blueprints for collaboration instead of mere exhortations to work together. But there is a real space for intermediary organizations, sponsored by interdenominational religious groups or civil rights organizations, to facilitate the collaboration of congregations within and across localities. One of the many reasons the IAF has had so much success over so many years is because the organizers transmit knowledge of structures and processes that have worked elsewhere, while allowing local communities to set their own agendas. There is no need to reinvent the wheel.

Another example of this kind of coordination work can be found in research that Kimberly Roberson, a project officer with the Charles Stewart Mott Foundation in Flint, Michigan, has done on churches that provide services to the poor. She finds that intermediary organizations are absolutely crucial in this effort; they create projects and then divide them into manageable pieces that can be adopted by individual congregations. Such projects include a soup kitchen, where different congregations are responsible for different nights, and an organization that screens individuals who request assistance and then matches them with the resources at a particular church. They succeed because the intermediary organization administering each project becomes the go-between for the congregations, minimizing denominational differences and providing the expertise and ideas that might be hard for any one congregation to acquire on its own. To extend this finding to the civil rights movement, one could imagine an intermediary organization working with congregations to identify areas of persistent racism within the local community, to design a strategy to combat one specific problem, and then to organize and distribute specific tasks to each participating congregation.

The Harvard Civil Rights Project could play an important role in creating these intermediary organizations and in collecting ideas for grass-roots projects that have been effective in communities around the United States. It cannot, of course, provide the theological foundation or the re-imagining of sacred symbols and rituals necessary to anchor civil rights within strong faith communities. But it can help answer the perennial problem of civil rights organizing: What is to be done, and how can we begin to tackle all that needs doing? The information and coordinating activity it could provide is perhaps especially useful because it is not denominationally specific; having no religious agenda, it cannot be suspected of promoting one. Instead, it can create common ground for different religious communities, each strong in its own faith, to work toward the same goal in coordinated but theologically specific ways.

The vision this presents is not that of a "beloved community," where differences of background and belief are erased in the crucible of common work and struggle. Such communities may indeed be created in a new civil rights movement; they may even be necessary to it. But as special and, yes, even sacred as they are, the vision of one beloved community cannot be the whole of the civil rights struggle. Such a struggle would rely too much on the dedication of activists who put civil rights first and foremost, who are willing to let those ideals take precedence over their other ideals, and who inevitably burn out as they face setback after setback. Instead, a new civil rights struggle must also incorporate a vision of "beloved communities": multiple faith communities, grounded in their own traditions, which incorporate civil rights as an essential element of that tradition, and which do so in order to invigorate their own faith as well as the wider society. Such a vision presents challenges of collaboration and structure. But it also allows the flame of civil rights to burn in many candles and lamps, in sanctuaries too numerous to ever be totally extinguished.

$\mathcal{N}otes$

NOTES TO INTRODUCTION

1. Frederick M. Wirt, 'We Ain't What We Was': Civil Rights in the New South (Durham: Duke University Press, 1997).
2. Martin Luther King, Jr., Where Do We Go From Here: Chaos or Community? (Boston: Beacon Press, 1968).
3. Charles Fager, Uncertain Resurrection: The Poor People's Washington Campaign (Grand Rapids, Mich.: William B. Eerdmans, 1969).
4. Richard H. Sewell, Ballots for Freedom: Antislavery Politics in the United States, 1827–1860 (New York: Norton, 1976).
5. Aldon D. Morris, The Origins of the Civil Rights Movement (New York: Free Press, 1984); Adam Fairclough, To Redeem the Soul of America: the Southern Christian Leadership Conference and Martin Luther King, Jr. (Athens: University of Georgia Press, 1987).
6. Robert Mann, The Walls of Jericho (New York: Harcourt Brace and Co., 1996).
7. William Greider, The Education of David Stockman and Other Americans (New York: E.P. Dutton, 1982).
8. Washington Post/Henry J. Kaiser Family Foundation/Harvard University survey, July 29-August 18, 1998, Washington Post Opinion Archive, http://dbweb.washingtonpost.com/wp . . . polls/vault/.
9. Ibid.
10. Laurie Goodstein with Marjorie Connelly, "American Teenagers Are Both Worldly and Devoid of Cynicism, Poll Indicates," New York Times, April 30, 1998.
11. After trying to write an abstract introduction to these powerful papers, I decided to say something personal about the origin of this project. This violates the tradition in social science, where religious values are private matters, not mentioned in our writings, a tradition I have observed in three decades of writing about social issues. In general, I think that this is a good idea, since our trade very largely concerns evidence, not values, and our audience crosses the spectrum of religious beliefs. Our conclusions should not be accepted or rejected on

the basis of what others think about our values. On the other hand, what we choose to study and whether or not we go beyond our research to try to apply it in the world are often matters of values, sometimes of religious values, but we rarely acknowledge that. Also, I think that scholars who understand and share religious values probably have some responsibility to try to help people in their tradition to think about the relationship between those values and choices we face in public life. Since I am making what is probably my only appearance in the company of theologians, I decided to set aside my normal practice and say something about my own experience in print, since religious experience was the original source of this enterprise.

12. Ralph Reed, *Active Faith: How Christians Are Changing the Soul of American Politics* (New York: Free Press, 1996).

13. Laurie Goldstein, "For Christian Men's Group, Racial Harmony Starts at the Local Level," *New York Times,* September 29, 1997, p. A12. Promise Keepers was founded in 1990 and brought 2.6 million men to religious conferences in stadiums during the next seven years.

14. John Yinger, *Closed Doors, Opportunities Lost: The Continuing Cost of Housing Discrimination* (New York: Russell Sage Foundation, 1995); Margery Austin Turner, Michael Fix, and Raymond J. Struyk, *Opportunities Denied, Opportunities Diminished: Racial Discrimination in Hiring* (Washington, D.C.: Urban Institute Press, 1991); Katheryn M. Neckerman and Joleen Kirschenmann, "Hiring Strategies, Racial Bias, and Inner City Workers," *Social Problems* 38 (November 1991). pp. 433–47; William Julius Wilson, *When Work Disappears: The World of the New Urban Poor* (New York: Alfred A. Knopf, 1996), chapter 5.

15. Norman C. Amaker, *Civil Rights and the Reagan Administration* (Washington, D.C.: Urban Institute Press, 1988); Gary Orfield and Susan Eaton, *Dismantling Desegregation: The Quiet Reversal of* Brown *v.* Board of Education (New York: New Press, 1996).

NOTES TO CHAPTER 1

1. See James M. Washington, ed., *I Have a Dream: Writings and Speeches that Changed the World* (San Francisco: Harper San Francisco, 1992), p. 102.

2. Ibid., p. 104.

3. Ibid., p. 105.

4. Paraphrased in Lawrence W. Levine, *Black Culture and Black Consciousness: Afro-American Folk Thought from Slavery to Freedom* (New York: Oxford University Press, 1977), pp. 31–32.

5. Walter Bruggemann, *The Prophetic Imagination* (Minneapolis: Fortress Press, 1978), p. 14.

6. Washington, *I Have a Dream,* p. 97.

7. William Galston, *Justice and the Human Good* (Chicago: University of Chicago Press, 1980).

8. Martin Luther King, Jr., *Where Do We Go From Here: Chaos or Community?* (Boston: Beacon Press, 1967), p. 187.
9. King Center Archives.

NOTES TO CHAPTER 2

1. Except for the war in Vietnam, essays on these subjects can be found in his collection of Essays on Human Existence entitled *The Insecurity of Freedom* (New York: Noonday Press, 1967). For Vietnam, see "The Moral Outrage" in *Vietnam: Crisis of Conscience*, R. Brown, A. Heschel, and M. Novak, eds. (New York: Association Press, 1967).
2. Both appear in *The Insecurity of Freedom;* "Religion and Race" on pp. 85–100 and "The White Man Is on Trial" on pp. 101–111. From this point on, citations from the two essays will be noted parenthetically in the body of the text. On the special relationship between Heschel and King on both personal and theological planes, see the beautiful portrait by his daughter, Susannah Heschel, "Theological Affinities in the Writings of Abraham Joshua Heschel and Martin Luther King, Jr.," in *Conservative Judaism* 50, no. 2–3 (Winter/Spring 1998), pp. 124–46. Her sense (p. 138 ff.) that Heschel had an impact on King's eventful linking of the cause of civil rights with that against the war in Vietnam can be confirmed. After hearing King's April 4, 1967, address at New York's Riverside Church, I met my teacher Heschel walking out. He mentioned how relieved he was that King had taken his counsel to link the two great evils that America was then involved in. King had accepted Heschel's position that one must apply across the board the principle that indifference to evil is as insidious as evil itself.

NOTES TO CHAPTER 3

1. Richard King, *Civil Rights and the Idea of Freedom* (New York: Oxford University Press, 1992), p. 99. For an interesting discussion of the term's philosophical antecedents, see John E. Smith, "Royce: The Absolute and the Beloved Community Revisited," in Leroy S. Rouner, ed., *Meaning, Truth and God* (Boston: Boston University Press, 1982), pp. 135–153.
2. Martin Luther King, Jr., "An Experiment in Love," in *A Testament of Hope: The Essential Writings of Martin Luther King, Jr.,* edited by James M. Washington (San Francisco: HarperCollins Paperback, 1986), p. 20.
3. Martin Luther King, Jr., *Strength to Love* (Cleveland: William Collins, 1963), p. 50.
4. "The Student Nonviolent Coordinating Committee (as revised in conference, April 29, 1962)," *The Charles Sherrod Papers* (file 24, State Historical Society of Wisconsin).
5. Ibid. John Lewis, SNCC's chairman in 1965, illustrated the spiritual divide between the young activists and the older religious generation, in describing the sources of his own activism: "So many black church ministers talked about the

way over yonder and the afterlife. But when I heard Dr. King preaching on the radio one Sunday afternoon, I was amazed that he did not talk about the pearly gates and the streets paved with gold. He was concerned about the streets of Montgomery, the highways and byways of America." (John Lewis, interview with author, November 19, 1993.)

6. John Lewis interview.

7. See Cleveland Sellers, *The River of No Return: The Autobiography of a Black Militant and the Life and Death of SNCC* (Jackson: University Press of Mississippi, 1990); and George M. Fredrickson, *Black Liberation: A Comparative History of Black Ideologies in the United States and South Africa* (New York: Oxford University Press, 1995), pp. 277–318.

8. See Doug McAdam, *Freedom Summer* (New York: Oxford University Press, 1976), pp. 171–178.

9. See Sara Evans, *Personal Politics: The Roots of Women's Liberation in the Civil Rights Movement and the New Left* (New York: Random House, 1979).

10. See Steven M. Tipton, *Getting Saved From the Sixties: Moral Meaning in Conversion and Cultural Change* (Berkeley: University of California Press, 1982).

11. The best accounts are memoirs. For example, see James H. Cone, *My Soul Looks Back* (Nashville: Abingdon, 1982) and Will D. Campbell, *Brother to a Dragonfly* (New York: Continuum Books, 1977).

12. Clayborne Carson, *In Struggle: SNCC and the Black Awakening of the 1960s* (Cambridge: Harvard University Press, 1981), p. 305.

13. See Joe Klein, "In God They Trust," *The New Yorker*, June 16, 1997, pp. 40–48.

14. Kay Mills, *This Little Light of Mine: The Life of Fannie Lou Hamer* (New York: Dutton, 1993), p. 78.

15. The Citizens' Council primer for third and fourth graders explains this concept: "God wanted the white people to live alone. And He wanted colored people to live alone. The white man built America for you. White men built America so they could make the rules. George Washington was a brave and honest white man. . . . The white man has always been kind to the Negro. . . . Negro people like to live by themselves. Negroes use their own bathrooms. They do not use white people bathrooms. . . . This is called our Southern Way of Life." (Cited in Nicholas von Hoffman, *Mississippi Notebook* [New York: David White Company, 1964], p. 46.)

16. John Dittmer, *Local People: The Struggle for Civil Rights in Mississippi* (Urbana: University of Illinois Press, 1994), p. 58.

17. Cited in Dittmer, *Local People*, p. 266.

18. Mills, *This Little Light of Mine*, p. 82

19. Lawrence Guyot and Mike Thelwell, "The Politics of Necessity and Survival in Mississippi," *Freedomways* 6 (Spring 1966), p. 132.

20. See William H. Chafe, *Never Stop Running: Allard Lowenstein and the Struggle to Save American Liberalism* (New York: Basic Books, 1993), pp. 187–210.

21. Cited in Dittmer, *Local People*, p. 209.

22. Willie Peacock, cited in Dittmer, *Local People,* p. 210.
23. Cleveland Sellers interview with author.
24. These sometimes disputed numbers are based on the statistics of the *Congressional Quarterly,* week ending July 5, 1963, pp. 1091–93 (Mississippi Archives and History).
25. John Lewis interview.
26. Bob Moses cited in Eric R. Burner, *And Gently He Shall Lead Them: Robert Parris Moses and Civil Rights in Mississippi* (New York: New York University Press, 1994), p. 129.
27. Carson, *In Struggle,* p. 99. Bob Moses cited in Burner, *And Gently He Shall Lead Them,* p. 129.
28. Moses cited in Carson, *In Struggle,* p. 101.
29. Richard Lischer points out that King's phrase, with its clear Hegelian resonances, was borrowed from the American philosopher Josiah Royce "to evoke the period of brotherhood that would follow the current social struggle." (Richard Lischer, *The Preacher King: Martin Luther King, Jr. and the Word that Moved America* [New York: Oxford University Press, 1995], p. 234.) Yet King placed less emphasis on the specific details of the ideal, less emphasis on techniques of engineering the beloved community, than on the character of life required to foster the coming of a new social order. King was a preacher, not an economist or political theorist. Importantly, Lischer shows that as his rhetoric became tempered by a keener understanding of social realities, King's use of the phrase was eventually replaced by specific reference to the Kingdom of God. The former phrase, the beloved community, carries overtones of utopian idealism; the latter, Lischer says, "acknowledges God's claim upon all human achievement." However, one should add that to many local people in the movement, the beloved community itself acknowledged the prevenience of divine grace inasmuch as it represented, in one activist's words, a "tiny taste of the Kingdom to come."
30. Fannie Lou Hamer cited in Carson, *In Struggle,* p. 99. Clayborne Carson claims (p. 99) that most of the supporters of the proposed Summer Project were veteran SNCC volunteers. In her study *A Case of Black and White: Northern Volunteers and the Southern Freedom Summers, 1964–1965* (Westport, Connecticut: Greenwood Press, 1982), p. 99, Mary Aickin Rothschild adds, "Fannie Lou Hamer believed that the 'bridge' built between white volunteers and black children was one of the greatest achievements of the summers. Never again would southern blacks be so separated from the white community. Likewise, the white community simply could not continue to maintain many of the myths about the 'necessity' of separation of the races, which, of course, had never existed anyway when there was work to be done" (p. 172).
31. James Forman cited in Carson, *In Struggle,* p. 99.
32. Cited in Sellers, *River of No Return,* p. 56.
33. SNCC document cited in Sellers, *River of No Return,* p. 56.
34. Sellers, *River of No Return,* p. 51.

35. Leslie Burl McLemore, *The Mississippi Freedom Democratic Party: A Case Study of Grass-Roots Politics,* (unpublished dissertation, University of Massachusetts, 1971), p. 128.

36. Charles M. Payne, *I've Got the Light of Freedom: The Organizing Tradition and the Mississippi Freedom Struggle* (Berkeley: University of California Press, 1995), p. 258.

37. Ibid., p. 258.

38. Fannie Lou Hamer in *Freedom on My Mind,* a documentary film produced and directed by Connie Fidd and Marilyn Mulford (Berkeley, California: Clarity Educational Productions, 1994).

39. "Verbatim transcript of interview by phone by Jack Minnis with Mrs. Fannie Lou Hamer" (SNCC Papers, Martin Luther King Center, Atlanta).

40. Cited in Payne, *I've Got the Light of Freedom,* p. 259.

41. Cited in ibid., p. 258.

42. Ibid., p. 256.

43. Ibid., p. 263.

44. Ibid., p. 261.

45. Ibid., p. 260.

46. Jean Wheeler Smith cited in Payne, *I've Got the Light of Freedom,* p. 259.

47. Danny Collum, "Stepping Out into Freedom: The Life of Fannie Lou Hamer," *Sojourners* (December 1982), p. 15.

48. Payne, *I've Got the Light of Freedom,* p. 260.

49. John Lewis cited in Lischer, *The Preacher King,* p. 244.

50. Lischer, *The Preacher King,* p. 245. See also Stanley Hauerwas, "Remembering Martin Luther King, Jr., Remembering," *The Journal of Religious Ethics* 23, no. 1 (Spring 1995), p. 141.

51. Hamer appears altogether untroubled by a theological matter that has preoccupied and often perplexed many Christian theologians. How can certain people, ideas, or experiences not directly associated with Jesus Christ or Christian symbolism nonetheless become expressions of God's goodness?

    Paul Tillich, whose Protestant liberal cool seems a long way from Ruleville, Mississippi, offered an experiential description of the "New Creation" of Christ that is close to the spirit (though not the rhetoric) of Hamer's account. Tillich's idea of the New Being illuminates the "confessing church" of the civil rights struggle. "Where one is grasped by a human face as human, although one has to overcome personal distaste, or racial strangeness, or national conflicts, or the differences of sex, age, of beauty, of strength, of knowledge, and all the other innumerable causes of separation—there New Creation happens" (*The New Being* [New York: Charles Scribner's Sons, 1955] p. 22). As such, the invisible church, the church within the church, includes many women and men who come to God by other names than Jesus.

    For his part, the contemporary Jesuit theologian Karl Rahner coined the term "anonymous Christians" to refer to people who exhibit moral responsibility and goodness but who are not Christian in an explicitly confessional sense.

Hamer's sympathy with various parts of these descriptions is interesting not only for the fact that she had never heard of these men, but more for the way she freely combines themes that academic theologians have long deemed incompatible, stretching them in new and exciting directions with no worry about incommensurabilities and conflicts. Hamer's theology makes sense of the lived experience of faith and of the theological and existential complexities of a movement calling. The "Christlike" young people were willing to give up their lives for the sake of black freedom; and in the case of James Chaney, Andrew Goodman, and Mickey Schwerner did so. "If Christ were here today, He would be just like these young people who the Southerners called radicals and beatniks. Christ was called a Beelzebub, called so many names. But He was Christ." What could be less difficult to accept than the proposition that Christ is present in an interracial fellowship linked together in the struggle for justice, bearing witness in a variety of ways to the reconciling God in the segregated South?

Implicit in Hamer's rich theological imagination is the notion that the created and social orders continually confront human history with an inner teleology; in creation and preservation, in acts of compassion and mercy, and in the manifold array of beauty, God not only declares himself, but also arouses and stimulates the world and history. There is an inner richness, a spirit, in creation that always and everywhere bears witness to the divine mystery within which it is concealed. When that richness is exhibited in compassionate acts, it attests to the aliveness of that spirit—however concealed—in a way that must be taken seriously. Your anonymous Christian and New Being are too interior or private, Hamer might say to Rahner and Tillich.

52. Fannie Lou Hamer, "Foreword," in Tracy Sugarman, *Stranger at the Gates* (New York: Hill and Wang, 1966), p. vii.
53. Ibid., vii.
54. Ibid., vii.
55. On the religious motives of the summer volunteers, see McAdam, *Freedom Summer,* pp. 46–49, 62–65.
56. Hamer, *Stranger at the Gates,* vii.
57. She was in good theological company. John Lewis, the former seminarian at the American Baptist Seminary in Nashville and chairman of SNCC until the spring of 1966, liked to describe the spreading flame of the movement as a convergence of wills, a coming together of the God whose righteousness flows as a mighty stream with a people readied by time and cruelty. Lewis explained, "Some people might want to call this [the movement] the spirit of history or some other force but I believe the movement happened because we were in step with the Creator. Personally, I believed that I had been called by God to enter the struggle. I had to learn to turn myself over and follow; to be consistent and follow, and somehow trust that it was all going to be taken care of; it was all going to work out. My faith in God was at the heart of what I did . . . I heard the minister preaching, saying that if I believed in Jesus, then my hands and my

feet must become the hands and feet of other men and women. I knew that if I was going to be a follower, I must do the work of the movement."

Like Martin Luther King, Jr., Lewis preached an interracial movement—a "circle of trust, the band of brothers"—the heart of which was the belief that "the movement was based on the simple truth of the Great Teacher: love thy neighbor as thyself." King may have more closely identified his use of the "beloved community" with the biblical concept of the Kingdom of God than did SNCC; still, for a while, both waves of the movement identified this interracial fellowship in terms of a theological reality that gathered its moral and spiritual energies from the God who reconciles.

58. As Michael Walzer writes, "God's promise generates a sense of possibility (it would be rash, given the fearfulness of the Israelite slaves, to say that it generates a sense of confidence): the world is not all Egypt. Without that sense of possibility, oppression would be experienced as an inescapable condition, a matter of personal or collective bad luck, a stroke of fate" (*Exodus and Revolution,* [New York: Basic Books, 1985], pp. 21–21).

59. In his excellent book, *Civil Rights and the Idea of Freedom,* Richard King explains (p. 29), "The centrality to black theology of the Exodus story meant that slavery/freedom was understood on a figural-spiritual level by many black Christians. Thus slavery and freedom referred to more than 'just' a secular experience or status, for they were also spiritual or sacred experiences of a people whose experience was part of God's purpose and plan. Freedom, according to this spiritual interpretation, was a destination in sacred history as well as a goal of action within secular history; it was a future condition implying a fundamental transformation in individual and group life."

60. Because this dialect was so exuberantly at play in Hamer's theology, she did not need to replace the first person singular pronoun "I" with the plural "we." C. Eric Lincoln and Lawrence H. Mamiya's claim would not hold in her case, that "the creators of the civil rights songs always used the first person plural pronouns 'we' and 'our,'" in order to foster a sense of solidarity, of acting together "as one consolidated body" (Eric Lincoln and Lawrence H. Mamiya, *The Black Church in the African American Experience* [Durham: Duke University Press, 1990], p. 370). For Mrs. Hamer, the "I" included both the individual self and the beloved community; as the writer Zora Neale Hurston once said of the ritual of "shouting," it is both "absolutely individualistic" and "a community thing" (cited in Joseph M. Murphy, *Working the Spirit: Ceremonies of the African Diaspora* [Boston: Beacon Press, 1994], p. 173).

61. Bob Moses, in *Freedom on My Mind.*

62. Cited in Mills, *This Little Light of Mine: The Life of Fannie Lou Hamer,* p. 79.

63. Cornel West describes prophetic Christianity as an utterly honest confrontation with the tragic character of human history "without permitting the immensity of what is and what must be lost to call into question the significance of what may be gained." At the same time, prophetic religion elevates "the notion of struggle"—not just individual, but collective and thus redemptive—to the high-

est priority. West explains, "To be a prophetic Afro-American Christian is to negate what is and transform prevailing realities against the backdrop of the present historical limits. In short, prophetic Afro-American Christian thought imbues Afro-American thinking with the sobriety of tragedy, the struggle for freedom, and the spirit of hope" (*Prophesy Deliverance! An Afro-American Revolutionary Christianity* [Philadelphia: Westminster Press, 1982], p. 19).

64. Consider bell hooks' words of advice, "To live in anti-racist society, we must collectively renew our commitment to a democratic vision of racial justice and equality. Pursuing that vision we create a culture where beloved community flourishes and is sustained . . . The interracial circle of love that I know can happen because each individual present in it has made his or her own commitment to living an anti-racist life and to furthering the struggle to end white supremacy will become a reality for everyone only if those of us who have created these communities share how they emerge in our lives and the strategies we use to sustain them" (*Killing Rage* [New York: Outlet, 1996], p. 271).

65. The Voice of Calvary Ministry in Jackson, Mississippi (and its sister community in Pasadena, California), founded by civil rights worker Reverend John M. Perkins, continues to serve as the influential model of grass-roots African-American evangelical social activism, embodying a peculiar mix of black nationalist self-reliance, "Bible-centered" piety, and Anabaptist social radicalism.

66. Andrés Topia, "Can Anything Good Come Out of the Hood," *Christianity Today,* May 16,1994, p. 28.

67. Ibid.

68. John Perkins, *Resurrecting Hope: Powerful Stories of How God Is Moving to Reach US Cities* (Ventura, California: Regal Books, 1995), p. 111.

69. John Perkins and Wayne Gordon, "What Is Christian Community Development?" The Christian Community Development Association, n.d.

70. See John Perkins, *Let Justice Roll Down* (Ventura, California: Regal Books, 1976); John Perkins, *A Quiet Revolution* (Pasadena, California: Urban Family Publications, 1976); John Perkins and Thomas A. Tarrants, III, *He's My Brother: A Black Activist and a Former Klansman Tell Their Stories* (Grand Rapids, Michigan: Chosen Books, 1994).

71. Spencer Perkins and Chris Rice, *More Than Equals: Racial Healing for the Sake of the Gospel.* (Downers Grove, Illinois: Intervarsity Press, 1993), p. 17. See also Jody Miller Shearer, *Enter the River: Healing Steps from White Privilege Toward Racial Reconciliation* (Scottdale, Pennsylvania: Herald Press, 1994); Curtiss Paul DeYoung, *Reconciliation: Our Greatest Challenge—Our Only Hope* (Valley Forge, Pennsylvania: Judson Press, 1997).

72. See Ray Bakke, *A Theology as Big as the City* (Downers Grove, Illinois: Intervarsity Press, 1997); Robert D. Lupton, *Return Flight: Community Development Through Reneighboring Our Cities* (Atlanta: FCS Urban Ministries, 1997); Randy White, *Journey to the Center of the City: Making a Difference in an Urban Neighborhood* (Downers Grove, Illinois: Intervarsity Press, 1997).

73. Perkins and Rice, *More Than Equals,* p. 19.

74. My friend, the Reverend Eugene Rivers, has recently criticized evangelical reconciliation initiatives for their bland or etherealized notions of justice. "Real, genuine reconciliation would mean that Whites would start a war with Whites to
make sure that black people got what they needed in terms of justice." But that's
not happening, Rivers adds, for most evangelical initiatives are too often based
on personal or emotional relationships. He explains, "I had a meeting with the
editorial board of *Christianity Today* and they made an interesting observation,
that Blacks are apparently not interested in racial reconciliation. I agree with that
assessment. Black people want freedom. These kinds of emotional reconciliation
sessions, where we receive apologies and extend forgiveness, are mostly just temporary purgings. Reconciliation minus justice is of cathartic value, but it doesn't
go much beyond that." As a former philosophy student at Harvard, Rivers certainly knows of a richer and hard-earned reconciliation, one built on difference
and diversity, that refuses to consume or tyrannize. Eugene Rivers in Jennifer
Parker, "No Cheap Reconciliation," *Reconcilers* (Summer 1997), pp. 4–6.

75. For example, the Promise Keepers want to atone for the sins of evangelical hus-
bands and fathers, offering men the emotional space to reclaim the patriarchy of
evangelical suburbanites. A case in point is the advice of Tony Evans, an
African-American leader, in the Christian men's movement: "Sit down with your
wife and say something like this: "Honey, I've made a terrible mistake. I've
given you my role. I gave up leading this family, and I forced you to take my
place. Now, I must reclaim that role." . . . I'm not suggesting [to you men] you
ask for your role back, I'm urging you take it back. . . . there can be no compro-
mise here."

    Stokely Carmichael, the free-wheeling father of the Black Power movement,
during a discussion about the place of women in the civil rights movement, once
bragged to some of his male SNCC buddies, "A woman's place is supine." But
Carmichael's remark was male bravado; he knew how ludicrous it was. As
Cleveland Sellers said in his friend's defense, "Stokely knew that if he said that
in front of Mrs. Hamer or Mrs. Devine or Mrs. Blackwell or any of the feisty
women he worked with, they would have slammed him upside the head with an
iron skillet."

76. John Perkins, *With Justice for All* (Ventura, California: Regal Books, 1982), p.
107.

77. Victoria Gray Adams, interview with author.

78. Richard Rorty's recent book, *Achieving Our Country* (Cambridge: Harvard University Press, 1998), borrows material from the Southern struggle (and other
American progressive movements) to build a hard-hitting (and well-deserved) attack on the etherealized preoccupations of the contemporary academy, which he
thinks prefers cultural politics over real politics. Consider his description of the
difference between "the residual left" (primarily concerned about laws) and the
"academic left" (primarily concerned about culture) as "the difference between
the people who read books like Thomas Geoghegan's *Which Side Are You
On?*—a brilliant explanation of how unions get busted—and people who read

Fredric Jameson's *Postmodernism, or The Cultural Logic of Late Capitalism.* The latter is an equally brilliant book, but it operates on a level of abstraction too high to encourage any particular political initiative. After reading Geoghegan, you have views on some of the things which need to be done. After reading Jameson, you have views on practically everything except what needs to be done" (p. 78). But when Rorty further asks us to drop appeals to God (or Nature or History) as sources of social responsibility, I hear him asking Hamer and King to leave the table. The attempt to reconstruct Hamer or King's legacy—or the lessons of the civil rights movement—outside the context of the African-American Christian tradition is shaky (and quite possibly dishonest) business.

NOTES TO CHAPTER 4

1. A classic reflection on civil disobedience and its relation to civic community is found in Martin Luther King's "Letter from a Birmingham Jail." See Martin Luther King, Jr., "Letter from a Birmingham Jail," in James M. Washington, ed., *I Have a Dream: Writings and Speeches that Changed the World* (San Francisco: Harper Collins, 1992), p. 90.
2. Walter Rauschenbusch, *Christianity and the Social Crisis* (Louisville: Westminster/John Knox, 1991), p. 421.
3. For a more complete account of Niebuhr's career and his relationship to these formative events, see Richard Fox, *Reinhold Niebuhr: A Biography* (New York: Pantheon Books, 1985), pp. 41–110.
4. Reinhold Niebuhr, *Moral Man and Immoral Society* (New York: Charles Scribner's Sons, 1932), p. 253. King describes his encounter with Niebuhr's writing and its effects on his own thinking in Martin Luther King, Jr., *Stride Toward Freedom* (San Francisco: Harper & Row, 1958), pp. 97–100.
5. Reinhold Niebuhr, *The Children of Light and the Children of Darkness* (New York: Charles Scribner's Sons, 1972; first published, 1944).
6. Reinhold Niebuhr, "Liberty and Equality," in Ronald Stone, ed., *Faith and Politics* (New York: George Braziller, 1968), p. 197.
7. James Cone, *Black Theology and Black Power* (San Francisco: Harper & Row, 1969). Also Cone, *A Black Theology of Liberation* (Philadelphia: Lippincott, 1970).
8. Gustavo Gutiérrez, *We Drink from our own Wells* (Maryknoll, N.Y.: Orbis Books, 1984).
9. Glenn Tinder, *The Political Meaning of Christianity* (Baton Rouge: Louisiana State University Press, 1989), p. 142.
10. Niebuhr, *The Children of Light and the Children of Darkness*, pp. xiii-xiv.
11. John Howard Yoder, *The Politics of Jesus*, 2nd ed. (Grand Rapids: Eerdmans, 1994). Yoder, whose theology was grounded in the Mennonite tradition, died in January 1998 after a distinguished teaching career at the University of Notre Dame.
12. Stanley Hauerwas, *A Community of Character* (Notre Dame, Ind.: University of Notre Dame Press, 1981).

13. Stanley Hauerwas, *After Christendom?: How the Church Is to Behave If Freedom, Justice, and a Christian Nation Are Bad Ideas* (Nashville: Abingdon Press, 1991), pp. 45–68.

14. John Calvin, *Institutes of the Christian Religion,* ed. John T. McNeill (Philadelphia: Westminster Press, 1960), vol. 2, p. 1487.

15. For a more extended interpretation of Niebuhr's theological understanding of politics, see Robin W. Lovin, *Reinhold Niebuhr and Christian Realism* (Cambridge: Cambridge University Press, 1995), pp. 158–90.

16. See especially Robert N. Bellah, et al., *Habits of the Heart: Individualism and Commitment in American Life* (Berkeley: University of California Press, 1985), and Robert D. Putnam, "Bowling Alone: America's Declining Social Capital," *Journal of Democracy* 6 (January 1995), pp. 65–78.

17. See Gunnar Myrdal, *An American Dilemma: The Negro Problem and Modern Democracy* (New York: Harper and Brothers, 1944), p. xlvii.

18. Reinhold Niebuhr, "Liberty and Equality," p. 197. See note 6 above.

NOTES TO CHAPTER 5

1. Articles in the last decade include Taitetsu Unno, "Personal Rights and Contemporary Buddhism," and Robert Thurman, "Social and Cultural Rights in Buddhism," in Leroy Rouner, ed., *Human Rights and the World's Religions* (Notre Dame, Indiana: University of Notre Dame Press, 1988), pp. 129–163; Padmasiri de Silva, "Human Rights in Buddhist Perspective" and Masao Abe, "A Buddhist View of Human Rights," in Abdullahi A. An-Na'im et al., eds., *Human Rights and Religious Values: An Uneasy Relationship?* (Grand Rapids: William B. Eerdmans, 1995), pp. 133–153; and Robert Thurman, "Human Rights and Human Responsibilities: Buddhist Views on Individualism and Altruism," in Irene Bloom, J. Paul Martin, and Wayne Proudfoot, eds., *Religious Diversity and Human Rights* (New York: Columbia University Press, 1996), pp. 87–113. More significant, however, are the political protests of the Dalai Lama (political and religious leader of Tibet in exile), Thich Nhat Hanh (Vietnamese monk in exile), and Sulak Sivaraksa (Thai lay social activist), all of whom have been nominated for the Nobel Peace Prize as Buddhist champions of human rights. For Buddhist behavior in ethnic and political conflict, see K.M. de Silva et al., eds., *Ethnic Conflict in Buddhist Societies: Sri Lanka, Thailand and Burma* (Boulder: Westview, 1988); W.A.W. Warnapala, *Ethnic Strife and Politics in Sri Lanka* (New Delhi: Navrang, 1994); Ronald Swartz, *Circle of Protest: Political Ritual in the Tibetan Uprising* (New York: Columbia University Press, 1994); and Tessa J. Bartholomeusz and Chandra R. de Silva, eds., *Buddhist Fundamentalism and Minority Identities in Sri Lanka* (Albany: SUNY Press, 1998).

2. Buddhist priests first arrived in Hawaii in 1889 to start enduring groups, but Hawaii was not part of the United States until annexation in July 7, 1898. The earliest Buddhist priests in the mainland United States arrived in 1899.

3. The Buddhist priests who signed the protest letter represented a broad spectrum

of the major Buddhist denominations: Bishop Yemyō Imamura of Jōdo Shinshū (Nishi), Eikaku Seki of Shingon, Bishop Hōsen Isobe of Sōtō Zen, Bishop Ryōzen Yamada of Jōdo, Bishop Chōsei Nunome of Nichiren, and Kankai Izuhara of Jōdo Shinshū (Higashi), as well as two Shinto priests. For the best overview of the confrontation, see Louise Hunter, *Buddhism in Hawaii: Its Impact on a Yankee Community* (Honolulu: University of Hawaii Press, 1971), pp. 116–129.

4. The history by Rick Fields, *How the Swans Came to the Lake: A Narrative History of Buddhism in America* (Boston: Shambala, 1981), completely omitted the story of the arrival and history of Jōdo Shinshū in America, even though at that time it was the largest Buddhist group in the United States. Fortunately, he corrected his omission in later editions of his book (3d ed., 1992). The book compiled and edited by Don Morreale, *The Complete Guide to Buddhist America*, 2d ed. (Boston: Shambala, 1998), is even more startling since he was well aware of the Jōdo Shinshū and SGI movements, but chose to ignore them because he said he couldn't cover everything. Both authors have made marvelous contributions by collecting many obscure fragments from different parts of the country, but they have also shown how easy it to overlook major groups like Jōdo Shinshū and SGI-USA. Not to include these groups is like writing a complete guide to American Christianity and leaving out Roman Catholics and Mormons. The reason seems to be that both Fields and Morreale focused on styles of Buddhism that appealed to middle-class European Americans. The fact that Fields and Morreale could ignore these other groups shows that, unlike Islam and Roman Catholicism, Buddhism does not have an integrated structure, but has a variety of traditions shaped by local cultures. Buddhists of one type may have little knowledge or connection with Buddhists of other forms of practice.

5. Based on U.S. Census data, the U.S. population of Japanese ancestry increased dramatically after 1900, beginning with 148 in 1880, and increasing to 2,039 in 1890, 24,326 in 1900, 72,157 in 1910, 111,101 in 1920, 138,834 in 1930, 126,947 in 1940, 168,773 in 1950, 260,195 in 1960, and 373,983 in 1970. In 1930, about half of the Japanese in America were foreign-born (70,477), but by 1940 nearly two-thirds were born in the United States (79,642).

6. War Relocation Authority, *The Evacuated People—A Quantitative Description* (Washington, D.C.: U.S. Department of the Interior, 1942), Table 24, p. 79; quoted in Tetsuden Kashima, *Buddhism in America: The Social Organization of an Ethnic Religious Institution* (Westport, Conn.: Greenwood Press, 1977), p. 53.

7. "A conservative estimate of religious orientation among Japanese immigrants indicates that two-thirds came from prefectures dominated by the Jōdo Shinshū faith" (Kashima 13, quoting Kosei Ogura, "A Sociological Study of the Buddhist Churches in North America," [master's thesis, University of Southern California, Los Angeles, 1932], p.84). In the 1990s with the increasing popularity of Buddhism, there are 25 different Buddhist groups in Hawaii having a total of 96 temples, but 41 of these temples belong to Jōdo Shinshū, three times more than

any other single group. See *Unity in Diversity: Hawaii's Buddhist Communities* (Honolulu: Hawaii Association of International Buddhists, 1997).

8. From the library of Rev. Tetsuro Kashima and quoted by his son, Tetsuden Kashima, in *Buddhism in America*, p. 52.

9. The patriotism of the Japanese Americans was most vividly demonstrated by the record of the 442nd Regiment of *nisei* who served in Europe and became one of the most bloodied and decorated units in the U.S. Army. Japanese Americans emphasized loyalty and duty, rather than protest and dissent. It is no accident that a major book by Bill Hosokawa on the first generation of Japanese born in America should be entitled *Nisei: The Quiet Americans* (New York: William Morrow and Company, 1969).

10. In July 1942, Purcell brought a test case on behalf of Miss Mitsuye Endo, an employee of the state of California. On December 18, 1944, the Supreme Court ordered that Endo be released.

11. Hosokawa, *Nisei: The Quiet Americans,* p. 328. For a fuller discussion of the legal issues, see the collection of articles, edited by Charles McClain, *The Mass Internment of Japanese Americans and the Quest for Legal Redress* (New York: Garland, 1994).

12. Eric K. Yamamoto, "Korematsu Revisited—Correcting the Injustice of Extraordinary Government Excess and Lax Judicial Review: Time for a Better Accommodation of National Security Concerns and Civil Liberties," *Santa Clara Law Review* 26, no. 1 (Winter 1986), p.2. For their assistance in providing information about the incarceration of Japanese Americans in World War II, I wish to express my gratitude to Lawrence Foster and Eric Yamamoto of the William S. Richardson School of Law, University of Hawaii.

13. See Yamamoto, "Korematsu Revisited," p. 4.

14. The doctrine of karmic retribution in the next lifetime for misdeeds committed in this lifetime is vividly illustrated in popular tracts, such as the *Scripture of Cause and Effect* (*Yinguo Jing*) distributed in Chinese Buddhist temples, and is a standard part of Buddhist manuals of practice, and the *Upāsaka Sūtra,* translated by Shih Heng-ching, *The Sūtra on Upāsaka Precepts* (Berkeley: Bukkyo Dendo Kyokai, 1991), pp. 151–178.

15. This attitude was conveyed to me in conversation by Nechung Rinpoche in the mid-1970s when he came to Hawaii after lengthy imprisonment by the Chinese. As head of the Nechung Monastery, the official oracle of the Tibetan government that reviewed major government decisions, he had held an important religious and political post in Tibet prior to Chinese occupation. As a result, after their takeover, the Chinese had imprisoned and tortured him for many years to provoke a confession for what his communist jailers considered to be an abuse of power. Similarly, the Dalai Lama of Tibet, Tenzin Gyatso, displays no anger against the Chinese, even though they are brutalizing his people and trying to destroy much of Tibetan Buddhist culture.

16. Treatise on the *Two Entrances and Four Practices* attributed to Bodhidharma. The translation contains some editorial changes, but is based on John McRae,

The Northern School and the Formation of Early Ch'an Buddhism (Honolulu: University of Hawaii Press, 1986), pp. 103–104.

17. Fields, *How the Swans Came to the Lake,* p. 193.
18. For an excellent introduction to the primary Mahayana values, usually translated as the six perfections of a bodhisattva, see Har Dayal, *The Bodhisattva Doctrine in Buddhist Sanskrit Literature* (London: Routledge & Kegan Paul, 1932), pp. 165–269. For contemporary American Zen writings on these virtues (increased now to ten), see Robert Aitken, *The Practice of Perfection: The Paramitas from a Zen Buddhist Perspective* (New York: Pantheon Books, 1994) and Taigen Daniel Leighton, *Bodhisattva Archetypes* (New York: Penguin Arkana Books, 1998), chapter 3. Similarly, see the chapter "On Endurance" in *The Sūtra on Upāsaka Precepts,* pp. 179–182, a precept text still actively used by Chinese Buddhists. As a consequence of their Zen training, students of unethical Buddhist masters have been reticent about complaining against abuse, although a Korean Sŏn (Zen) Buddhist nun, Sungaku Sunim, has recently brought a sexual harassment suit against the former abbot of Daewan Temple in Hawaii. Such complaints are usually dismissed by the Buddhist hierarchy in Korea, and this suit is the first legal sexual harassment case in Korean Buddhist history. Sungaku Sunim's lawyer, who specializes in civil rights cases, is a former Zen student of Robert Aitken, founder of Buddhist Peace Fellowship. The case was settled out of court in 1999.
19. The classic paradigm of church-state relations was developed in China's Tang Dynasty (A.D. 618–907) law codes, which then were adopted in Korea and Japan. Stanley Weinstein, in *Buddhism Under the Tang* (New York: Cambridge University Press, 1987), writes of the state progressively curbing the power of Buddhist monasteries, the state management of the clergy, the use of Buddhism for political goals, and the violent persecution of Buddhism under Emperor Wu (A.D. 840–846).
20. See Angelo N. Ancheta, *Race, Rights, and the Asian American Experience* (New Brunswick, N.J.: Rutgers University Press, 1998) and Elmer Clarence Sandmeyer, *The Anti-Chinese Movement in California* (Urbana: University of Illinois Press, 1939).
21. See Roger Daniels, *Prisoners Without Trial: Japanese Americans in World War II* (New York: Hill and Wang, 1993), especially chapter 1; Bill Hosokawa, *Nisei: The Quiet Americans* (New York: William Morrow, 1969), pp. 41–132; Paul R. Spickard, *Japanese Americans: The Formation and Transformation of an Ethnic Group* (New York: Twayne, 1997). The federal Commission on Wartime Relocation and Internment of Civilians concludes that "The broad historical causes which shaped these [relocation] decisions were race prejudice, war hysteria and a failure of political leadership." (Quoted in P.T. Nash, "Moving for Redress," reprinted in McClain, ed., *The Mass Internment of Japanese Americans,* p. 181.) See also Charles McClain, ed., *Japanese Immigrants and American Law: The Alien Land Laws and Other Issues* (New York: Garland, 1994).

22. This information was given to the author by Alfred Bloom in a telephone conversation on July 28, 1998.

23. Civil rights was the theme of the Spring 1993 issue of *Turning Wheel,* and related topics can be found in other issues, such as those dealing with sexual misconduct (Spring 1996), homelessness (Fall 1966), health care (Winter 1998), and work (Spring 1998).

24. See my article, "Racial Diversity in Soka Gakkai International-USA," in Christopher Queen, ed., *Engaged Buddhism in the West* (forthcoming).

25. A case involving same-sex marriage, which has received a great deal of publicity, is being argued before the courts by Dan Foley, a lawyer who happens to be a member of SGI-USA in Hawaii.

26. See Henry Rosemont's analysis of the American dilemma in "Human Rights: A Bill of Worries," in W.T. deBary and Tu Weiming, eds., *Confucianism and Human Rights* (New York: Columbia University Press, 1998), p. 57.

27. This idea is elaborated by Peter D. Hershock, "Dramatic Intervention: Human Rights from a Buddhist Perspective," to appear in a forthcoming issue of *Philosophy East and West.*

28. The world community has recognized these three Buddhists by awarding the Nobel Peace Prize to the Dalai Lama in 1989, to Aung San Suu Kyi in 1991, and by nominating Sulak at least twice and then awarding him the Right Livelihood Award in 1995.

29. See a recent translation of "The Scripture of Brahma's Net" by Hubert Nearman in *Buddhist Writings on Meditation and Daily Practice* (Mount Shasta, Calif.: Shasta Abbey, 1994), pp. 49–188.

30. See Shih Heng-ching, *The Sūtra on Upāsaka Precepts.* Buddhist ethics are designed for two kinds of people: monastics and the laity. Since Buddhism has been dominated by the monastic community more than any other religion, principles of behavior for lay society are underdeveloped and have tended to urge laity to mimic monastics or to enter the monastery. A very different approach is taken by the Upāsaka Sūtra an important early Mahayana treatise for lay Buddhists. It elevates the life of the laity above that of the monastic community since the laity can give food, medicine, and practical help, whereas the monks can give only words.

31. Even though the monastic model has dominated Buddhist history, the importance of laity emerged at the beginning of the Western era with the rise of Mahayana, in the fifth and sixth century in China, and now again in modern Japan and America. In comparison to the many regulations for monastics, the materials outlining a social ethic for lay Buddhists that are relevant to civil rights are not large. See my article on "Searching for a Mahayana Social Ethic," *Journal of Religious Ethics* 24, no. 2 (Fall 1996), pp. 351–375.

32. *The Lotus Sutra: The White Lotus of the Marvelous Law,* tr. Tsugunari Kubo and Akira Yuyama (Berkeley: Bukkyo dendo kyokai, 1991), p. 269.

33. These are the first two verses of the Prakrit version. See John Brough, *The Gāndhārī Dharmapada* (New York: Oxford University Press, 1963), p. 290, and Nārada Thera, *The Dhammapada* (London: John Murray, 1954), p. 85.

34. K. N. Jayatilleke, *The Principles of International Law in Buddhist Doctrine* (Leiden, Netherlands: A.W. Sijthoff, n.d.), summarized by Taitetsu Unno, "Personal Rights and Contemporary Buddhism," in Rouner, ed., *Human Rights and the World's Religions,* p. 132. Similar points are made by G.P. Malalasekera and K.N. Jayatilleke in *Buddhism and the Race Question* (Paris: UNESCO, 1958), pp. 32–79.

35. "The Book of Octads," *Sutta Nipata,* v. 772–803, generally considered to be the oldest Buddhist scriptural text.

36. Sulak Sivaraksa, *Loyalty Demands Dissent: Autobiography of An Engaged Buddhist* (Berkeley: Parallax Press, 1998), p. 186. Winston King reports that Thich Nhat Hanh further discussed the phrase in his 1963 book *Engaged Buddhism*. See Winston King, "Engaged Buddhism: Past, Present, Future," *The Eastern Buddhist* 27 (Autumn 1994), p. 14.

37. Thich Nhat Hanh, "Foreword," in Chan Khong, *Learning True Love: How I Learned and Practiced Social Change in Vietnam* (Berkeley: Parallax Press, 1993), p. ix.

38. Ken Kraft, *Inner Peace, World Peace* (Albany: SUNY Press, 1992).

39. In 1966 when Thich Nhat Hanh was confronted by a questioner in an American audience about how difficult the war was for people in America, he became enraged when he thought of the countless villagers who had died. Instead of lashing out, he excused himself and went outside to focus on his breathing so that he could understand his anger and why the person provoked it. Only after regaining his composure, did he return to respond to the question. For other examples, see Daniel Berrigan and Thich Nhat Hanh, *The Raft Is Not the Shore* (Boston: Beacon, 1975).

40. For a history of the School of Youth for Social Service, see Khong, *Learning True Love,* pp. 70–128.

41. Summarized from Thich Nhat Hanh, *Interbeing: Fourteen Guidelines for Engaged Buddhism* (Berkeley: Parallax Press, 1987; revised 1993), pp. 17–20.

42. Thich Nhat Hanh left Vietnam in 1966 to lobby for the end of the war. Many of his speeches were collected in *Vietnam: Lotus in a Sea of Fire,* (New York: Hill and Wang, 1967). Later he led the Buddhist peace delegation in Paris and now lives in exile in rural France. An excellent overview of his work is provided by Sallie King, "Thich Nhat Hanh and the Unified Buddhist Church: Nondualism in Action," in Christopher Queen and Sallie King, eds., *Engaged Buddhism: Buddhist Liberation Movements in Asia* (Albany: SUNY Press, 1996), pp. 321–364.

43. I am greatly indebted to Judith Simmer-Brown for sending me a copy of her unpublished manuscript on "Buddhist Peace Fellowship: 'Speaking Truth to Power,'" which is to appear in a volume edited by Christopher Queen on *Engaged Buddhism in the West* (forthcoming) and from which this quote is taken. Many young Americans who served their country in Vietnam came to see parts of their lives as unacceptable, and being unable to accept themselves, committed suicide. When Thich Nhat Hanh, who knows the horror American soldiers

committed against him and his people, is able to accept and embrace these men, a great healing takes place.

44. See Ken Kraft, "Prospects of a Socially Engaged Buddhism," *Inner Peace, World Peace,* and Ken Tanaka, "Concern for Others in Pure Land Soteriological and Ethical Considerations: A Case of *Jōgyō Daihi* in Jōdo Shinshū Buddhism," in Kenneth K. Tanaka and Eisho Nasu, eds., *Engaged Pure Land Buddhism: Challenges Facing Jōdo Shinshū in the Contemporary World* (Berkeley: WisdomOcean, 1998), pp. 88–110.

45. Dennis Hirota, *Tannishō: A Primer: A Record of the Words of Shinran Set Down in Lamentation over Departure from his Teaching* (Kyoto: Ryukoku University, 1982), p. 25.

46. In a doctrine that foreshadowed modern ecology, Zhan-ran (A.D. 711–782) extended the concept of Buddha nature not just to all people, but also to all things: "a blade of grass, a tree, a pebble, and a particle of dust each has a Buddha-nature." See Linda L. Penkower, *T'ien-t'ai During the T'ang Synasty: Chan-jan and the Signification of Buddhism* (Ann Arbor, Mich.: UMI Press, 1993), p. 510. For modern studies of Buddhism and ecology, see Allan Hunt Badiner, ed., *Dharma Gaia: A Harvest of Essays in Buddhism and Ecology* (Berkeley: Parallax Press, 1990); Nancy Nash, ed., *Tree of Life: Buddhism and Protection of Nature* (Geneva: Buddhism Protection of Nature Project, 1987); Mary Evelyn Tucker and Duncan Ryūken Williams, eds., *Buddhism and Ecology: The Interconnection of Dharma and Deeds* (Cambridge: Harvard University Center for the Study of World Religions, 1997); and Amy Morgante, ed., *Buddhist Perspectives on the Earth Charter* (Boston: Boston Research Center for the 21st Century, 1997).

47. Harvey Aronson, *Love and Sympathy in Theravada Buddhism* (Delhi: Motilal Banarsidass, 1980), pp. 14–16. For a study of similar themes in Mahayana Buddhism, see my "Buddhist Compassion (*ci-bei*) and Zhiyi's *Mohozhiguan,*" in Yusho Muranaka, ed., *Tendai daishi kenkyf (Studies on The Great Master of Tendai, Zhihi)* (Kyoto: Tendai Gakkai, Kahoku insatsu kabushiki kaisha, 1997), pp. 1–23.

48. Anguttara-nikāya 1.22, translated by Aronson, *Love and Sympathy,* p. 3.

49. His Holiness the Dalai Lama, *The Good Heart* (Boston: Wisdom, 1996).

50. "Bhikkhus, even if bandits were to sever you savagely limb by limb with a two-handled saw, he who gave rise to a mind of hate towards them would not be carrying out my teaching," the Buddha is reported to have taught. (*Middle Length Discourses of the Buddha,* tr. Bhikkhu Nanamoli and Bhikkhu Bodhi [London: Wisdom Publications, 1995], p. 223.)

51. David Chappell, "Searching for a Mahayana Social Ethic," *Journal of Religious Ethics* 24, no. 2 (Fall 1996), pp. 368–369.

52. Daisaku Ikeda, *Humanity and the New Millennium: From Chaos to Cosmos* (Tokyo: Soka Gakkai International, 1998), p. 35. Compare *The Lion's Roar of Queen Śrīmālā A Buddhist Scripture on the Tathāgata-Garbha Theory,* tr. Alex and Hideko Wayman (New York: Columbia University Press, 1974), p. 65.

53. Political controls often prevented Buddhists from organized social action. For example, during a period of political disunion in China in the sixth century, Buddhist social welfare programs flourished. (See Michihata, Ryōshū, *Chūgoku bukkyō to shakai fukushi jigyō* [Kyoto: Hōzōkan, 1967].) After reimposition of state control Buddhist activities were restricted until it became illegal to be active outside the monastery. As a result, for the last millennium Chinese Buddhists may have been free to chant vows to save all beings, but they have not been active in society, except in recent decades in Taiwan. See Stanley Weinstein, *Buddhism Under the T'ang* (Cambridge: Cambridge University Press, 1987) and Whalen Lai, "Chinese Buddhist and Christian Charities: A Comparative History," in *Buddhist-Christian Studies* 12 (1992), pp. 5–33.

54. Article 23 reads: "Everyone has the right to work, to free choice of employment, to just and favourable conditions of work and to protection against unemployment." This article asserts a "second-generation" human right, meaning that it reaches beyond protection from abuse by the government (articles 2–21) to embrace economic, social, and cultural goals based on the socialist tradition in France (articles 22–27). Henry Rosemont has argued that virtually all first-generation rights can be achieved without regard for the welfare of a person, whereas second-generation rights require taking active responsibility for others.

55. Bernard Glassman and Rick Fields, *Instructions to the Cook: A Zen Master's Lessons in Living a Life That Matters* (New York: Bell Tower, 1996), pp. 18–19. For a biography of Glassman, see Helen Tworkov, *Zen in America: Profiles of Five Teachers* (San Francisco: North Point Press, 1989), pp. 109–151.

56. Ibid., p. 58.

57. Jeremy Rifkin, *The End of Work: The Decline of the Global Labor Force and the Dawn of the Post-Market Era* (New York: Putnam, 1995), pp. 236–274.

58. See David C. Korten, *When Corporations Rule the World* (West Hartford: Kumarian, 1995) and Benjamin Barber, *Jihad* vs. *McWorld* (New York: Viking, 1997).

59. The most recent assault in this regard globally has been the effort by the World Trade Organization to establish a Multilateral Agreement on Investment (MAI) that would allow foreigners unrestricted access to local property and markets in all countries, thus denying local communities control over their own destinies. The director-general of the World Trade Organization, Renato Ruggiero, has said that the MAI would be the "constitution for the global economy." See Maude Barlow and Tony Clark, *MAI and the Threat to American Freedom* (New York: Stoddart, 1998).

60. For the Alternatives to Consumerism Project, see Sulak Sivaraksa, *Loyalty Demands Dissent: Autobiography of An Engaged Buddhist* (Berkeley: Parallax Press, 1998), pp. 208–209.

61. David Loy, an American Buddhist living in Japan, has written "The Religion of the Market," *Journal of the American Academy of Religion* 65, no. 2 (Summer 1997), pp. 275–290.

62. For a biography of Robert Aitken, see Tworkov, *Zen in America*, pp. 25–62.

63. For an overview of the Vipassana meditation movement and its main American or-

ganization, the Insight Meditation Society (IMS) in Barre, Massachusetts, see Gil
Fronsdal, "Insight Meditation in the United States: Life, Liberty, and the Pursuit of
Happiness," in Charles Prebish and Kenneth Tanaka, eds., *The Faces of Buddhism
in America* (Berkeley: University of California Press, 1998), pp. 164–180.

64. See George Bond, "A.T. Ariyaratne and the Sarvodaya Shramadana Movement
in Sri Lanka," in Queen and King, eds., *Engaged Buddhism,* pp. 121–146. This
book is a core text for the master's degree program in engaged Buddhism at the
Naropa Institute. A survey of American socially engaged Buddhist movements
will be outlined in Christopher Queen, ed., *Engaged Buddhism in the West*
(forthcoming).

65. "Contemplation and Revolution: An Interview with Joanna Macy," *Turning
Wheel* (Summer 1998), p. 21.

66. Tanaka and Nasu, eds., *Engaged Pure Land Buddhism.*

67. Rev. Yoshiaki Fujitani, a Jōdo Shinshū minister in Hawaii, is now a member of
the national board of NFIVC. As a contribution to the White House Conference
on Aging in 1995, Project Dana organized an interfaith meeting at the largest
Christian church in Hawaii on January 28, 1995, on the topic of "Aging: Gath-
ering a Spiritual Perspective," in order to formulate input for the conference on
the spiritual values of the elderly.

68. Beginning in the United States only in 1960, SGI-USA rapidly grew through active proselytizing in the 1960s and 1970s. Over 300,000 joined, although today
less than a third of these are active. Its headquarters are at 525 Wilshire Boulevard, Santa Monica, California 90401–1403.

69. Among the almost one hundred Buddhist temples in Hawaii, each one has a
clear ethnic identity except Soka Gakkai (see *Unity in Diversity*). The national
board of directors of Jōdo Shinshū has only three non-Japanese lay directors
out of forty-one, and only five European American ministers out of sixty-two
(Kenneth Tanaka, "Issues of Ethnicity in the Buddhist Church of America," in
Queen, ed., *Engaged Buddhism in the West* [forthcoming]).

70. Although most immigrant Buddhist groups in the United States have remained as
support groups for the culture of their countries of origin—whether China, Japan,
Korea, Vietnam, Laos, Sri Lanka, or Thailand—the two exceptions have been Zen
and Tibetan Buddhism. The leaders of these two latter groups are primarily Japanese and Tibetan, respectively, but their membership consists largely of educated
middle-class European Americans (virtually no African Americans, Latin Americans, or Asian Americans from other parts of Asia are active in the groups). For
data on the number of African American and Hispanic local leaders in SGI-USA,
see my forthcoming article "Race and Diversity in Buddhism: Soka Gakkai International-USA," in Queen, ed., *Engaged Buddhism in the West,* where I analyze
the ethnic identity of 2,449 local SGI-USA district leaders in eight cities and find
654 African Americans (26.7 percent) and 139 Hispanics (5.7 percent).

71. Examples of topics related to civil and social rights that have been discussed in
the *World Tribune* in recent months are: diversity in the workplace (December
26, 1997); consumption and responsibility (January 2, 1998); black baseball

player and humanitarian, Roberto Clemente (January 9, 1998); black photographer Gordon Parks (January 16, 1998); U.S. Postal Service's Black Heritage series (January 30, 1998); child labor (April 24, 1998); the first woman social activist in Colorado, Frances Jacobs (May 8, 1998); creatively working with disabilities (May 15, 1998); Paul Robeson, singer, actor, and social activist (May 22, 1998); the gay, lesbian, bisexual, and transgender movement (June 19, 1998); and talks by SGI President Ikeda against abuses of power in "What Is Real Democracy?" (July 17, 1998) and "Against the Powerful" (July 31, 1998); and so on.

72. For Nichiren's social and political activism, see Masaharu Anesaki, *Nichiren: The Buddhist Prophet* (Cambridge: Harvard University Press, 1916), and Phillip Yampolsky, ed., *Selected Writings of Nichiren* (New York: Columbia University Press, 1990).

73. Several articles from the monthly magazine, *Seikyo Times*, no. 408 (July 1995), featured articles that challenged the idea of race as a myth and social construct.

74. The nineteen members of the national committee in May 1998 included Native American, Pakistani, Japanese, Hispanic, Korean, European, Chinese, African American, and lesbian members. (Fax listing the members from Greg Martin and Carrie Rogers, SGI-USA Headquarters, May 15, 1997.)

75. YPC is now renamed the Youth Peace Committee and its current organization and activities were outlined in the *World Tribune* (July 24, 1998).

76. In postwar Japan, Soka Gakkai formed its own political party, the Komeito (Clean Government Party), and Soka Gakkai members ran for political office, but recently it has cut its ties with the party. For its early history, see Kiyoaki Murata, *Japan's New Buddhism: An Objective Account of Soka Gakkai* (New York: Weatherhill, 1969), chapter 9.

77. The Daewon Korean Temple in Hawaii sponsored a series of peace conferences in the 1980s and 1990s led by Glenn Paige, and often involving Johan Galtung, in which the "structural violence of institutions" was a frequent theme. These began in October 1983 in Hawaii, but included later meetings in Mongolia (1989) and Korea (1991), ending with a meeting in Hawaii in 1993. See Glenn D. Paige and Sarah Gilliatt, *Buddhism and Nonviolent Global Problem-Solving* (Honolulu: Matsunaga Institute for Peace, 1991).

78. Legal corporations have sometimes been considered "fictive persons," and this became even more true with the recent ruling by the Supreme Court (June 26, 1998) that corporations must be vigilant in eliminating sexual harassment in the workplace. This ruling demonstrated once again that corporations in the United States are not considered impersonal and passive structures, but must be vigilant in monitoring the actions of their managements and safeguarding the welfare of their employees. Ignorance is no longer an excuse.

79. The publications and tapes of Thich Nhat Hanh and the Order of Interbeing can be purchased through Parallax Press, P.O. Box 7355, Berkeley, California 94707. The editor of Parallax Press, Arnold Kotler, usually organizes Thich Nhat Hanh's American schedule each year.

80. The Naropa Institute was very active in organizing annual summer conferences

on Christian and Buddhist Meditation in the early 1980s. For a summary report
of the first five events, see Susan Walker, ed., *Speaking of Silence: Christians and
Buddhists on the Contemplative Way* (New York: Paulist Press, 1987).

81. See Robert Aitken and David Steindl-Rast, *The Ground We Share: Everyday
Practice, Buddhist and Christian* (Liguori, Missouri: Triumph Books, 1994), a
book recording conversations between Aitken Roshi, a Zen master, and Brother
David, a Benedictine. The two first collaborated as retreat leaders as part of the
first international Buddhist-Christian Conference held in Hawaii in the summer
of 1980.

82. Sulak first began collaborating with Christians and Muslims as part of the Coordinating Group for Religion and Society in the mid-1970s in response to the
killing and kidnapping of community leaders in Thailand, and has served as an
active participant with the Society for Buddhist-Christian Studies in the 1980s
and 1990s, being a speaker at most of their international conferences, plus being
a regular member of the Theological Encounter With Buddhism group that
began meeting in 1984.

83. See His Holiness the Dalai Lama, *The Good Heart: A Buddhist Perspective on
The Teachings of Jesus* (Boston: Wisdom, 1996).

84. See Daniel Berrigan and Thich Nhat Hanh, *The Raft Is Not the Shore,* and,
more recently, Thich Nhat Hanh, *Living Buddha, Living Christ* (New York:
Riverhead Books, Putnam, 1995), recording observations made over many years
of interfaith collaboration.

85. For an overview of Buddhist interfaith activity, see David W. Chappell, "Buddhist Interfaith Dialogue: To Build A Global Community," in a memorial volume edited by Sallie King and Paul Ingram in honor of Frederick Streng, to be
published by Curzon Press.

86. The Glassman group includes at least one priest, Robert Kennedy, S.J., and two
Christian nuns.

87. SGI-USA was active in sponsoring the Social Engaged Buddhist-Christian International Conference in Chicago in August 1996 and now is coordinating regular
interfaith activity in the Los Angeles area through its national headquarters at
606 Wilshire Boulevard, Santa Monica.

88. In order to develop programs for a civil society, in 1993 SGI headquarters in
Japan created an institute not under the SGI-USA religious organization, but affiliated with it, that is called the Boston Research Center for the Twenty-first
Century. Its statement of purpose reads in part: "Human rights, nonviolence,
ecological harmony, and economic justice are focal points of the center's work."

NOTES TO CHAPTER 6

1. The general hypothesis offered in the opening pages is the fruit of reflection on
American race relations over the past 35 years. Many books and articles as well
as personal experiences have shaped my thinking. Among the most important
books are Shelby Steele, *The Content of Our Character* (New York: St. Martin's

Press, 1990); Andrew Michael Manis, *Southern Civil Religions in Conflict* (Athens: University of Georgia Press, 1987); Stephen B. Oates, *Let the Trumpet Sound: The Life of Martin Luther King, Jr.* (New York: New American Library, 1982); Columbus Salley and Ronald Behm, *Your God Is Too White* (Downers Grove, Ill.: InterVarsity Press, 1970); Stokely Carmichael and Charles V. Hamilton, *Black Power: The Politics of Liberation in America* (New York: Vintage Books, 1967); William H. Grier and Price M. Cobbs; *Black Rage* (New York: Bantam Books, 1968); and Eldridge Cleaver, *Soul on Ice* (New York: Dell, 1968).

I was a student at Wheaton College (Illinois) from 1962 to 1966 where more attention was paid to the Vietnam War than to the climactic phases of the civil rights movement. Nevertheless, before the 1960s were out, black evangelicals like Tom Skinner (*Black and Free* [Grand Rapids, Mich.: Zondervan, 1968]) and William Pannell (*My Friend the Enemy* [Waco, Tex: Word, 1968]) were becoming known in white evangelical circles. Evangelicals had no excuse for ignoring Salley and Behm's *Your God Is Too White* and John Perkins' *A Quiet Revolution* (Waco, Tex.: Word, 1976), and in the 1970s there were more efforts to bring black and white evangelicals together in the cause of social justice. An example of the latter was the movement that produced *The Chicago Declaration*, Ronald J. Sider, ed. (Carol Stream, Ill.: Creation House, 1974).

2. One can make distinctions between the relative significance of the court decisions compared to congressional legislation, as has Gerard N. Rosenberg in *The Hollow Hope* (Chicago: University of Chicago Press, 1991). He concludes that court decisions such as the U.S. Supreme Court's *Brown v. Board of Education* (1954) had virtually no direct effect on segregation before Congress took action. This is not to underestimate the significance of executive action, such as Eisenhower's calling out of the National Guard in Little Rock.

3. See, for example, Joseph C. Hough, Jr., *Black Power and White Protestants* (New York: Oxford University Press, 1968), which shows the very limited ability of white Protestants to respond to the Black Power movement. In this respect, it is worth considering Charles A. Lofgren's argument in *The Plessy Case: A Legal-Historical Interpretation* (New York: Oxford University Press, 1987) that the Supreme Court's 1890s "separate but equal" ruling nonetheless contained seeds of the civil rights transformation of this century.

4. See Oates, *Let the Trumpet Sound*; Manis, *Southern Civil Religions in Conflict*; and Jesse L. Jackson, *Straight from the Heart* (Philadelphia: Fortress Press, 1987), passim.

5. As the background for what follows, see my *The Scattered Voice: Christians at Odds in the Public Square* (Grand Rapids: Zondervan, 1990), esp. chapter 6, "Civil Rights Reformers"; and my *Recharging the American Experiment: Principled Pluralism for Genuine Civic Community* (Grand Rapids: Baker Books, 1994), esp. chapter 7, "Individual and Institutional Rights."

6. I make no attempt here to discuss the history of racial discrimination and the reform efforts in American education that led to court-ordered busing. For the his-

tory of *Brown v. Board of Education* see Richard Kluger, *Simple Justice* (New York: Vintage Books, 1975).

7. On September 1, 1998, federal district court judge Peter J. Messitte ordered an end to mandatory busing in Prince George's County, Maryland. The ruling met with approval on all sides, reflecting changed circumstances since the 1970s when court-ordered busing went into effect. Janette Bell, an African American and president of the county's education association, commented that "one of the negatives [of busing] was that when kids were moved so far away from home, parents were no longer involved in the schools" (*Washington Post*, Sept. 2, 1998).

   In the fall of 1998 in Washington, D.C., an increasing number of parents were seeking access to new charter schools. One reason, as Angelia Orr explained, is that she "dreaded September, when [her daughter] Ashlee would have to travel six miles through notoriously dangerous streets to Roper Middle School in Northeast" (*Washington Times*, Aug. 28, 1998).

8. The diverse range of cultures, communities, towns, school districts, and rural and urban ethnic enclaves across America is astounding, and thus no generalization about the relation between family and school will hold up everywhere. An early opponent of segregation in the South, novelist and critic Walker Percy, offers remarkable insight into the difference in the social meaning of the school for whites in the North in contrast to whites in the South in his essay "The Southern Moderate," in Patrick Samway, ed., *Walker Percy: Sign-Posts in a Strange Land* (New York: Noonday Press, 1991), pp. 94–101. In the South, Percy wrote in 1957, the school body corresponded far more to the social body than it did in the North. Especially in Northern urban areas, the school was a place where people sent their children to receive certain services. In the South, the school was much less differentiated from the community. This is one reason why the desegregation of schools required different approaches and sensitivities in different parts of the country.

9. This is, of course, the heart of the problem in the struggle over affirmative action. See Drew S. Days III, "Affirmative Action," in Larry Gostin, ed., *Civil Liberties in Conflict* (New York: Routledge: 1988), pp. 85–101; Glenn C. Loury, "Affirmative Action: Is It Just? Does It Work?" in Shlomo Slonim, ed., *The Constitutional Bases of Political and Social Change in the United States* (New York: Praeger, 1990), pp. 109–39; Stephen L. Carter, *Reflections of an Affirmative Action Baby* (New York: Basic Books, 1991); and Steele, *The Content of Our Character*. A good collection of views on all sides of the affirmative action debate can be found in George E. Curry, ed., *The Affirmative Action Debate* (Reading, Mass.: Addison-Wesley, 1996).

   When Eldridge Cleaver was about to return to the United States after years in exile, he explained his motive: "Those of us who developed a psychology of opposition must take a pause and sum up our experiences. We must recognize that in a sense we are playing in a brand new ball game. The slogans of yesterday will not get us through the tasks at hand" (*New York Times*, Nov. 18, 1975).

10. Compare, for example, the different emphases of the following authors: Glenn C. Loury, *One by One, From the Inside Out: Essays and Reviews on Race and Responsibility in America* (New York: The Free Press, 1995); Nicholas Lemann, *The Promised Land: The Great Black Migration and How it Changed America* (New York: Knopf, 1991); Jim Sleeper, *The Closest of Strangers: Liberalism and the Politics of Race in New York* (New York: W.W. Norton, 1990); Andrew Hacker, *Two Nations: Black and White, Separate, Hostile, Unequal* (New York: Scribners, 1992); and Steele, *Content of Our Character.*

11. When it comes to seeing Christianity as either a liberating force or a restrictive weight in the struggle to overcome racism, see the contrast between Salley and Behm, *Your God Is Too White* (liberating) and Forrest G. Wood, *The Arrogance of Faith: Christianity and Race in America from the Colonial Era to the Twentieth Century* (New York: Knopf, 1990) (restrictively oppressive).

12. My debt to the reformed stream of evangelical Protestantism is heavy. See Al Wolters, *Creation Regained: Biblical Basics for a Reformational Worldview* (Grand Rapids: Eerdmans, 1985); Brian J. Walsh and Richard J. Middleton, *The Transforming Vision: Shaping a Christian Worldview* (Downers Grove, Ill.: InterVarsity Press, 1984); Herman Dooyeweerd, *Roots of Western Culture: Pagan, Secular, and Christian Options* (Toronto: Wedge Publishing Foundation, 1979); Peter S. Heslam, *Creating a Christian Worldview: Abraham Kuyper's Lectures on Calvinism* (Grand Rapids: Eerdmans, 1998); Lesslie Newbigin, *The Gospel in a Pluralist Society* (Grand Rapids: Eerdmans, 1989).

13. My understanding of the seventh day of creation as both the climax of creation and the day of eschatological redemption and fulfillment owes a debt to many authors: Abraham Joshua Heschel, "The Sabbath: Its Meaning for Modern Man," in Heschel, *The Earth Is the Lord's; and The Sabbath* (New York: Harper Torchbooks, 1951); Oliver O'Donovan, *Resurrection and Moral Order: An Outline for Evangelical Ethics* (Grand Rapids: Eerdmans, 1986); Jurgen Moltmann, *God in Creation* (San Francisco: Harper San Francisco, 1985); Wolfhart Pannenberg, *Systematic Theology,* vol. 2, chap. 7, "Creation of the World" (Grand Rapids: Eerdmans, 1991), pp. 1–174; Henri Blocher, *In the Beginning: The Opening Chapters of Genesis* (Downers Grove, Ill.: InterVarsity Press, 1984); Geerhardus Vos, *The Teaching of the Epistle to the Hebrews* (Nutley, N.J.: Reformed and Presbyterian Publishing Co., 1974).

14. On the meaning of the resurrection, see Herman Ridderbos, *Paul: An Outline of His Theology* (Grand Rapids: Eerdmans, 1975), pp. 44–90, 205–252, 487–562; and N.T. Wright, *The Climax of the Covenant* (Minneapolis: Fortress Press, 1991), esp. pp. 26–35.

15. See, for example, Christopher J.H. Wright, *An Eye for An Eye: The Place of Old Testament Ethics Today* (Downers Grove, Ill.: InterVarsity Press, 1983); Waldron Scott, *Bring Forth Justice* (Grand Rapids: Eerdmans, 1980); and O'-Donovan, *Resurrection and Moral Order.*

16. Coming from quite different points of view, all of the following can nonetheless be considered "common rationality" ethicists: Robert N. Bellah, et al., *The*

Good Society (New York: Knopf, 1991); Gary J. Dorrien, *Reconstructing the Common Good: Theology and the Social Order* (Marynoll, N.Y.: Orbis Books, 1990); and Michael Novak, *Free Persons and the Common Good* (Lanham, Maryland: Madison Books, 1989).

17. Consider, for example, Alasdair MacIntyre, *Whose Justice? Which Rationality?* (Notre Dame: University of Notre Dame Press, 1988), and Stanley Hauerwas, *Dispatches from the Front: Theological Engagements With the Secular* (Durham: Duke University Press, 1995).

18. See my *The Scattered Voice*, pp. 1–95, and Mark A. Noll, *The Scandal of the Evangelical Mind* (Grand Rapids: Eerdmans, 1994), pp. 149–76.

19. For expression of, or assessment of, civil-religious nationalism, see Manis, *Southern Civil Religions in Conflict*; Jackson, *Straight From the Heart*; Ruth H. Bloch, "Religion and Ideological Change in the American Revolution," in Mark A. Noll, ed., *Religion and American Politics: From the Colonial Period to the 1980s* (New York: Oxford University Press, 1990), pp. 44–61; Sidney E. Mead "The 'Nation with the Soul of a Church,'" and David Little, "The Origins of Perplexity: Civil Religion and Moral Belief in the Thought of Thomas Jefferson," both in Russell E. Richey and Donald G. Jones, eds., *American Civil Religion* (New York: Harper Forum Books, 1974), pp. 45–75 and 185–210; and Walker Percy, "Stoicism in the South," in *Walker Percy*, pp. 83–88.

20. On the idea of the political community as a pluralist unity or community of communities, see Michael Walzer, "A Community of Communities," in *Debating Democracy's Discontent: Essays on American Politics, Law and Public Philosophy*, Anita L. Allen and Milton C. Regan, eds. (New York: Oxford University Press, 1998); and James W. Skillen and Rockne M. McCarthy, eds., *Political Order and the Plural Structure of Society* (Atlanta: Scholars Press, 1991), pp. 1–27 and passim.

NOTES TO CHAPTER 7

1. Guillermo Gomez-Peña, "The Two Guadalupes" in *Goddess of the Americas/La Diosa de las Américas: Writings on the Virgin of Guadalupe,* ed. Ana Castillo (New York: Riverhead Books, 1996), pp. 178–79.

2. In this essay, the terms "Latino" and "Hispanic" will be used interchangeably. As theologian Fernando Segovia points out, there is no one satisfactory label for U.S. Latinos. Though some may argue that, etymologically speaking, "Latino" does not glorify the European (particularly, the colonizing Spanish colonial) dimension of personhood as does the word "Hispanic," Segovia correctly notes that both terms are labels derived from the Latin language, both referring to territories of the Roman Empire, Hispania and Latium. In this way, both terms—Hispanic and Latino—point to Europe and, by extension, to a contentious history of colonization. "Introduction: Aliens in the Promised Land: The Manifest Destiny of U.S. Hispanic American Theology," in *Hispanic/Latino Theol-*

ogy: *Challenge and Promise,* ed. Ada María Isasi-Díaz and Fernando F. Segovia (Minneapolis: Fortress Press, 1996), pp. 15–42.

3. Some specific figures include the following: (1) today Hispanics number more than twenty-nine million people, accounting for 11 percent of the U.S. population; (2) of this total, nearly two-thirds are of Mexican origin, while Central and South Americans account for 13 percent, Puerto Ricans, 11 percent, and Cubans, 5 percent; (3) adjusting for inflation, the median income of Hispanic households was $27,737 in 1989, compared with $24,906 in 1996; (4) while graduation rates for African Americans are approaching those of Anglo Americans, Hispanic graduation rates do not show much improvement; (5) young, U.S.-born Hispanics have a high-school dropout rate of 18 percent, which is twice as high as that for whites; (6) immigrant Hispanic youth have a dropout rate of 46 percent; (7) more than a third of Hispanic households are headed by a person who is not a U.S. citizen, and the median income of these households was roughly 20 percent lower in 1996 than for households headed by U.S.-born Latinos. R. A. Zaldivar, "Census Indicates Hispanics Falling Behind in Economy," *Boston Sunday Globe,* October 12, 1997.

4. Theologically speaking, our point of departure in many ways follows David Tracy's two-pronged treatment of praxis, "the critical relationship between theory and practice whereby each is dialectically influenced and transformed by the other." At its best, Christian praxis not only takes into account the neo-orthodox theological insistence that "the real power of Christian symbols in their full existential meaning" can illuminate and change the actual historical situation of humanity, but also takes seriously the critical relationship between theory and practice. If praxis is indeed distinct from everyday practice, then it must always relate to, in some form or other, "a critical theory applicable to all infra-structural and super-structural factors of human reality." David Tracy, *Blessed Rage for Order: The New Pluralism in Theology* (New York: Harper and Row, 1988), pp. 242–44.

5. Orlando Espín, *The Faith of the People: Theological Reflections on Popular Catholicism* (Maryknoll, N.Y.: Orbis Books, 1997), p. 119.

6. See especially William A. Christian, *Local Religion in Sixteenth-Century Spain* (Princeton: Princeton University Press, 1981) and Inga Clendinnen, *Aztecs: an Interpretation* (Cambridge: Cambridge University Press, 1995).

7. See Luis Maldonado, *Introducción a la religiosidad popular* (Santander: Sal Terre, 1985), pp. 30–34.

8. See Joseph M. Murray. *Santería: An African Religion in America* (Boston: Beacon Press, 1988).

9. Orlando Espín and Sixto Garcia, "'Lilies of the Field': A Hispanic Theology of Providence and Human Responsibility," *Proceedings of the Catholic Theological Society of America* 44 (1989), p. 73.

10. Ada María Isasi-Díaz, *En la Lucha/In the Struggle: a Hispanic Women's Liberation Theology* (Minneapolis: Fortress Press, 1993), p. 48.

11. See Roberto S. Goizueta, *Caminemos con Jesús: Toward a Hispanic/Latino Theology of Accompaniment* (Maryknoll, New York: Orbis Books, 1995); Orlando Espín, *The Faith of the People*, (Maryknoll, New York: Orbis Books, 1997); Alejandro García-Rivera, *St. Martín de Porres: The Little Story and the Semiotics of Culture*, (Maryknoll, N.Y.: Orbis Books, 1996) and *The Community of the Beautiful: A Theological Aesthetics*, (Collegeville, Minn: Liturgical Press, 1999); Ana María Díaz-Stevens and Anthony M. Stevens-Arroyo, *Recognizing the Latino Resurgence* (Boulder, Colorado: Westview Press, 1998). See also Allan Figueroa Deck, S.J., *The Second Wave: Hispanic Ministry and the Evangelization of Cultures* (Mahwah, N.J.: Paulist Press, 1989).

12. Roberto S. Goizueta, *op. cit.*, pp. 53–65.

13. Similar formulations on the memory of suffering and dangerous memory can be found in the important work of Johannes Baptist Metz. See especially *Faith in History and Society: Toward a Practical Fundamental Theology*, tr. David Smith (New York: Seabury Press, 1979) and *Faith and the Future: Essays on Theology, Solidarity, and Modernity*, coauthored with Jurgen Moltmann (Maryknoll, N.Y.: Orbis Books, 1995).

14. Roberto S.Goizueta, "U.S. Hispanic Popular Catholicism as Theopoetics," in *Hispanic/Latino Theology: Challenge and Promise*, ed. Ada María Isasi-Diaz and Fernando F. Segovia (Minneapolis: Fortress Press, 1996), p. 274.

15. In theology, this point has been taken up extensively by Virgilio Elizondo, especially in *Galilean Journey: The Mexican-American Promise* (Maryknoll, N.Y.: Orbis Books, 1983) and *The Future Is Mestizo: Life Where Cultures Meet* (Oak Park, Ill.: Meyer-Stone Books, 1988). In literature, the theme abounds. A good place to start would be Gloria Anzaldua, *Borderlands/La Frontera: The New Mestiza* (San Francisco: Aunt Lute Books, 1987), and Jose Antonio Burciaga, *Drink Cultura: Chicanismo* (Santa Barbara: Joshua Odell Editions, 1993).

16. Guillermo Gomez-Peña, "The Multi-cultural Paradigm: Essays, Performance Texts, and Poetry," in *Warrior for Gringostroika* (Saint Paul: Graywolf Press, 1993), p. 47.

17. See Walter J. Ong, S.J., *The Presence of the Word* (New York: Simon and Schuster, 1967), pp. 111–75.

18. See Segundo Galilea, *Religiosidad Popular y Pastoral Hispano-Americana* (New York: Northeast Hispanic Catholic Pastoral Center, 1981), p. 17.

19. Juan Lorenzo Hinojosa describes the movement away from traditional popular Catholicism in "Culture, Spirituality and U.S. Hispanics," in *Frontiers of Hispanic Theology in the United States,* ed. Allan Figueroa Deck, S.J., (Maryknoll, N.Y.: Orbis Books, 1992), pp. 154–68.

20. See María Pilar Aquino, *Our Cry for Life* (Maryknoll, N.Y.: Orbis Books, 1993), pp. 109–77, and Ada María Isasi-Díaz, *En la lucha/In the Struggle* (Minneapolis: Fortress, 1993).

21. See Díaz-Stevens and Stevens-Arroyo, *The Latino Resurgence, op. cit.*

22. Rodolfo "Corky" González, "Yo Soy Joaquín," quoted in Anthony Stevens-

Arroyo, *Prophets Denied Honor: An Anthology on the Hispano Church in the United States* (Maryknoll, N.Y.: Orbis Books, 1980), p. 20.

23. Ibid., p.20. Simiarly, as Cristián Parker writes: " . . . the popular mentality, in its option for life, preserves a dose of rebellion deep down—a sane, sound way of resisting the sudden attacks of a dominant culture that, at every step, threatens the integrity of its culture and human existence as well." Cristián Parker, *Popular Religion and Modernization in Latin America* (Maryknoll, N.Y.: Orbis Books, 1996), p. 261.

24. Gustavo Gutierrez, *A Theology of Liberation: History, Politics, and Salvation* (Maryknoll, N.Y.: Orbis Books, 1973), pp. 1–15.

25. Christine Lehmann, "Latin American Liberation Theology and the Problem of Popular Religion" (Brown University Senior Thesis, December 1994), p.38. See also Michael Candelaria, *Popular Religion and Liberation: The Dilemma of Liberation Theology* (Albany: State University of New York Press, 1990), pp. 5–6.

26. Louise Michael Colonnese, ed.,*The Church in the Present-day Transformation of Latin America in the Light of the Council: Second General Conference of Latin American Bishops,* (Bogota: General Secretariat of CELAM, 1970–73), pp. 91–92.

27. One should note that though César Chávez (California) was perhaps the most visible Latino prophetic luminary in the past half-century, he is not the only one. Two other important (Chicano) contemporaries of Chávez, who also brought together sprituality and politics, are particularly worthy of mention: Rodolfo "Corky" Gonzalez and Reis López Tijerina. Not only did Gonzalez (Colorado) write the inspirational poem "Yo Soy Joaquín," as we have already noted, but in 1969 he helped create *El Plan Espiritual de Aztlán,* which called for a revival of Mexican-American values and the creation of a new political party based on self-determination. Reis López Tijerina (New Mexico) organized a separatist movement in 1963 called *Alianza Federal de las Mercedes,* which demanded from the U.S. government the return of millions of acres originally owned by the Hispanic (originally, Spanish) community of the Southwest. One should further note that both Gonzalez and Tijerina were Protestants (Congregational and Pentecostal, respectively). For a more comprehensive look at these men as well as many other Latinos and Latinas whose histories have been long overlooked, see Stevens-Arroyo's *Prophets Denied Honor.*

28. Chávez himself said: "I was convinced [that my ideology was] . . . very Christian. That's my interpretation. I don't think it was so much political or economic." Richard Griswold del Castillo and Richard A. Garcia, *César Chávez A Triumph of Spirit* (Norman: University of Oklahoma Press, 1995), p. 111. See also Jennifer Reed-Bouley, *Guiding Moral Action: A Study of the United Farm Workers' Use of Catholic Social Teaching and Religious Symbols* (Ph.D. dissertation, Loyola University of Chicago, 1998), and Frederick John Dalton, *The Moral Vision of César E. Chávez: An Examination of His Public Life from an Ethical Perspective* (Ph.D. dissertation, Graduate Theological Union, 1998).

29. Ibid., p. 98.

30. As Chávez notes, when most of UFW's Catholic "friends" forsook the organiza-
    tion as it began to stirke in 1965, "the California Migrant Ministry held a meeting
    with its staff and decided that the strike was a matter of life or death for farm
    workers everywhere, and that even it it meant the end of the Migrant Ministry
    they would turn over their resources to the strikers. The political pressure on the
    Protestant Churches was tremendous and the Migrant Ministry lost a lot of
    money. But they stuck it out, and they began to point the way to the rest of the
    Church." César E. Chávez, "The Mexican-American and the Church," in Stevens-
    Arroyo's *Prophets Denied Honor,* p. 119.
31. Susan Ferris and Ricardo Sandoval, *The Fight in the Fields: César Chávez and
    the Farmworkers Movement,* ed. Diana Hembree (New York: Harcourt Brace
    & Co., 1997), p. 128.
32. Griswold del Castillo, *César Chávez: A Triumph of Spirit,* p. 46.

Notes to Chapter 8

1. Malcolm X, *The Autobiography of Malcolm X* (New York: Ballantine Books,
   1965), p. 340.
2. Ibid., p. 334.
3. Unused refers to the amount not used for the expenses of daily living. Hence it is
   not obligatory for everyone, but rather for those whose wealth exceeds their
   daily needs.
4. Islamic orthodoxy defines *shirk* as the association of equals, spouses, offspring,
   or any anthropomorphic qualities with God.
5. Matthew 7:12, *Holy Bible: New Revised Standard Edition* (New York: American Biblical Society, 1991).
6. Analects of Confucious, 15:23, in *A Sourcebook in Chinese Philosophy*, tr.
   Wing-tsit Chan (Princeton, N.J.: Princeton University Press, 1963), p. 44.
7. *An-Nawawi's Forty Hadith* (Damascus: The Holy Koran Publishing House,
   1976).
8. Martin Buber, *I and Thou,* 2nd ed. (New York: Collier Books, 1958).
9. Chapter 42, Verse 11. Hereafter Qur'anic quotations will be written in the body
   of the text and follow the form of two numbers with a colon between them to
   indicate chapter and verse (e.g., 42:11).
10. As quoted by Ali Shariati in "The World-View of Tawhid" in his *On the Sociol-
    ogy of Islam* (Berkeley: Mizan Press, 1979), p. 83n.
11. "*Wa min kulli shay'in khalaqanaa zawjayn*"and from all "things" we have cre-
    ated pairs (51:49).
12. Buber, *I and Thou,* p. 3.
13. Ibid.
14. "And your Lord said to the angels, Verily I am creating a *khalifah* on the earth"
    (2:30).
15. Muslims are commanded "To worship Allah as if you were observing Him and
    you cannot achieve this state of devotion you must consider that He is looking

at you." M. M. Khan, *The Translation and Meaning of Sahih Bukhari,* 2nd ed. (Pakistan: Sethi Straw Board Mills Ltd., 1974), p. 42.

16. Ada Maria Isasi-Diaz in *Women's Consciousness, Women's Conscience: A Reader in Feminist Ethics,* Barbara Hilkert Andolsen, Christine E. Gudorf, and Mary D. Pellauer, eds. (Minneapolis: Winston Press, 1985), p. 79.

17. Ibid., p. 51.

18. Ibid., p. 54.

19. Ibid., p. 56.

20. Ibid., p. 57.

21. Martha Minow, *Not Only for Myself* (New York: New Press, 1997), p. 54.

22. See Farid Esack, *Qur'an, Liberation and Pluralism* (Oxford: One World Press, 1997), esp. pp. 207–61, for an articulation of the relationship between Islamic principles and the struggle against apartheid in South Africa.

23. *An-Nawawi's Forty Hadith,* p. 110.

NOTES TO CHAPTER 9

1. Alan Wolfe suggests that most middle-class Americans have added an eleventh commandment to the biblical decalogue, "Thou shalt not judge," and that tolerance has become their highest value. See Alan Wolfe, *One Nation After All: What Middle-class Americans Really Think about God, Country, Family, Racism, Welfare, Immigration, Homosexuality, Work, the Right, the Left, and Each Other* (New York: Viking, 1998), p. 54.

2. In the words of Orlando Patterson, "In almost all areas of life, progress—sometimes quite dramatic—has been made in surmounting the ingrained and institutional evils of racism and oppression. . . . [T]here is no gainsaying the clear trend lines of progress in changing ethnic attitudes and in the improved condition of the vast majority of Afro-Americans." Orlando Patterson, *The Ordeal of Integration: Progress and Resentment in America's 'Racial' Crisis* (Washington, D.C.: Civitas Counterpoint, 1997), p. 1. See all of chapter 1 of this book for the data and analysis on which Patterson bases his statement.

3. William Julius Wilson has argued that poor city neighborhoods are increasingly cut off from basic opportunities to act on the values they hold due to this social isolation. Wilson defines social isolation as "lack of contact or of sustained interaction with individuals and institutions that represent mainstream society." The lack of job opportunities ("the disappearance of work") is the most damning evidence of this isolation. See Wilson, *When Work Disappears: The World of the New Urban Poor* (New York: Knopf, 1996), passim.

4. See Michael Walzer, *On Toleration* (New Haven: Yale University Press, 1997), esp. pp. 10–13.

5. John Rawls, "The Idea of an Overlapping Consensus," *Oxford Journal of Legal Studies* 7 (1987), pp. 12–13.

6. See John A. Coleman, "Religious Liberty in America and Mediating Structures," in his *An American Strategic Theology* (New York: Paulist Press, 1982), p. 226.

7. See Aristotle, *Nicomachean Ethics,* 1167a, b, trans. Martin Ostwald (Indianapolis: Bobbs-Merrill, 1962), p. 257.

8. Pope John Paul II, "Sollicitudo rei socialis," in David J. O'Brien and Thomas A. Shannon, eds., *Catholic Social Thought: The Documentary Heritage,* no. 38. (Maryknoll, N.Y.: Orbis Books, 1992).

9. The Protestant theologian H. Richard Niebuhr traces the destructiveness that human beings are capable of wreaking upon one another to a defensive posture toward the brokenness of human lives and human communities. In the face of these divisions, "The color of our lives is anxiety, and self-preservation is our first law. Hence we divide our world into the good and the evil, into friends who will assist us to maintain ourselves awhile and foes intent on our reduction to beings of no significance or to nothingness." This sort of anxiety, therefore, is a major threat to the civil rights of those who appear different, and faith in a loving God becomes a source of overcoming such threats. See H. Richard Niebuhr, *The Responsible Self: An Essay in Christian Moral Philosophy* (New York: Harper and Row, 1963), pp. 140–44.

10. See my essay, "A Communitarian Reconstruction of Human Rights: Contributions from Catholic Tradition," in *Catholicism and Liberalism: Contributions to American Public Philosophy,* Cambridge Studies in Religion and American Public Life, ed. R. Bruce Douglass and David Hollenbach (Cambridge University Press, 1994), pp. 127–50.

11. See Sidney Verba, Kay Lehman Schlozman, and Henry Brady, *Voice and Equality: Civic Voluntarism in American Politics.* (Cambridge: Harvard University Press, 1995), chapter 5, esp. 145–49, and chapter 13 on church-based recruitment for political involvement; also chapter 14 on motivation for political engagement on specific issues, some of which are related to religious belief.

Index

About the Contributors

David W. Chappell is professor and graduate chair of the Department of Religion at the University of Hawaii. His doctorate at Yale University was on Tao-Ch'O (563-645), a Chinese pioneer of Pure Land Buddhism. One of his major publications is *T'ien-T'ai Buddhism: An Outline of the Four-Fold Teachings* (Daiichi-Shobo, 1983). After coediting *Unity in Diversity: Hawaii's Buddhist Communities* (Hawaii Association of International Buddhists, 1997), he is focusing more on Buddhist roles in modern society and preparing a book on Buddhist peace work.

Jesuit Father Allan Figueroa Deck is the director of the Loyola Institute for Spirituality in Orange, California. He is adjunct professor of theology at Loyola Marymount University. Father Deck specializes in Hispanic religion and spirituality. A cofounder of the Academy of Catholic Hispanic Theologians of the United States (ACHTUS), he is a writer and speaker on Hispanic ministry and the emerging leadership potential of Hispanics in the churches and American society.

Robert M. Franklin is president of the Interdenominational Theological Center in Atlanta—the nation's foremost center for African-American graduate theological education. He has served at Harvard Divinity School, Colgate-Rochester Divinity School, Candler School of Theology, and the Ford Foundation. Dr. Franklin is author of *Another Day's Journey: Black Churches Confronting the American Crisis* (Fortress Press, 1997) and *Liberating Visions: Human Fulfillment and Social Justice in African-American Thought* (Fortress Press, 1990).

David Hollenbach, S.J. is the Margaret O'Brien Flatley Professor of Theology at Boston College, where he teaches theological ethics and Christian social ethics. His interests are in the foundations of Christian social ethics, particularly in the areas of human rights, theory of justice, and the role of religion in social and political life.

Reuven Kimelman is a professor of Talmud and Midrash at Brandeis University. He has published widely in journals of scholarly and popular interest on history, ethics, liturgy, and current affairs. He is currently writing two books, *The Jewish Ethics of Power* and *The Rhetoric of Jewish Prayer*.

Michal Kurlaender works at The Civil Rights Project at Harvard University and is a doctoral student at the Harvard Graduate School of Education.

Holly J. Lebowitz is a religion writer living in Cambridge, Massachusetts.

Ann Chih Lin is an assistant professor in the School of Public Policy and the Department of Political Science at the University of Michigan. She writes on policy implementation, on immigrants, and on crime. She has also been active in the Catholic Common Ground Initiative, an effort to foster dialogue and understanding on issues important to the life of the Roman Catholic Church in the United States.

Robin W. Lovin is dean and professor of ethics at Perkins School of Theology at Southern Methodist University in Dallas, Texas. He holds B.D. and Ph.D. degrees from Harvard University. He taught at Emory and the University of Chicago and was dean of the Theological School at Drew University prior to moving to SMU in 1994. His writings include *Christian Faith and Public Choices: The Social Ethics of Barth, Brunner, and Bonhoeffer* (Fortress Press, 1984) and *Reinhold Niebuhr and Christian Realism* (Cambridge, 1995).

Charles Marsh is the director of the Project on Theology and Community and associate professor of theology at Loyola College in Baltimore, Maryland. His most recent book, *God's Long Summer: Stories of Faith and Civil Rights* (Princeton, 1997), won the 1998 Louisville Grawemeyer Award in Religion.

Gary Orfield is professor of education and social policy at Harvard University. He is codirector of The Civil Rights Project at Harvard University. His most recent books are (with Susan Eaton) *Dismantling Desegregation: The Quiet Reversal of* Brown *v.* Board of Education (New Press,

1996) and (with Edward Miller) *Chilling Admissions: The Affirmative Action Crisis and the Search for Alternatives* (Harvard Educational Publishing, 1998).

James W. Skillen is the executive director of the Center for Public Justice, Washington, D.C., and editor of the center's *Public Justice Report*. He earned his Ph.D. in political science at Duke University. He is the author of *Recharging the American Experiment: Principled Pluralism for Genuine Civic Community* (Baker Book House, 1994) and *The Scattered Voice: Christians at Odds in the Public Square* (Zondervan, 1990), and coauthor with Rockne McCarthy of *Political Order and the Plural Structure of Society* (Scholars Press, 1991).

Christopher Tirres (A.B., Princeton University) is a doctoral candidate in religion at Harvard University. Tirres is a native of El Paso,Texas.

Amina Wadud is associate professor of Islamic studies in the Department of Philosophy and Religious Studies at Virginia Commonwealth University. Author of *Qur'an and Woman: Rereading the Sacred Text from a Woman's Perspective* (Oxford, 1999), which focuses on the importance of gender-inclusive interpretation of the sacred text, she travels extensively to address international audiences on issues of Islam and social justice.

Preston Noah Williams is Houghton Professor of Theology and Contemporary Change at Harvard University. Williams received his B.D. from Johnson C. Smith University, S.T.M. from Yale Divinity School, and Ph.D. from Harvard University. In addition to teaching introductory and advanced courses in Christian ethics, he is particularly interested in issues of social and economic justice, human rights and nondiscrimination, and Afro-American religion.